D1519862

THE STATE
OF SOVIET STUDIES

THE STATE
OF SOVIET STUDIES

Walter Z. Laqueur and Leopold Labedz
Editors

The M.I.T. Press
Massachusetts Institute of Technology
Cambridge, Massachusetts

These essays originally appeared in *Survey: A Journal of Soviet and East European Studies*, Nos. 50 and 51 (London, January and April 1964).

Library of Congress Catalog Card Number 65–15749
Printed in the United States of America

CONTENTS

THE STATE
OF SOVIET STUDIES

IN SEARCH OF RUSSIA

Walter Laqueur

SOONER or later it was bound to happen—the emergence of the student of Soviet affairs as a fictional character. 'Who stole Punnakan? ', a long short story (a ' pamphlet ', as the author prefers to call it) in *Oktyabr* (1963, No. 10), the Soviet literary periodical, is a fascinating account of the work and, above all, the *moeurs* of Western students of Soviet affairs. It is the story of a Thai Court Chamberlain who finds himself caught up in the gang warfare between various Western institutions of higher learning. I do not want to say much more about the tale, not wishing to spoil the enjoyment of others. I had looked forward a long time to its appearance, for the author was known as a man of powerful imagination. True, I had not been quite sure whether he was a bacteriologist or a writer, since the only other work of his that I knew was published some twelve years ago, describing how the Americans waged germ warfare on the people of Korea and China. Roman Kim, we are told, has done much research work for his new *opus* in a number of places, including Africa. Ideologically, the Western student of Soviet affairs as he emerges from this novel can be placed somewhere between Porfirio Rubirosa, Allen Dulles, and the late Madame Blavatsky, but ideology is of very little importance really. Most of his time is spent in the bars of luxury hotels, beautiful women abound, and only the poorer members of the profession drive a Jaguar E; but all of them are experts on drinks, perfumes, French cooking, men's clothes, and generally speaking the better things in life. Arguments among experts and research centres are settled not in scholarly journals but with the help of a Beretta 25. This glamorous image of the student of Soviet affairs, James Bond and Lemmy Caution rolled into one, will make him the envy of academic colleagues toiling away in less favoured domains, such as patristics or medieval economic history. And yet the picture painted by Mr Kim does not seem quite complete. To fill in the necessary details one has to go back rather far in time, and the point of departure should preferably be a major library, not the Stork Club. I do not know whether at the end Mr Roman Kim will be with us, but this for once cannot be helped.

*   *   *   *

THE traditional fascination which Russia has had for the West has not always been matched by exact knowledge. Regular contacts between Russia and the West date back to the seventeenth century. Yet fifty years or so later, one of Peter the Great's envoys to a West European court reported that he found it exceedingly difficult to enlist specialists for work in Russia; not only was it generally believed that the country bordered on Red Indian territory; it was thought to be, quite literally, the end of the world. Most Russians' notions of Europe at the time—and for many years to come—were even more fanciful.

Many foreigners went to Russia in the seventeenth century—British traders, French and Austrian diplomats, Italian churchmen, and some of them wrote useful and entertaining accounts of their stay there. But it was only after the Petrine reforms and the influx of more foreigners in the eighteenth century that Russia became an object of systematic study. Most of the foreigners who had settled in Petersburg and Moscow were Germans, and this, and its geographical nearness, made Germany the centre of early Russian studies. It is a sobering thought that almost 200 years ago there was a German periodical which provided a critical bibliography of *all* books published in Russia; there was no such compilation in Russia itself at the time, nor for many years after, and there is none now in the West.

The early nineteenth century was the heyday of historical-philosophical theories and constructions, formulated not only by travellers and historians, but also by men of such widely different background, outlook, and interest as Donoso Cortes, Moses Hess, Victor Hugo, and Nietzsche, who all commented at length on the present state and future destiny of Russia; most of them had never been near the country, but what they wrote was not necessarily more misleading than the accounts of the experts, for even their knowledge was slight. What Herzen knew about Russian agrarian institutions he had learned from the account given by that well known visitor the Baron from Westphalia.

Russian language and literature were taught in very few European universities. The first great expansion in political-historical studies, what would now be called ' area study ' or *Zeitgeschichte*, came only around 1880. Mackenzie Wallace's *Russia*, subsequently translated into many languages, first appeared in 1877; the following year saw the publication of Rambaud's *Histoire de Russie* and Brueckner's *Culturhistorische Studien*, and soon after the first volume of Anatole Leroy-Beaulieu's famous work was published. The first modern periodicals devoted to the study of Russia and Eastern Europe appeared only on the eve of the first world war. The Germans were first off the mark with Schiemann's *Zeitschrift für Osteuropäische Geschichte*, which did not, however, strictly speaking, deal with contemporary Russia; there had been such a journal, the *Russische Revue*, but it folded up in the early nineties. Bernard Pares' *Russian Review*, launched in Liverpool in 1912, was less academic, more lively, and far more concerned with contemporary affairs. It should therefore be regarded as the first of the modern journals devoted to the study of Russia—as distinct from the study of Russian history.

Great power rivalries contributed much to the development of Russian studies; the other day I read a long memorandum dated 1912 or 1913, submitted by Professor Hoetzsch to the German Foreign Ministry, in which he urged the need to establish a German society for the study of Eastern Europe. One of his main arguments was the reference to Bernard Pares' activities in Liverpool, which he somewhat exaggerated (German Foreign Ministry Archives 1867–1920, University of California microfilm 159). Obviously, Germany could not possibly lag behind Britain.

IT is instructive to compare the editorial statements in the first numbers of these journals. There was the brisk, optimistic, no-nonsense attitude of Bernard Pares, who announced in the first number of the *Russian Review* that 'the Russian people does not as a whole share the idiosyncrasies whether of extreme reactionaries or extreme revolutionaries, and seeks both the steady and normal progress of the Russian empire and the goodwill of our own country'. This was in 1912; when, ten years later, the *Russian Review* was reborn as the *Slavonic Review*, the same writer had lost most of his illusions, and had at least stopped projecting British mental attitudes on the unsuspecting Russians. In his new preface he simply stated that it was important to know about Russia, because through the world war England had come into closer contact with that country. He also promised an impartial hearing to all schools; but this apparently did not extend to the communists themselves, for as he put it elsewhere, 'it was never a question whether the vain experiment of Bolshevism could succeed in Russia'. He complained (as he had done in 1912) about the abysmal lack of knowledge in England of things Russian, as revealed in debates in Parliament, in the press, and elsewhere.

The *Monde Slave* was founded during the first world war, in 1917 to be precise; it is not surprising to find in its first editorial statement, fuller and more elegant than the British, many references to the German danger. *Osteuropa*, the German monthly devoted to Russian affairs, came into being at the time of the Soviet-German rapprochement, and soon became the leading periodical of its kind in any language. Its editor, Otto Hoetzsch, was a pro-Russian conservative, not unlike Bernard Pares in the scope of his interests, which were by no means limited to academic life. Usually a most prolific writer and speaker, he preferred on this occasion to be very brief; there is nothing quotable at all in his short introduction. Soviet-German relations were still a very fragile plant, and Hoetzsch probably thought, no doubt correctly, that whatever he said was likely to be misconstrued and give rise to suspicions.

Perhaps even more anti-climactic was the emergence of a journal of Russian studies in the United States—one day it simply existed. A project had been afoot in 1939 to establish an American review, but when preparations had almost been completed, a cable from Sir Bernard Pares from blitzed London induced the American editors to play host to the *Slavonic and East European Review* during the war. If America found itself without due preparation drawn to play a leading role in world affairs, its initiation into the field of Russian studies was similarly abrupt.

The study of Russian and other East European languages was, of

course, the precondition for all other research. There was no lack of
teachers in Germany or the United States; instruction in Russian was first
given at Harvard in 1896, at the University of California in 1901. In
England, on the other hand, there were very few men or women with the
necessary qualifications; Forbes at Oxford and Goudy at Cambridge were
well known, but the list of teachers and translators of Russian in the
whole of Britain could still be printed on a single page of the *Russian
Review,* and it included a reference to the Russian vice-consul in West
Hartlepool These linguists and students of literature were not as a rule
deeply interested in contemporary Russia, being more attracted to
language than to politics. But there were a few who had chosen recent
history, economics, or Russian institutions as their field of study, and who
were themselves actively engaged in politics. Archibald Coolidge, Prince,
Harper, Pares, all spent years in government service. Theodor Schiemann, the Nestor of Russian studies in Germany, was an adviser to
Kaiser Wilhelm on East European affairs, and an editorial writer on the
arch-conservative *Kreuzzeitung.* Of Baltic origin, he was violently anti-
Russian, very much in contrast to his successor Otto Hoetzsch, who like-
wise played a prominent part in German politics. It is no exaggeration
to say that all leading students of Russia at the time advised their governments in an official or unofficial capacity, though not all rose as high in
rank as their erstwhile colleague Thomas Garrigue Masaryk.

Whether historians are superior to other observers in judging current
political situations is open to doubt. The Russian experts, almost without
exception, under-rated the importance of the revolutionary movement.
After the revolution their difficulties increased; they had now to deal
with a country that in many essential respects had undergone radical
change. Little had been known in the West about Russian socialism and
communism; the comments on this subject published by German and
British experts during the first world war must be read to be believed;
one of them translated ' Trudoviki' as ' The Weary Ones' (this was
not intended as a joke); another introduced Trotsky as a Ukrainian
nationalist. In Germany, Staehlin, the leading historian of modern
Russia, interpreted the Bolshevik revolution and subsequent events in
terms of religious philosophy; Pares, after prolonged and bitter opposition to Lenin's Russia, came to display as much enthusiasm for Stalin's
Russia as he had for Nikolai II's; in America Samuel Harper, the only
American scholar to deal with contemporary Russian affairs, began by
declaring the Sisson papers, that crudest of anti-Bolshevik forgeries,
authentic, and twenty years later described the big purge as a necessary
stage on Russia's road to constitutional government.

Such naïveté was unfortunately very widespread; the judgment of
intelligent journalists, from Mackenzie Wallace onward, has on the
whole been more reliable than that of the academics. The real merits of
men like Pares or Hoetzsch lay in a different field altogether; they tried to
explain to their governments and to the reading public that Russia was
a very important country, that detailed information on things Russian

was urgently needed. They fought an uphill struggle, and in doing so laid the foundations for the extensive and systematic study of Eastern Europe at a time when its need was scarcely recognised.

Today it is easy to under-rate the difficulties faced by these men; financing Russian studies, for instance, was a major problem. Universities in the Western world were as a rule marked by an attitude of detachment from the life around them. Fashions might come and go, but why change the syllabus? Why study Russian, why not Assyrian? In Germany most of the money for Russian studies came from business men, particularly from exporters from the iron and steel concerns, who were interested in accurate economic and political information in connection with their trade. In America, after the second world war, the Foundations stepped in and made the rapid expansion of Russian studies possible. There were no such foundations in Britain, and big business showed little interest. As a result Russian studies in Britain were constantly faced with financial difficulties; it was a foreign government (Czechoslovakia) that paid for the building of the permanent home of the School of Slavonic Studies, and even rich American universities needed Polish and Czechoslovak subsidies until well after the second world war to maintain chairs for the study of the literatures of Eastern Europe.

THE inter-war period was not a happy one for Russian studies in England or the United States. The institutions that had been founded before the first world war continued to exist, but did not really grow. In America the academic experts were enlisted into government service for long stretches of time, while those who continued to teach, such as Patrick, Noyes, and Karpovich, had few students. Russian studies were moreover impeded by an unfavourable political climate which reinforced the prejudice and resistance in the academic world to area studies. Nor were there enough qualified men at the time in the United States; despite the presence of so many millions of immigrants from Eastern Europe and their descendants, interest in Russian and East European affairs was selective and strictly limited.

In Britain there was similar stagnation, though a School of Slavonic Studies had been founded in the nineteen-twenties. There were close relations with many East European countries (owing to the contacts of such men as R. W. Seton-Watson), but there was much less activity in the Soviet field. There were individual historians, economists, philosophers, theologians, and linguists studying specific aspects of Russian history, philosophy, etc., but their work was uncoordinated and taken all together did not add up to 'Russian studies'. In his efforts to introduce Russian studies in Britain before the first world war, Pares had had the active support of leading personalities and friends of Russia outside the academic world like Mackenzie Wallace, Aylmer Maude, Constance Garnett, Maurice Baring. After the war, these old friends dropped out; the new friends of Russia were not interested in making the country they admired a subject of study and detached investigation. As a result

Russian studies were pursued on strictly academic lines, that is, with hardly any reference to contemporary affairs.

The Slavonic Review went through a similar development; originally founded to study contemporary Russia and its institutions, it became less and less interested in topical problems and was gradually transformed into an eminently respectable academic journal. Much of the stagnation in Russian studies in the West was due to the difficulties of communication with Russia, of obtaining Russian books and newspapers, not to mention the obstacles to visiting the Soviet Union for many years after 1917. Not that this prevented the Germans from forging ahead; the years 1920–33 were the heyday of Russian studies in Germany. A society of sponsors similar to the English in scope had already been founded before the first world war; subsequently a number of Russian and East European research institutions came into being at German universities at Breslau (1918), Koenigsberg (1922), and Leipzig (1928). Hoetzsch pursued very actively his policy of cultural exchange; *Osteuropa* frequently published contributions by Soviet experts, German students of East European affairs often went to Russia. There were more 'Russian experts' in Germany than in any other country, and more publications—and these by and large on a fairly high level. The Germans before 1933 were on the whole the best informed people on Russia, meaning that those few thousands who had an interest in foreign affairs had a fuller and more realistic picture of the state of affairs in the Soviet Union than their counterparts in other countries.

After 1933 this changed very rapidly. Some leading students of Russian affairs were forced to emigrate; others (including Hoetzsch) had to resign their academic posts. With the progress of Nazification, the conditions for objective, scientific study disappeared. Some valuable research was still done in more specialised fields such as economics, but even those who did not believe in official Nazi doctrine on Russia and the Slavs had to pay lip service to the new dogma. Many German students of Russian affairs became involved in activities of a non-academic kind that they were later to regret. Even so, the orthodox Nazis were never quite satisfied with the state of affairs in the field of *Ostforschung*. They criticised their colleagues for not paying sufficient attention to racial factors in Eastern Europe, for regarding Russia as a national entity, neglecting the minorities, and, generally speaking, for being too well disposed towards Russia. Even Schiemann was posthumously hauled over the coals.

B Y the end of the thirties, with the growing involvement of the Soviet Union in world affairs, the demand in the West for information on Russian affairs expanded rapidly but the universities and other academic research institutes were quite unable to meet it. In consequence what information was available came largely from communists, or ex-communists, or from journalists who had been stationed in Moscow. Some of these men and women wrote excellent books, but their work could not replace systematic study, especially on the more technical aspects of Soviet development. Only the second world war brought a decisive change in this respect; it has been said that war gives (or used to give) a powerful impulse to discovery and technical advance. It certainly did so in the field of Soviet and East European studies, for hundreds of experts were now needed, and since only a few existed, they had to be produced as quickly and expediently as possible.

It is not the intention here to provide a catalogue of Russian research, or even a review of the main stages of its development; those interested can refer to the detailed studies published in recent years.[1] The study of Russian, East European, and communist affairs has made great progress since the second world war, large research centres have come into being, libraries and other facilities have been developed, and the list of members of the various professional organisations have become longer and longer.[2] This growth has levelled off in recent years; the Soviet Union, however important, is not the only field of interest in today's world; Africa, Latin America, and the Far East have also figured prominently in area studies. Even so, the growth of Russian and East European studies has been astounding, especially in the United States, considering how ill-prepared academic institutions were for such an expansion before the second world war. Unfortunately, this quantitative growth has not always been matched by a parallel advance in quality. There are some basic shortcomings in contemporary Russian and East European studies, and in some respects developments over the last decade or so seem to have gone in the wrong direction. This has been due largely to prevailing customs and intellectual fashions in the academic world. Universities try to inculcate a spirit of objectivity and detachment, and put a high value on thoroughness; these are admirable qualities, but against this there are at present some very serious drawbacks, which sometimes provoke the question whether the universities are the best place to pursue Russian studies.

ONE of the most striking developments since the second world war, particularly in the United States and in Germany, but to a lesser extent also in other countries, is the gradual disappearance of the full professor as an active participant in these studies. Most of the articles and books published these days are dissertations or parts of dissertations, or 'papers' written by young lecturers aspiring to higher positions in the academic world. Since a brilliant writer is not necessarily a good

1 e.g. Harold Fischer on *American Research on Russia*; Manning's *History of Slavic Studies in the United States*; Seton-Watson's and Bolsover's essay on Russian studies in Britain; Jens Hacker's surveys of East European and Russian studies in West Germany and Austria; Berton-Langer-Swearingen on Japanese research in the Russian field; and the briefer notes on work in Italy (Hartmann), Spain (Ronay), and France (Kerblay and others).
2 Between 1850 and 1950 some 250 doctoral dissertations on Russia and the Soviet Union were approved in American universities. The number accepted since 1950 is estimated at 1,000 and has probably already exceeded this figure.

teacher, and vice versa, and since both teachers and writers are needed, the system which, as in America, insists that everyone shall publish seems both mistaken and wasteful. In the past the most important contributions to learning came from men at the height of their mental powers and experience; today the publication of a book or even an essay by a leading member of the profession is an event, and unfortunately not always a joyful event. Administrative responsibilities of various kinds have grown to such an extent that substantive work is often impossible. Trapped in countless board meetings, committees, and other extraneous activities, those who could and should be leaders in their field do not always find the time even to keep abreast with current developments. Hoetzsch was a scholar, a public lecturer who drew large audiences, a member of the German parliament, a well known editorial writer; he not merely found the time to follow current events but wrote for many years a monthly political survey in *Osteuropa*. Sir Bernard Pares' many public activities hardly affected his output as an historian and a student of current affairs. Today it is exceedingly difficult to imagine a professor anywhere in the world with enough time (and the urge) to achieve half as much as his predecessors; and since there is no reason to assume that academicians today are inferior to those of the twenties, it can only be concluded that something is very wrong with the whole system.

Partly it will be explained as the inevitable result of specialisation and fragmentation in the study of international affairs. It is certainly true that it has become much more difficult to master all the important material than it was forty years ago, what with the multiplication of books, journals, and other sources. Yet for all that, the need to do so, the need not to lose sight of the broad lines of development in each field, is no less pressing than it was. Unfortunately, the fashions prevailing in the groves of academe have aggravated the situation. There is a widespread belief that the study of contemporary problems is not a suitable subject for academic research. This is supposed to be the traditional approach, yet leading philosophers and historians of the eighteenth and nineteenth centuries would certainly not have assented to this doctrine. Today it has become accepted; a scholar who publishes a book on some present-day topic will frequently retreat in his next work to safer ground in order to re-establish his academic respectability. The trend towards specialisation is not combated but encouraged; it is much easier to obtain support in the academic world for a highly specialised project of doubtful value than for a work of a more general character. Obviously, there is no such thing as an ' all-round, all-purpose Soviet expert'; there is no earthly reason why a student of Soviet poetry should be well informed about current developments in Soviet agriculture. But it is disconcerting if the student of poetry is totally unaware of developments in the other arts, or if the student of agriculture approaches his subject in isolation from other socio-economic developments. This lack of broad perspective is frequently coupled with a false image of scholarship. The ' sound scholarship' praised in a book review often simply refers to the number of footnotes; no wonder that students want to conform and think it necessary to quote an authority for the bold statement that the first world war broke out in 1914. This concept of the scholar puts a premium not on fresh insights, on independent thought, on a contribution to knowledge, let alone on a clear intelligible style; its ideal figure is more likely to be the author of a monograph on an obscure subject, written in a professional jargon that will be intelligible at most to a small group of like-minded people, and of course plentifully supplied with footnotes. As a result, scholarship and academic standards have often become synonyms for sterility and irrelevance.

Often there is a breakdown in communication between the expert and the wider public; academics these days seem to be capable of producing books that are read only by fellow professors and occasionally by their students. (Only in Britain and West Germany have there been a handful of books with a wider appeal.) But there is perhaps no more urgent job to be done; intelligent popularisation and generalisation is needed not only to combat the dangerous trends towards over-specialisation; it would in many cases be a most useful intellectual exercise. Unsheltered by professional jargon and accepted methodology, those trying to expose their findings in intelligible terms may find themselves rethinking some of their basic assumptions.

INNOVATORS have been at work during the last decade and one feels reluctant to criticise attempts to experiment with new methods and concepts. Yet the sad truth is that the contribution to the field of Soviet studies of the more modern trends in sociology and political science has been on the whole negligible. Some of the early straight historical accounts, such as Louis Fischer's book on Soviet foreign policy or W. H. Chamberlin's *History of the Civil War*, have retained their value for thirty years or more. It is difficult to think of any book published in the fifties by a sociologist or a political scientist whose prospects are equally bright. Some sociological studies have broken fresh ground by marshalling and analysing new material on various aspects of Soviet life, but the contribution they have made to our knowledge comes from their broad factual content, not from their methodological approach, their model-building, theory of communication, quantification, and what not. One recalls even among the best samples of the species those great projects with their weighty emphasis on methodology and their even weightier discovery of the obvious. One recalls, on a different level, the sterile endeavours to find sundry operational codes and unravel rituals, or, in different fields, ill written pages upon pages of unmitigated trivialities, of pseudo-academicism and bogus scholarship, of a pomposity that passes for profundity. It has been a very sheltered world in which a professor's word carried great weight and an outside critic's very little, for he had neither academic standing nor academic patronage. This lack of a critical approach was often reflected in book reviews. Most irritating about much of this literature was not so much its content as the aura of academic respectability which concealed the poverty of its substance.

Seen in a broader context the picture is admittedly far less bleak; most of the shortcomings noted are common to many other fields of study, which suffer in addition from a number of disorders from which Soviet studies are free. And no one will deny that in comparison with the immediate post-war period tremendous progress has been achieved, particularly in the United States but also in England. One recalls that not so very long ago the late Professor Baykov's *Development of the Soviet Economic System* and Dr Schlesinger's *Spirit of post-war Russia* were considered the most authoritative works in the field of Soviet studies in Britain. Dr Schlesinger, it will be remembered, wrote: 'Our interpretation would put the 1936 Stalin Constitution into line with the Declaration of Rights, the American Declaration of Independence, and the French Rights of Man ' (p. 86).

That Eastern Europe has attracted less interest than Russia as a field of study is not surprising; Bulgarian foreign policy is intellectually not a very important topic and Albanian cultural life not a very stimulating one. Yet it is not only a neglected field of study; the lacunae are more glaring than in Soviet studies, standards seem to be lower, and, to put it very bluntly, the likelihood that outrageous nonsense may be produced considerably greater. The field of East European studies is to a considerable extent manned by friends and enemies of a certain country rather than by students who approach it with an open mind; personal considerations seem to play an important part. Nationalist passions in Eastern Europe have always run high and their impact on academic life has usually been disastrous; to see some of the old battles fought out over again on a new continent is a strain to which the uninvolved public should not be but is often subjected.

Soviet and East European studies in the United States require a fairly extensive appraisal, for since the second world war America has unquestionably taken first place in this field. In Britain, by contrast, new academic fashions have had singularly little effect. Individual writers have fortunately not hesitated to tackle large subjects; over-specialisation certainly has not been a major danger in this country. At one time in the fifties it appeared as if uncritical attitudes were to prevail. The one periodical existing at the time might be thought to resemble an English-language edition of *Voprosy Ekonomiki*. As such it had its merits. But subsequent events have not borne out these fears; prolonged exposure to the facts of life has a corrosive impact on all but the most tightly closed minds. Some of the old habits may linger on in certain quarters but this has to do with the general political and intellectual climate in Britain; it is certainly not peculiar to students of Soviet and East European affairs alone. More disconcerting, perhaps, is the narrow basis of Soviet and East European studies in Britain. The fact that some leading members of the profession are very much in demand as lecturers and writers abroad tends to make one forget that the number of students is very small indeed, and does not appear to be growing.

W EST GERMANY faces the opposite problem; a far greater proliferation of Soviet and East European studies, but an undistinguished performance with some exceptions by the leaders in the field. There has been some encouraging specialised work—for instance on Soviet medicine, and in legal studies—but at the same time the once so prolific German professors on the whole have stopped publishing. The burden of organisational and administrative duties weighs heavily there as it does in other parts of the world.

But there may be other reasons as well; a certain reluctance to express opinions on recent or current affairs; the recent past has taught them the great advantages of caution. Apart from some general textbooks and some compilations of documents it is difficult to think of any outstanding work done by Germans in a field in which they were once the undisputed masters. The visitor to the magnificently equipped West Berlin Osteuropa Institute cannot help comparing it with the discomfort and the cramped conditions at 16 Dunster Street. Yet the intellectual output seems to be in inverse ratio.

Many French intellectuals have shown interest in communism and some have studied Marxist and Marxist-Leninist philosophy. Yet this interest has not extended far into Soviet and East European affairs; Frenchmen have traditionally been less interested than other people in foreign countries; what interest there was has been restricted to immediate French preoccupations. Individual Frenchmen have made valuable contributions to our knowledge, but it is doubtful whether one can yet talk about a French school of Soviet studies.

In Italy publishers and newspapermen have shown more awareness and initiative than the academics. While the Italian press has had for some years now the best news coverage from Moscow, and while Milan and Rome publishing houses have brought out in Italian translations Soviet writers whose names were not even known to all the specialists in England and America, no comparable contribution has been made by Italian universities. Italy may be an extreme example, but its case raises one most important question, namely the impact of Soviet studies on public opinion. Does informed public opinion, do governments, take any notice of its achievements? To what extent do those with a general interest in politics now have a fuller and more realistic picture of things Russian and East European? Prevailing fashions in the academic world have made such communication difficult if not impossible.

*   *   *

Some recent critical comments of mine on the state of Western coverage of things Soviet have been approvingly quoted, mostly out of context, in Soviet publications. This has not deterred me from returning to this subject in greater detail. However grave the deficiencies of much that is published in the West, there is no doubt that the preconditions for unfettered study and publication exist in the countries I have mentioned. In other words studies in the West could improve. One does not have to say more.

*   *   *

I am not sure whether Mr. Roman Kim has followed us all the way. He may have found the theoretical digressions somewhat boring; they may not tally at all with his image of the student of Soviet affairs. Nicholas II, it will be recalled, believed the Protocols of the Elders of Zion to be gospel truth. We know, and the Barghoorn case merely confirms it, that Mr. Kim's fantasies are shared by others in the seats of power. In their eyes, too, the study of Soviet affairs appears at times as part of a conspiracy.

USA: SOME CRITICAL REFLECTIONS

Adam Ulam

WE who study Soviet affairs have—why try to conceal it—a skeleton in our filing cabinets. To describe this skeleton let me invoke a fictitious case of two fictitious characters, X and Y. In his attempt to learn as much as possible about the Soviet Union, X, between roughly 1930 and 1950, read nothing but the works of reputable, non-communist authors. He grounded himself on the writings of the Webbs and Sir John Maynard. Turning to the American academicians, he followed the studies of the Soviet government, law, and various aspects of Soviet society which might have come from the pen of a professor at Chicago, Harvard, Columbia, or Williams. This serious intellectual fare would be supplemented by the reading of the most objective non-academic experts on Russia, and finally of those few journalists who had no axe to grind, especially the ones who had spent a long time in the Soviet Union.

His friend Y had an equal ambition to learn, but his taste ran to the non-scholarly and melodramatic. Indifferent to objectivity, he would seek the key to Soviet politics in the writings of the avowed enemies of the regime, like the ex-Mensheviks; he would delight in the fictional accounts à la Koestler or Victor Serge. Sinking lower, Y would pursue trashy or sensational stories of the 'I was a Prisoner of the Red Terror' variety. He would infuriate X by insisting that there were aspects of Soviet politics which are more easily understood by studying the struggle between Al Capone and Dan Torrio than the one between Lenin and Martov, or the dispute about 'socialism in one country'.

Which of our fictitious characters would have been in a better position to understand the nature of Soviet politics under Stalin?

Of course this confrontation is not quite fair. There was a number of scholarly works which were realistic and dared to call a spade a spade. But in general it remains true that the average Anglo-American academician writing of the Soviet Union during the period under discussion approached categories like 'the police state', 'terror', 'totalitarianism', with the same trepidation and distaste as the Victorian novelist felt when he had to allude to the sexual act. The reasons for this attitude were not in the main political, but sprang from causes which affect all scholarship, and often take an exaggerated form when dealing with things Russian. It is a simple truism that if one works on something, one has to believe in the importance of one's subject. It is impossible to spend a lot of time and effort studying, say, the Supreme Soviet, without growing fond of the good old Supreme Soviet and admitting first to oneself, then more cautiously to one's readers, that, Stalin or no Stalin, the Supreme

Soviet *has* been of real importance in Russian politics. Can one undertake the appalling task of reading systematically through *Voprosy Filosofii*, only to conclude that one has wasted one's time? That if you want
to find out what Soviet philosophy is at the given moment you should
read the minutes of the most recent central committee meeting? Moreover, the social scientist is often afraid of appearing too sensational, too
journalistic, really rather low, if he allows a note of moral judgment
to be heard too stridently from beneath the mass of documentation. And
finally, and paradoxically, what most often inhibits the student of Soviet
affairs is the very example of his opposite number in Russia. If he cannot
discuss any aspect of the Soviet scene without mumbling ' totalitarianism ', ' Stalinism ', is he really different from a Soviet student of Western
affairs who, whatever he writes on, will employ the scriptural references
to ' monopoly capitalism ' or Wall Street?

THE reader will notice that I have shifted my tenses. Yes, some of the
old problems and difficulties still affect our research. But, in
general, American scholarship on Russia has come of age, having shed
much of its youthful illusions and adolescent fears.

A cynic will assert that the change has been due to two factors. The
atmosphere of the cold war has made the academician bolder (or, depending on one's point of view, more timid) in his conclusions; and, in the
second place, the flow of gold from the foundations has enabled American scholarship on Russia to achieve a breadth and coverage which
simply was not there before. To be sure. But, however cynical one is,
one should not overlook one great change which has affected Soviet
studies in America, and which, however mercenary or political its
ultimate sources, promises to transfer them to quite a different plane
from the one on which they dwelt fifteen or twenty years ago.

This has been the creation of a sizable cultural milieu in America
whose interest in Russia transcends Russia as a ' problem ' in United
States policy, Russia as an example of ' the planned society ', or even
Russia as the home of the great nineteenth century novel. Scholarship
cannot really flourish if there is an element of the exotic about it or if
it is produced exclusively in answer to this or that ' problem ' or ' threat '.
Some will deplore that for many an American student a topic in
Russian history or in Marxist ideology is not a matter of passionate
commitment, but a Ph.D. thesis. But we need and we are getting sober
and prosaic professionalism, and our Belinskys and Dobrolyubovs,
believers in scholarship *engagé*, will take care of themselves.

Even when Russian studies in this country produced the smallest
harvest, between the two world wars, there existed small oases of scholarship. There was a handful of excellent historians at a handful of
institutions, notably Columbia, Harvard, and Yale, who devoted themselves to Russia. Perhaps fortunately, the focus of their interest was
not recent Soviet history; but their work provided the necessary under-
pinnings for Soviet studies, and the influence of their missionary work

is still strongly felt, and not only in historiography. It is becoming unfashionable, as it should be, to write of the Soviet Union without knowledge of the mainstream of Russian history. The expansion in the teaching of the Russian language and Russian history in colleges is undoubtedly creating a more sophisticated reading public, and this in turn is having a beneficial effect not only on journalism but also on scholarly investigations of the Soviet Union.

In the last ten to fifteen years we have seen a number of respectable or interesting (often both) monographs on Russian history. That their focus has been mainly on intellectual history, largely of a biographical nature, and almost always within the nineteenth century (1800–1917) is both understandable and characteristic. Understandable because anyone in the West who wants to write about Russian social history is confronted with almost insuperable practical difficulties, and the exchange programme with the Soviet Union is not likely to bring a fundamental change in this respect. The same difficulty, the problem of access to the archives, local data, etc., hampers, though not nearly in the same degree, the work of an institutional or diplomatic historian. Historical treatment of the Soviet period has unique dangers and pitfalls. It is a brave soul, usually a political scientist or sociologist in the borrowed clothes of an historian, who will venture into this jungle of disappearing and reappearing documents, personalities, and reputations.

The state of affairs in intellectual history is much better. The writer, unless he is a frightful pedant (but *he* usually does not write books; he reviews them), will find abundant sources in the main libraries of America. The great and the near-great writers and figures of nineteenth-century Russia have been portrayed, assessed, and reappraised in an ever growing volume of books and articles. But there is more behind the popularity of Russian intellectual history than just the convenience of subject and the influence of one particularly talented and attractive teacher, now no longer with us. In many ways the young academician finds himself very much at home in the milieu of the nineteenth-century intelligentsia. They wrote and talked a lot, usually well. They were interested in broad ethical, as well as political questions, and even the more fanatical among them possessed a wide culture and a certain charm. It would be invidious to try to assess the great volume of work which was and is being done on nineteenth-century thought. But certain observations are in order.

Among the most successful works have been biographies. We have had for instance a biography of Herzen remarkably free from the usual dull weightiness of a doctoral thesis turned into a book, in which a psychological vignette of the writer is blended with insight into the intellectual atmosphere of his day. Even a biography of Speransky falls into the genre of intellectual rather than administrative and political history. Books, articles, papers, have illuminated more general topics like Pan-slavism, Slavophilism, the connection between the government and

intellectual life during Nicholas I's reign, etc. The common characteristics of the great majority of these works are solidity and competence.
The authors have made full use of the scrupulous and ponderous techniques of research which we have inherited from German scholarship.
Occasionally there is a bow in the direction of Dr Freud. But the
manner of writing is usually relaxed. Unless he writes about a figure or
subject near the end of the period, the author does not try to demonstrate a lesson, and so avoids the 'grading' of the figures and movements
of the past which is indulged in with such zeal by Soviet historians.
(Herzen barely a passing grade, Chernyshevsky very good, Plekhanov
very good in philosophy, unsatisfactory in deportment.)

I do not mean to imply that American historical scholarship is blood-
less. On the contrary, we have little enclaves of 'personality cults' of
Plekhanov, Herzen, Struve, etc. This is all to the good. How unappetis-
ing to make an historical figure merely a collage of footnotes and
influences. But it is true that academic disengagement has certain dangers
and deficiencies. It avoids cosmic indignation and transports, but it
breeds a certain timidity of conclusions and style. The American scholar
is not, as his caustic transatlantic colleague sometimes implies, fearful of
the foundations which grant money for research or of currents of public
opinion. But he does spend an undue amount of time and effort in the
vain attempt to make himself invulnerable to the professional critic. As
a result his work is more often competent than readable.

THE studies of the pre-revolutionary and revolutionary periods form a
link between history proper and sovietology (a terrible word but how
not to use it?). Here both the virtues and weaknesses are much less
pronounced. How can one fail to like the Mensheviks, or resist the
temptation to whisper a warning to them to do this or that at this or
that moment in their march to the 'garbage heap of history'. Trotsky,
who consigned them there, would be surprised to see young American
scholars today rummaging enthusiastically in that heap. We grow fond
of or impatient with the Kadets (we recognise them all around us). Even
that heterogeneous group, the Socialist Revolutionaries, have found
passionate chroniclers. We relive with them the heroics of Savinkov and
Chernov's indecision. The tone is much more *engagé* than in studies of
the preceding period. Our Soviet visitors are really puzzled by our
interest in something so *passé* and 'impractical'. But this is as it should
be, and in time the Soviets will see the point.

The closer we get to the Revolution and to the immediate post-
revolutionary period, the more we must admit that some of the most
enlightening and readable work has been done by people outside the
academic fraternity.

The years of the Revolution, the Civil War, and the NEP have a
special attraction for the research worker because, unlike the bleak
1930s, they offer a mass of documentation. Their inherent drama has

produced some of the most eloquent writing in the whole field. There is
no doubt that much remains to be done in the way of interpretation, for
we still have even in the scholarly world a cluster of myths and inaccura-
cies about events and concepts such as the role of foreign intervention,
' socialism in one country ', etc., and they do not yield easily even in the
face of the most scrupulous and eloquent argument. For the 1920s we
have a veritable mine of information whicn is far from exhausted;
writers investigating such major topics as Stalin's rise to power, the
decision to collectivise, etc., have not always paid enough attention to
the flavour and tone of communism of those years, as revealed in the
reports of party congresses and conferences. Trotsky will never lack
biographers; he appeals to the hidden Napoleonic impulse of the intellectual, but we have rather slighted figures like Zinoviev and Bukharin. The
Civil War and intervention have yielded first rate historical writing, but
it has inevitably partaken more of an enquiry into ' who was guilty ' and
' what was to be done ', rather than of an attempt to see it within the
context of Soviet politics. Everything considered, the writing here has
bridged the gap between the unreadable and the unfootnoted, but this
cannot yet be said of all branches of our sovietology.

As to the role of political science and social relations in Soviet studies,
it is tinged with an element of peculiarly American tragedy. Within the
last decades American social scientists have been stirred by the rise of
a new and militant faith called behaviourism. Like most new faiths, its
content is vague, but its ritual rather precise; and this ritual requires the
solemn abjuration of history, and the use of various techniques dragged
by the hair from the realm of mathematics, etc. Now in the Soviet field,
alas, the present is very often a mirage. The most firmly established data
of administration and industrial organisation dissolve magically after a
sudden speech by Khrushchev or a meeting of the central committee. We
students of Soviet affairs would like to participate in the triumphant
march of behaviourism. But most often we can't. We have to refer to
the history of Bolshevism, of Soviet administration, etc., rather than
make a word-content analysis of speeches by Khrushchev, or attempt a
description of the decision-making process at the oblast level (try to do
it without beginning ' under Stalin. . . '). The historians look at us with
suspicion. Our history is too recent. Our behaviourist colleagues treat us
almost with pity. And the foundations show an increasing propensity to
allocate their largesse to fields where behaviourism is flourishing, as in
the study of underdeveloped territories.

WHAT saves us is thát by now the student of Soviet affairs occupies
a firm position in American society, if not in the esteem of his
colleagues, and he will not be dislodged just because he does not know
games theory. For all of our technical obsolescence, and our persistence
in the use of historical tools (as *they* would say), we find readers who
do not feel cheated because a book on Soviet *government* deals largely
with events of the past, because an eminent sociologist injects his

philosophico-historical predilections into a study of terror and progress in the Soviet Union, or even because the 20th CPSU congress or the Sino-Soviet dispute are discussed in essays and without a single set of statistics.

I do not mean to imply that our morale is uniformly good. Many of the younger social scientists (the attrition rate is especially high among the sociologists) break down under the strain and pass over to the behaviourist camp. That is usually the first step in what is known as ' retooling '. The student of Soviet affairs, having been purged of historicism, emerges after a period as an expert on Latin America or Africa. These academic Janissaries, it must be admitted, are very often the most effective students of the underdeveloped countries. Soviet studies thus fertilise other fields, bringing an element of perspective and caution to the ' straight ' Africanist's discipline. In general this cross fertilisation has its serious and beneficial role.

As for the old guard, it holds to its historico-analytical investigation of the Soviet system and society. The sociologist is of course particularly hampered by the inherent difficulty of studying social phenomena in the Soviet Union, but the political scientist also has to work on the basis of evidence which often is far from satisfactory. Some of the best work has been done in terms of unpretentious pedagogical effort: it is no mean achievement that we have a dispassionate and scholarly accumulation of materials and texts on Soviet politics and society which familiarise the college student with the basic facts and tone of Soviet social life, and which counteract the stale and superficial journalistic stereotypes. But beyond those solid foundations we have gathered in the last fifteen years the products of research and of sophisticated speculation on subjects like the structure of the Communist Party, the managerial class in the USSR, the role of the armed forces, etc. Much more frequently than before, the specialist knows the language and has a familiarity with Russia's cultural and political history as well as with his own subject.

This brings me to another dimension of Soviet studies, and the dangers thereof. This is the field of Soviet foreign policy, which often merges into the area of the worldwide communist movement. A worker in this field is most apt to be classified—and even a medievalist or a specialist on the Old Slavonic aorist is not immune—as a Soviet expert. A wretched term! Nicholas II wanted the word ' intelligentsia ' removed from the Russian language. We must wish that the terms ' Soviet expert ' and its fellow monstrosity ' kremlinologist ' should disappear from usage. For in the popular mind the word has come to denote not only the man who knows what is happening or what did happen in his field in Soviet Russia, but also what *will* happen. The newspapers, television, clubs devoted to this ever-spreading pastime of discussing world affairs, one's friends in Washington, they all lack interest in the doings of the Central Control Commission in the 1920s, but are burning to know who will be Khrushchev's successor and what will be the final outcome of the Sino-Soviet difficulties. Along with prophetic power, the expert is also required to demonstrate his knowledge of 'what really is going on' in the Soviet Union, i.e., not what is in the minutes of the central committee, but what Suslov said to Brezhnev while they were taking tea.

It would be pleasant to report that in the face of this pressure our students of Soviet affairs have presented an unbreakable front of scholarly virtue. Alas, there are some who have fallen, and who along-side some good work are also writing and talking as if they were under the table when the Party presidium was conducting its most secret deliberations. The prophet is traditionally a would-be policy maker, and many a scholar has fallen prey to this weakness, unmindful of the predicament of the 'old China hands' and of their predictions and suggestions of circa 1945-49.[1]

I am not demanding, which would be absurd, that the scholar should barricade himself behind his speciality, have no preferences as a citizen, feel no obligation to enlighten the public on a matter within his speciality, eschew as beneath contempt the public media of communication. But the focus of his interests and competence should be sharply delimited.

Other, more technical but not unrelated, problems of American scholarship on Soviet foreign policy and the communist movement at large demand compassionate treatment from the outsider. 'Journalism', shouts the academic critic; 'ivory tower scholarship', says the general reader reproachfully. To pass unscathed by either of these charges requires more skill than a communist does to escape being branded as a dogmatist or a revisionist. But, at the cost of being slightly inconsistent, I shall assert that it is one of the virtues of the American social scientists that, armed with their research apparatus, they boldly advanced into this no-man's land. Whereas before we had mainly journalistic accounts of travels in various communist countries, we now have a plethora of well documented studies on the communist parties of Poland, Hungary, etc.; on their relations with the Soviet Union, studies of social change wrought by the revolutions and foreign dominance, and so on. Insofar as possible, the various shifts and continuities in the Soviet Union's foreign relations have been amply documented and discussed.

There is an unavoidable tendency in these fields to be guided to some extent by the political importance of the subject. Unfortunately, not all the important problems of the world are intellectually interesting. It is also a heartening but unproved article of belief, in the American social sciences, that every important problem can be more easily resolved if submitted to scholarly scrutiny. There are, right now, many people and many research institutions scrupulously investigating the previous record and utterances of the Soviets on the subject of disarmament. Agreed that

---

[1] To be sure, if you wait long enough most prophecies come true, but in an unexpected way. We can see *now* that the Chinese communists *are* different from the Russian ones.

few things are as important as the future Soviet attitude towards disarmament. But is much light thrown on the question, or much profit derived
for scholarship in general, by the repeated assessment of what Lenin
said on the subject in 1916 and how and why it was different from what
he said in 1922? Many of the people thus employed would be more
happily and usefully engaged in rummaging through some relatively
unexplored aspects of Soviet policies in the 1920s. The Sino-Soviet
dispute has launched many books and articles, some of them excellent,
works of love and precision, but many tediously shoddy. In any case,
too many in relation to the paucity of monographs on a variety of topics
which are not 'hot'. It may be argued that the mere saturation of the
public mind with reading material which at least observes some rules of
scholarship is all to the good, but I doubt it. A perceptive monograph on
Sino-Russian relations between 1860 and 1914 will ultimately contribute
more to the general reader's sophistication, even on current issues, than
the repeated exegeses of the voluminous and angry insults exchanged by
the two sides. The danger of continued exposure to this barrage is that
after a while it induces a condition akin to shell shock even among the
analysts. Mr Khrushchev, through repetition, has undoubtedly convinced himself and many Russians that he has been fighting the Stalinists,
and not, in the main, the people who just want his job; and we half
believe it ourselves. The same hypnotic condition is becoming noticeable
among the students of the current dispute: muttering 'dogmatism' and
'revisionism', some of them will soon persuade themselves that it is really
Eduard Bernstein who is at the bottom of the trouble.

*   *   *   *

IT is clearly impossible to attempt a survey of this kind without resort-
ing to the questionable practice, on the one hand, of criticising people
for the general direction of their work, and on the other of 'indicating
the gaps in our knowledge'. This practice smacks of bureaucratic pomposity, and the only excuse is that it is preferable when performed by a
defenceless individual who himself has sinned, rather than by a collegium
of academic and foundation oligarchs. I must repeat what I have ham-
mered at throughout: the basis for Soviet studies in this country must
remain historical. We need more good historical writing. It is instructive
to see how the study of the politics and sociology of Eastern Europe has
suffered in this country, because we don't have yet, where Eastern
Europe is concerned, what we are beginning to have in the case of
Russia: an abundant body of historical studies. The study of even
Poland and Yugoslavia remains in the nature of a somewhat exotic off-
shoot of Soviet studies. We need courses and works dealing with their
history and culture.

    What we don't need is an artificially stimulated interest in 'Soviet
science, 'Soviet' music, or even 'Soviet' art. If a scientist, artist, or
sociologist is interested in what is happening in those fields in the Soviet

Union, this is all to the good, but let no foundation or research institution encourage a wholesale migration into such a mutilated speciality.

Soviet studies in the United States are mirrors of American society: wealth, which means a lot of money, is spent on research, which often leads to waste, but which sometimes lays the quantitative basis for an improvement in quality. The search for novelty, which often results in a strange jargon or a preposterous technique, not infrequently suggests a fresh approach. Democracy is increasingly tempered by a bureaucratic spirit, with the result that while we don't have great masters who lay down the canons of taste and study, we are spared the academic seignorial system which still lingers elsewhere; and with the further result that there is too much stress on 'production' and not enough on style. Bureaucratisation of American academic life has undoubtedly brought forth a new type, that of the academic entrepreneur, who, often without high scholarly credentials himself, distributes research funds, indicates 'gaps in our knowledge', etc. But we are still free. The last fifteen years have, in general, created a favourable atmosphere for academic endeavour. The rest is up to the scholar himself.

USA: WORK AT THE UNIVERSITIES

Robert F. Byrnes

THE enormous expansion of research and instruction throughout the United States concerning Russia and Eastern Europe has been one of the most constructive achievements in American education since the end of the second world war. Indeed, this development, and the parallel but later expansion of Chinese studies, and of the growth of interest in the Middle East, Latin America, and Africa, constitute a genuine intellectual revolution, one which is far from having run its course. The centres or institutes, variously called, have brought together an impressive array of scholars from a number of disciplines, have created effective multi-disciplinary programmes and libraries, and have provided stimulating and thorough training for hundreds of graduate students. There is general agreement in the academic world and in those circles of government most affected, that the quality of the young men and women attracted to and turned out by these graduate centres has been remarkably high, and that the published products of both the established faculties and the newly trained students have contributed enormously to our understanding of Russia and of the other areas under such intensive study. Moreover, the concept of the area programme is widely accepted, and has even had considerable influence within the social sciences and humanities beyond the foreign area fields. Instruction concerning Russia and other so-called non-Western areas has spread from the major centres into many universities and colleges, and is even beginning to affect social science courses and foreign language instruction programmes in high schools.

Programmes for research and instruction on Russia and Eastern Europe have produced other benefits for American education. For example, the ingenuity and skill developed in the study of a society which was closed to American scholars until the mid-1950s created new techniques of research which are of benefit in many disciplines where the basic data are more freely available. Finally, of course, the intensive study of a society so different from ours has clearly increased our understanding of our own system and of other societies, past and present, as well.

This revolution has been accomplished gradually and peacefully, with the understanding and support of faculties and trustees, of foundations, and of the government. The United States owes a particular debt to the sound judgment of those who launched this movement, because the main lines for development were laid out so wisely, and because specialists in the Russian and East European fields were never subject to the pressures which afflicted those who studied the Far East, especially China, during the 1940s and 1950s.

THE story of the study of Russia and of Eastern Europe in the United States since it first began in Oberlin College in 1885 can be divided into several stages, the most important of which was that between the end of the second world war and 1955, when a number of major universities, with substantial support from several foundations, notably the Rockefeller and Ford Foundations and the Carnegie Corporation, and with some assistance from the federal government, founded successful centres for research and training on this critical part of the world. The achievements of these institutes in a time of international crisis and educational ferment were so signal that other universities followed their example by establishing centres organised on the same lines, and by creating institutes for research and training on other parts of the world reflecting the practices and spirit of these pioneering institutions.

A new stage in this intellectual revolution has unfolded gradually since 1955, when the Soviet government began to allow scholars and even tourists into the Soviet Union for brief periods of time under carefully controlled conditions. By the time this essay appears, approximately 200 American scholars will have spent from a semester to two years conducting research in a Soviet academic institution, and probably twice as many will have spent a shorter period, generally a month, visiting the country which is the principal object of their research. The countries of East Central Europe, especially Poland and Yugoslavia, have opened up in the same way, so that new opportunities for training and research have appeared there as well.

Basically, the structure and curriculum of our centres and the research completed reflect the simple fact that we knew little about the Soviet Union and Eastern Europe, and that these areas were in effect closed when the centres were established. In their formative years, these institutes properly placed their emphasis upon training scholars, as distinct from scholar-teachers or teachers. To study effectively a society different in many ways from ours and closed as well, they established multi-disciplinary programmes and placed heavy emphasis upon critical examination of printed materials. The weaknesses of our library collections on the history of the years before the second world war, the difficulty of acquiring materials, and the natural concern with current crises, led to a heavy concentration upon recent developments. Disciplines in which field work is essential, such as sociology and anthropology, failed to develop the interest and vigour of others, such as history, economics, government, and literature. Language instruction emphasised reading ability because there was so little apparent need to understand and speak the languages of the closed areas. In other words, the circumstances of the formative years were quite unusual and profoundly affected the programmes, the curricula, and the spirit of both instruction and research. The opportunity now for training and research within the Soviet Union and Eastern Europe, the presence of a significant number of Americans who have already benefited from this opportunity, and the great thirst for knowledge in the American public as a whole and in higher education in particular, have established new levels, marking a stage at which we should pause to reflect concerning our strengths and weaknesses and the policies under which we should operate in the future.

American achievements have indeed been impressive. We have approximately twenty centres staffed with highly qualified scholars and providing first-rate training to carefully selected graduates of considerable ability and promise. American publications, both books and articles, are of remarkable quality, particularly when one considers how recent our interest in Russia and Eastern Europe is. Some of the specialists, such as Bergson, Black, Fainsod, Harris, Mosely, and Simmons, are clearly among the very best men in their disciplines, and some of the younger men and women now rising to the top show unusual promise.

At the same time, our libraries have enormously improved in quality and in the services they provide. A generation ago, a specialist in these areas would have had to work in the libraries of Western Europe. Now, at least five American collections are larger and better organised than any library in Western Europe, and one can carry on research in the United States in a number of fields of study more effectively than even in the Soviet Union or Eastern Europe.

In addition, Russian and East European studies have made great organisational progress, without surrendering control to men more interested in organisation than in teaching and scholarship. The American Council of Learned Societies and the Social Science Research Council, particularly through their Joint Committee on Slavic Studies, have provided loose but effective policy guidance and a channel for obtaining funds for research and travel. The newly reorganised American Association for the Advancement of Slavic Stud es has attracted the interest and support of more than 1,500 scholars and teachers, while the *Slavic Review* and the other journals especially interested in this area, such as the *Journal for Central European Affairs*, have substantially raised the quality of scholarly articles and reviews. Since 1955 the inter-University Committee on Travel Grants has effectively coordinated the work of the forty universities interested in scholarly exchanges with the Soviet Union and Eastern Europe, and has collected funds and provided the bridge over which hundreds of American scholars have visited the countries of their special interest. Above all, the striking advances made in every way have won the admiration and respect of scholars and administrators and have strengthened the conviction that research and teaching concerning Russia and Eastern Europe offer exciting possibilities for useful and productive careers. In fact, when one compares our progress in these areas with that of other countries which were considerably ahead of us twenty-five years ago, or with Soviet study of the United States, one is astonished at our progress.

A T the same time any objective observer would agree that Russian and Eastern European studies in the United States are hampered by several serious shortcomings and face a number of difficult problems in the years ahead. Most of them are obvious and have no doubt been recognised by many American and foreign scholars, and some progress towards their resolution has already been made. Even so, we should not let the considerable achievements blind us to the difficulties and hazards, and we should recognise that research and instruction in these areas has reached a turning-point something like that of 1946–47 and of 1955.

I shall ignore a number of shortcomings which are significant but not of the same magnitude as the central issues. For example, our approach to Russian literature seems far too sociological. Our multi-disciplinary programmes generally fail to achieve their goal of arousing fruitful interest in the techniques of other than the one discipline in which the graduate student does his major work. Our exchange programme with the Soviet Union has given the Soviet authorities an unwelcome influence over the direction of our research. Their refusal to countenance work on the Communist party and on the central government has forced scholars to work on peripheral subjects. Soviet control of American research in Moscow and Leningrad into the Soviet economy may also distort the direction of our study in that discipline as well.

Perhaps the most dangerous flaw or weakness is the heavy over-emphasis in both scholarship and instruction on recent developments. The situation may be less unbalanced than it was eight or eighteen years ago, but in general we respond to current events and to headlines and follow the trends of the cold war. Thus, approximately half the scholarly volumes published in the United States since 1945 which deal with Eastern Europe are related to developments there since the second world war. Since practically all the journalistic and other popular books and articles on this area are concerned only with recent developments, the American public, and the American student in particular, has a sadly unbalanced diet. Research, publication, and teaching in the Soviet field as well reflect the same kind of emphasis, though not to the same degree because interest in pre-revolutionary Russian history and literature serves as a powerful counter-force.

Another kind of imbalance is geographical or cultural. Thus, most of our research in the Russian field concentrates on Russia west of the Urals and on Russians, as compared to non-Russians and areas inhabited largely by non-Russians. Similarly, considerably more than half of our scholarly publications on Eastern Europe deal with only three countries, Poland, Czechoslovakia, and Yugoslavia, in part for historical reasons and in part because of the roles Poland and Yugoslavia have played in recent years. Eastern Germany has been almost entirely neglected. Even Greece, which attracts or creates headlines, is little noted by scholars, perhaps for the simple reason that American fellowship programmes and research and training centres generally exclude it from both Eastern Europe and the Middle East.

Any scholar could rattle off a long series of subjects which have been neglected or ignored in his particular field. These curious gaps—such as the remarkable neglect of Russian foreign policy—can all be explained when they occur in a field relatively new to American scholarship. More serious than these gaps, which will almost certainly be filled as teachers within particular disciplines direct their graduate students into new areas of interest, are the weaknesses within entire disciplines. Briefly, the fields of study in which we were relatively strong eight or eighteen years ago have thrived, while those in which we were particularly weak are still underdeveloped, are, in fact, relatively weaker than before. More than half the books and articles on Eastern Europe deal with either history or politics. More than half of our scholars and teachers, of our fellowship applicants, and of those who have studied in the Soviet Union are in history, government, and literature. These fields grow stronger and stronger, because scholars naturally reproduce themselves. On the other hand, we not only have perilously few specialists in some disciplines, but prospects for remedying these shortcomings are painfully slight. Thus, even though we have a number of truly distinguished men working in this area in economics, geography, geology, and sociology, and even though we have a smaller number of able men in other fields, such as anthropology, demography, education, philosophy, and the fine arts, there are no bright hopes for strengthening these fields gradually and soundly over the next ten years. Unless we do make significant progress soon, our scholarship and instruction will be as sadly out of balance as they are now because of our preoccupation with current affairs.

It is no doubt impossible to judge the quality of our scholarship in this area, as compared with that on France or England, for example; but I suspect that the scholarly publications on Russia and Eastern Europe are remarkably sound, given the newness of the field and the difficulties under which our scholars must work. However, we generally lack a conceptual framework, except that imposed by the cold war, and we are far weaker on interpretation than we are in description and analysis.

WE must in fact begin to face some of the larger issues and to seek a deeper understanding of the Soviet Union and of Eastern Europe in a framework unmarred by the current crises or by what has happened in these areas in the twentieth century. As Professor Black of Princeton put it, '. . . the senior scholar should assume the responsibility for exploring such problems of interpretation as the comparative study of institutions, the interaction of the traditional and the modern, the role of leaders and ideas, and the relationship of forms and functions, without which no understanding beyond a factual level is possible. If shepherds do not shepherd, the flock is likely to get lost '.

Related to this great need is that for more materials and tools for the college and high-school teacher and for the American citizen and government official, all eager to know more and all as a rule limited to popular and journalistic accounts. Several years ago Raymond Aron remarked that he was enormously impressed by the quality of American research on the Soviet Union, but puzzled and dismayed by the gap between the knowledge thus produced and public attitudes and policies.

A number of scholars are trying to fill this gap in the fields of history and government, but American scholarship in general must take a new direction if it is to fulfil its proper function in a democratic society.

It is now not only possible, but absolutely essential, for American scholars, young and old, to study in Russia and Eastern Europe for extended periods. Indeed, all of our scholars should plan to spend at least a semester every four or five years living and working in the area of their special interest. Consequently, the direction of our training and research programmes should be shifted from the bases on which they were established during the years when it was impossible to travel and work in the Soviet Union and Eastern Europe. They should be organised on the assumption that every graduate student will spend a semester or a year in the country of his interest. In particular, we should change the system of instruction and the requirements concerning foreign languages so that all of our scholars acquire and retain the essential ability to understand, speak, read, and write at least one of the languages of Russia and Eastern Europe.

A final problem we face reflects the uncertain position Russian and East European studies, and the study of other non-Western areas as well, hold in the university structure. The financial contribution of the universities themselves in these fields is generally not recognised, because it is hidden in ' invisible ' expenses, such as those for library, physical facilities, and salaries, and most of us tend to believe that the investments of the various foundations have considerably outweighed those of the universities. Generally, Russian and East European studies rely on foundation grants for graduate student fellowships, for faculty travel, and for study abroad by both graduate students and faculty. Indeed, our university administrators have come to rely entirely on outside sources for these purposes and often regard their institutes or centres largely as fund-raising devices which will ' wither away ' whenever the current crisis ends. In particular, administrators by and large have not been educated to recognise that the foundation grants were only temporary and that the universities must assume the obligation to finance fellowships and research abroad just as they support new appointments and laboratories. In retrospect, never since the Renaissance has research been so lavishly financed as it has been in the United States since the second world war. These splendid days are coming to an end as the foundations turn their attention to other interests. If when that happens the universities remain unprepared to act, Russian and East European studies will suffer a shattering blow.

Every American scholar and teacher can contribute significantly to reducing and even eliminating the shortcomings which hamper us. Some of these issues should naturally be taken up by particular institutions, and others tackled by the coordinated efforts of all interested universities. For instance, the perpetual shortage of scholars and teachers in geography could best be overcome if an institution such as the University of

Wisconsin, which has a good area programme and a distinguished Department of Geography, should appoint another geographer to work with Professor Robert Taaffe and make a particular effort to attract and train young geographers as specialists on Russia and Eastern Europe. Other institutions, such as Harvard and Indiana, with particular strength in early Russian history, should undertake special programmes for that neglected period. Finally, the major universities could and should coordinate their efforts more thoroughly to ensure a cooperative purchasing programme for their libraries, eliminating the cut-throat competition which has raised book prices enormously, and ensuring that every field of knowledge is systematically covered by at least one library. This kind of cooperative effort, not unknown in other periods of American history, would help us to maintain the remarkable rate of progress achieved since the second world war.

WESTERN RESEARCH INTO THE SOVIET ECONOMY

Peter Wiles

WHAT we do know is a catalogue, that can however be more or less sensibly drawn up. But the list of what we do not know is incomplete, since it includes what we do not know we do not know. There is of course a catalogue of desiderata, but there are also those data that will simply crop up, and the discoveries we shall owe to some genius whose interests we cannot anticipate. It follows that all delineations of ' the state of the subject ' are very ephemeral. Moreover they suffer excruciatingly from the ' honoris causa problem ': whom am I not to mention? To the dead the surveyor can only do too little or too much justice. To the living, however, he can give offence, which moreover can be repaid when it comes to reviews, research grants, and openings for promotion.

Sovietological economics is, in this respect, like any other subject. We don't know what will happen next in it; if we did, it would already have happened. But we know its history and some, at least, of the present gaps. We also, of course, know each other. The reader may rest assured that I have already given offence to nearly every one of my colleagues; that by the time this reaches print their reviews of my latest book will be in page-proof; that I've just got my grant, and don't want another. References here to any Sovietologist living or dead are purely coincidental, so to speak. The names that occur are strictly and only those that happen to fit the structure of the article. Those who have not been mentioned are cleverer and wiser and nicer and sillier and stupider and nastier than those who have.

Western economists as an undifferentiated group took an interest in War Communism, and drew from its collapse the expected lesson that a market was indispensable. They saw in the NEP only a return to the market, and paid little attention to the extremely interesting policy discussions of that period. Thus in the early twenties there was no Sovietological economics, and Soviet experience had merely been used to fortify a particular Western prejudice [1]—a prejudice that before linear programming and computers was largely justified.

The first good, specific work by Westerners merely anxious to understand was, naturally, on institutions and policy. One thinks of Maurice

---

[1] Compare Boris Brutzkus' excellent but narrow-minded book, *Economic Planning in Soviet Russia* (London, 1935), and the use made of it in F. A. von Hayek's very similar work, *Collectivist Economic Planning* (London, 1935).

Dobb,[2] W. F. Reddaway,[3] Otto Schiller.[4] But already then there was a greater man, combining institutional with quantitative insight: the exiled Social-Revolutionary S. N. Prokopovich,[5] whose general view of the Stalin period has never been overthrown or even seriously amended by later research. A similar figure, about equally great when we consider his total oeuvre, is another exile, the Menshevik Naum Jasny, who first counted every egg laid under Stalin in 700 pages,[6] and then blazed a trail in the jungle of wholesale prices. This is our Grand Old Enfant Terrible, whose guesses are nearly always right but whose quarrels sometimes distress us.

What Prokopovich and later Jasny lacked was statistical rigour and a grasp of theory. They were characteristic products of pre-revolutionary Russian economics: down to earth, devoid of technique, and mainly ' legal Marxist '. Statistical rigour was provided by the Americans, as a mere necessity of policy. When, during the second world war, there were negotiations and disagreements over Lend-Lease, American civil servants had perforce to examine the statistical basis of Soviet claims. From this there developed naturally a cold-war interest in the same topic. The great name in this field has been from the beginning that of Abram Bergson, now at Harvard. What is impressive here is, despite the original motivation, the extreme objectivity of this analysis. It has been attacked from the right as overstating Soviet achievements, by very competent statisticians. But it is easy to show, if the arguments and objections are pursued *jusqu'au bout*, that it is the critics whose technique is at fault and whose ' passions are showing '.[7]

Indeed, to anyone privileged to know Abram Bergson, the notion that he could be other than objective is ludicrous. The same spirit rules even in the RAND and the CIA themselves; their publications on communist economic statistics, and often on more imponderable matters too, are as fair and as technically perfect as any in the field. I shall not easily forget the first of the CIA publications. I was travelling to Washington from New York in Spring 1958, and chanced to meet a Polish economist on the same train. He opened his *New York Times* to see, under the name of Allen Dulles, a disquisition on the high rate of Soviet economic growth. Instinct as he was with the wry self-contradictions and humorous half-avowals of Polish communism, he yet could not accommodate this

---

2 *Russian Economic Development* and *Russian Economic Development since 1917*. The earlier work, belonging to Mr Dobb's Bukharinite phase, is in most ways better than the more widely quoted revision, which is distinctly *stalinisant*.

3 *The Russian Financial System* (London, 1935).

4 *Die Kollektivbewegung in der Sowjetunion* (Berlin, 1931).

5 His works, appearing in various languages since about 1921, are too numerous to mention.

6 *The Socialized Agriculture of the USSR* (Stanford, 1949).

7 Cf. Colin Clark, ' The Soviet Crisis ', *Encounter*, August 1935 (rebutted by myself in ' La Trahison du Clark ', *Encounter, October* 1955); Warren Nutter, *The Growth of Industrial Production in the Soviet Union* (Princeton, 1962) (critically reviewed by myself in *Challenge*, New York, July 1962, and in *Soviet Planning; Essays in Honour of Naum Jasny*, Blackwell, 1964).

phenomenon with his residual Marxism. I gleefully pointed out that it was just bourgeois objectivism in a so-called democracy.

THE latest branches of the subject to grow have been the study of Marxist theory and its practical relevance; and the determined application of Western theory to the new facts, not to mention the modification or extension of this theory in the light of these facts. When in the early thirties Stalin's centrally planned economy did not collapse like War Communism, there was a most culpable failure of courage and curiosity. Really no work was done on this central question until the fifties. I can remember as late as 1958 talking in San Francisco about the withering away of the state, to be gaped at by a new fledged D.Phil. who wondered why I thought it was relevant. Today he would not get past his orals without it. The confrontation of the two types of theory is also being increasingly pressed, notably by Alexander Erlich in his study of policies for economic growth during the NEP.[8] As to the application of Western theory, 1958 is perhaps also the last year in which I got into trouble for asserting (a) that Soviet prices are quite irrational, and (b) that it doesn't matter all that much. (a) is now trumpeted from Soviet roof tops, (b) has gained acceptance this side of the Iron Curtain while losing it on the other. A fairly satisfactory picture? In all fields but two, yes.[9] The first is statistical projection. It is curious to have to report that after all the work done, and in particular after the flood of new information provided, we are still very much in the dark. In the appendix I give a summary, a crême de la crême, of the figures that Soviet handbooks and Western re-working (where necessary) have produced. It will be seen that we still have no serious figures for forced labour or for arms output; and therefore no really reliable figures for industrial output or the labour force. Income distribution is also virtually a closed book to us.

Now, important as these gaps are, they are quite inevitable. The Soviet government must be expected to wish to *conceal* such figures, and success is not too difficult. *Deception* is, to be sure, also still practised, but with encouragingly little success. Only recently, for instance, a new index of construction was published which deliberately exaggerated the achievements of the thirties in order to accommodate the old exaggerations in the index of industrial production, which have never been corrected. This particular manoeuvre was easily seen through, and more honest figures are not difficult to find. More seriously, we suspect a watering of the figures for current agricultural output; here the truth will be much harder to discover. It remains however true, that at the mere level of quantitative factology we are well informed about the Soviet and indeed most European communist economies; certainly better than about underdeveloped countries.

---

[8] *The Soviet Industrialization Controversy* (Harvard, 1960).
[9] Though we still need a general work on communist foreign trade policy and theory.

My principal feeling of uncertainty, however, is engendered by our failure to foresee things. Specialists have constantly behaved—and no one has been more guilty than myself—as if economic prediction were much easier in a command than in a market economy. In the past it has been more successful, but perhaps only by chance. One of the earliest predictions that communist economies would outstrip all others was made in 1953 [10]; it has been unassailable for seven short years only, and now I have only very limited confidence in it.[11]

As economic predictions go, validity for seven years is extremely good but it is very serious that no one really foresaw the recent deceleration. The facts are that since 1958 Soviet agricultural output has not risen, and Chinese agricultural output has declined; Chinese industrial output has declined in many branches; since 1959 Cuban output of nearly everything has declined; since an uncertain date DDR agricultural output has declined; the Czechoslovak emergency plan for 1963 envisages nearly no growth in construction or industry (and the agricultural plan for 9·5 per cent growth will doubtless be unfulfilled); the Soviet national income as a whole has risen at about 4 per cent since 1958, or more slowly than that of Germany, Italy, and Japan, and indeed, during 1961–63, USA!

In Czechoslovakia and Cuba at least these failures can be attributed to widespread mismanagement in transport, industry, construction, and planning; things that have no relation to agriculture, and that according to Sovietological economics ought not to have happened. The Soviet system creaks and groans, we used to say, but it does at least move, except in agriculture. If Che and Fidel made so great a hash of it that output fell, that might be written off to the US blockade and to Latin American *Schlamperei*; but one cannot so easily explain why the impeccable Comrade Novotny has failed.

Nor did specialists truly foresee the *extent* of agricultural failure, or its consequences. In all the countries mentioned it has led to emergency imports from the West, which have meant a recasting of export plans; and now a prime question is whether Soviet, Czech, etc. manufactures can really be sold to the countries with grain surpluses, or with convertible currencies that can buy such surpluses. Why would the West need such inferior goods, when it has its own better ones? An alternative is to export minerals—but that lowers home manufacturing production. Another is a really big crash programme of investment in domestic agriculture—but that would incur sharply decreasing returns. This chain of consequences is very serious indeed, and the outlook for communist growth is now distinctly gloomier than the ' slower than before but double the United States rate ' so long predicted. It is probably true that the trade cycle is the most difficult of all economic phenomena to predict. The Sovietologist has still the right to smile at the expensive econometric models and computers and simulation games that always come out wrong;

---

10 P. Wiles, ' The Soviet Economy Outpaces the West ', *Foreign Affairs*, July 1953.
11 Less, that is, than when writing my contribution to this journal in April 1963.

at the balance of payments crises and stock exchange tumbles that no one foresees, and at the extreme variety of the forecasts made. But it must now be a quiet smile. Soviet-type economies suffer every other disease and accident than the trade cycle, so that long-term prediction remains very hazardous indeed.

Two other statistical errors merit mention—another ' honoris causa problem '. In 1955, before the Soviet census, Westerners were utterly in the dark as to the Soviet population. Soviet sources hinted at 220 million, and most of us bought that figure.[12] It is very strong criticism indeed of Soviet statisticians that the true figure turned out to be about 200 million, but the outsiders too were culpable; they should have been more wary.

Secondly, there was the famous ' missile gap ' of 1960. No doubt the USSR was capable of out-producing the USA to the extent then predicted in the Pentagon—a view that gravely affected the Presidential elections and the US defence budget. But it would appear that the experts grossly underestimated the sacrifice this would have imposed on the Kremlin's other goals and the welfare of the Soviet population. As time rolled by, the USSR produced a mere fraction of the predicted number of missiles. These matters are of course top secret, but the outsider wonders whether the economic evidence was placed in the centre of the Pentagon's intelligence picture, both when the prediction was made and when it had to be checked against events. Either this type of evidence was not used, or it was misleading. This may very well be nobody's fault—missiles are in any case a small fraction of Soviet engineering output. The failure more probably proves unavoidable ignorance than incompetence.

THE other field of failure, to my mind, is the use to which general economists put Sovietological findings. This is at the same time a failure of the Sovietologist's own imaginative concern for his society in suggesting applications of what he has learned. It is surely lamentable indeed that the economic policies of Western countries of all complexions incorporate no communist elements at all. In adopting input/output and linear programming, in reforming their wholesale prices, in introducing hire purchase and much else, the communist countries have taken many a leaf out of the capitalist book. Even if much of this simply proves their erstwhile folly, they still emerge as having broader and more open minds than we. They take economic progress more seriously than we do, and are commendably free from our institutional *immobilisme*.[13]

To us, a Soviet-type economy is still a mysterious object, unrelated to our own problems. I give one instance. We have balance-of-payments crises, they on the whole do not. True, when things go wrong they are unable to pay for their imports, and that means that the consumer must go

---

[12] Especially myself, in ' La Trahison du Clark ', cited above. Mr Clark's criticisms on this point were absolutely valid.

[13] Cf. my ' Communist Economics and Our Economics Textbooks ', in *The Study of the Soviet Economy* (Indiana University Press, 1961).

without. If things get worse even producer goods are cut, so that
factories go without raw materials or new machines, and production falls.
But in either case the import cut has few effects other than these direct
ones. *Pravda* carries no leader lamenting the activities of the gnomes in
Zürich, lights do not burn late at the central bank, there is no attempt
to cut investment as a whole, no politician murmurs about the 'whole-
some discipline of unemployment', 'necessary shake-out', 'unhealthy
growth', 'period of readjustment', 'things were getting out of hand',
etc. I sometimes wonder if there would be any growth gap at all, or any
fear the West will lose the battle of competitive coexistence, if it were not
for balance-of-payments crises and the threat thereof. It has not been
shown that this single communist advantage is not in the long run an
all-sufficient explanation. Here, then, is a thesis subject for someone.

My final complaint is that although this branch of Sovietology is
commendably free from the direct political bias of individuals, it has
become an American monopoly. In the good old days there were the
English: Dobb, Reddaway, etc. Prokopovich sat in Prague and Geneva,
Schiller in Berlin. Now out of a vastly expanded number there are still
only three first-class workers in Britain and three in France. Germany,
by tradition and political necessity full of very scholarly *Ostforscher*, has
only just begun to produce promising young economists in this field,
but I can think of four. This is due to the general backwardness of
economics in Germany, and is no reflection on that country's achievement
on the political side. There can however be little doubt that Germany will
in a very short time outstrip Britain and France.

Even so, Germany is a very American country. 'Germans make the
best Americans', they say in the USA, 'but they make lousy Germans'.
The most serious statistical works on the DDR itself are by Americans—
Stolper and Pryor. The German-language journal *Ost-Probleme*, one of
the best in the field, is or was financed by the US embassy. Munich, the
great capital of day-to-day or journalistic Sovietology (it is the seat of
the two broadcasting stations Radio Free Europe and Radio Liberty),
is in this respect an *exclusively* American city. The stations employ
refugees, but hardly Germans. The university, with such splendid opportunities before it, has only just entered Sovietological economics
(Raupach). The local branch of the Ost-Europa Gesellschaft is no
bigger than any other in the country. En passant let a plug be put in for
the very scholarly working papers produced by the various stations that
broadcast to communist countries. Circulated also to outsiders, they are
an indispensable means of keeping intelligently up to date. Almost
irrespective of what they broadcast, these stations maintain internally a
high standard of freedom and intelligence.

What is required is not more American, or German-American, but
more *neutral* Sovietology. It is a scandal that little Sweden (with, it is
true, a very substantial Norwegian contribution), is doing more to this
end than the unnumbered masses in India, Japan, and the Spanish-
speaking world. The ECE is also neutral: the product of Swiss tradition

and Swedish enterprise. As a source of information, and a lever wherewith to extract more information from the Russians, the ECE is invaluable. But it is still an official body and must look over its shoulder as it writes. Its published work, which is all I know, is more inhibited in its way than the working papers of the Munich broadcasting stations in theirs.

Bias cannot be avoided. If communism is studied on NATO territory it has an obvious bias no one can deny. Neutrals, on the other hand, are very silly about communism, much sillier than they in their complacency and unjustified moral superiority are even able to imagine. It is also possible to have too much research, even on important subjects. But two biases are far fewer than one. It is clear that some means should now be found, other than American foundation money, to expand research in places like

Institutet för Internationell Ekonomi, of the Universitetet Stockholm

APPENDIX

Our statistical knowledge of Soviet economic history: the main facts as they are at present seen by most of us

	(1) Output of all industry	(2) % of (1) which is machinery for investment	(3) Annual rate of growth of (1)	(4) Arms (very approximate)	(5) Output of Agriculture	(6) Volume of construction	(7) Population (mns.)	(8) Rate of growth of (7) in % p.a.
1897	35	—	} 5	—	—		Jan. 106·1 }	} 1·66
1913	76	—		—	81		Jan. 140·4 }	
1916	83							
1917	54	—	—	—	71			
1921	23	—	—	—	48			0·35
1926	74	—	} 13	—	95		Dec. 147·0	
1927	84	—	} 19	—	98			
1928	100	8·1	}	3/7	100	59·5	Jul. 151·5	1·3
	1928 weights / *1937 weights*		} 18/7					
1929	— —	—		—	—	—	Jan. 153·0	
1932	194 132	—	}	—	86	140	—	
1934	— —	—	} 18/12	—	85	—	—	1·0
1937	{ 439 238 / 100 }	15·7	} ↑ 9	100	108	100	Jul. 165·2	1·17
old 1 terri- 9 tory	—	—	↓	—	114	—	Jul. c.173·0	
	—— 130 ——	——12·1——		——300——		——123——		
4 new 0 terri- tory	—	—	—	—	129		Jul. c.195·1	
1944	—	—	—	—	—	—	Jul. 175·0	
1948	130	21·1	} 24	—	124	—	Jul. 174·8 }	} 1·0
1950	191	26·0		500	128	172	Jul. 180·1 }	
1952	—	—	} 13	—	132	—	—	
1955	315	23·2	} 10	1000	157	239	Jul. 196·1	1·9
1958	421	—	}	—	201	—	—	
1959	—	—	} 7	—	189	—	Jan. 208·8	
1961	519	—	}	—	205			

	(9) Urban population (mns.)	(10) Number of peasant households (mn.)	(11) Workers and employees in agriculture	(12) Workers in industry ('000)	(13) Annual hours of work in industry
1913	24·7	—	—	2930	2548
1917	—	—	—	—	(48)
1926	26·3				
1928	—	24·4	1660	3773	2054(42)
1933	—	—	—	—	1798
1937	56·1	—	—	—	1830
1939					
1 old					
9 territory	—	19·3			
4 new					
0 territory	c.61·8	22·2	2697	10,967	2293(48)
1950	—	—	—	—	2349
1953	—	19·9			
1955	86·5	—			c.2185
1956	—	20·0	6095	18,500	(48)
1959	100·0	18·5	5855	20,205	—
1960	—	—	—	—	(41)

	(14) All other workers and employees ('000)	(15) Doctors at work ('000)	(16) All other graduates at work ('000)	(17) Urban cost of living	(18) Net money wages	(19) Real take-home pay of workers
1913	—	23	c.140	44	33	75
1916	—	—	—	90	72	80
1917	—	—	—	300	233	78
1921	—	—	—	*	*	28
1922-23	—	—	—	64	26	41
1925-26	—	—	—	96	73·5	77
1928	5357	63	170	100	100	100
				'28 '37 weights		'28 '37 weights
1937	—	103	—	⌈ 701 / 495 ⌉ ————— ⌊ 100 ⌋	402	⌈ 57 / 81 ⌉ ————— ⌊ 100 ⌋
1 old						
9 territory	—	—	—	c.162	531	66
		142	766			
4 new						
0 territory	7528					
1948	—	—	—	316	825	53
1950	—	—	—	232	864	75
1952	—	—	—	203	805	90
1955	—	—	—	186	931	101
1956	25,942	329	—			
1959	30,449	380	2647			

* Runaway inflation, succeeded by currency reform.

	(20)	(21)	(22)	(23)	(24)	(25)	(26)	(27)
	Total consumption per head of population	Urban housing (mn.m^2)	(21)/(9)	Prices of:			Annual rate of growth GNP, %	Volume of visible exports
				Basic industrial products	grain in Zagotovka and Zakupka	Machinery for Investment		
1913	—	180	7·3	—	—	—	(fell to 39% of 1913)	360
1921	—	—	—	—	—	—	23·0	5·0
1925	—	—	—	—	—	—	12·5	96·7
1926	—	216	8·2					124
1927	—	—	—	—	—	—		
1928	133/94	—	—	100	100	70/141	7·5	145
1929	—	—	—	98	—	68/138	9·0/3·0	171
1932	—	—	—	97	—	65/112		201
1934	—	—	—	149	—	65/101	12·0/4·5	165
1937	100	—	—	220	121	100		—
1938 old 1 terri 9 tory	—	—	—	—	—	— / 106	1·0	100
4 new 0 terri tory	—	421	6·8	266	121	—		
1944	67	—	—	—	—	—	3·0	—
1946	—	—	—	—	—	—		104
1948	—	—	—	282	—	138		—
1949	—	—	—	667	—	282		—
1950	122	—	—	563	—	197		303
1952	—	—	—	—	193	175	7·0	—
1954	—	—	—	—	471	175		—
1955	176	640	7·4	(488)	—	163		535
1958	—	—	—	—	—	—	6·5	—
1960	—	958	9·05	—	—	—	4·5	900
1961	c.234	—	—	—	—	—		—

(1)   1897-1916: boundaries of 1913, net weights of 1900, omitting machinery (then a very small component): source, Gerschenkron, *Journal of Economic History*, Supplement VII of 1947, pp. 146, 157.   1913-28: official, gross (*Narodnoe Khozyaistvo* 1956). 1928-37: Powell in ed. A. Bergson and S. Kuznets, *Economic Trends in the Soviet Union*, Harvard 1963.
1937-40: Wiles as in (4), making proper allowance for arms.   1940-55: Shimkin and Leedy, net, includes arms (*Automotive Industries*, Jan. 1958; with interpolations by me, using D. Hodgman; *Soviet Industrial Production*, Harvard, 1954).   1955-61: Green-slade and Wallace (in Joint Economic Committee of Congress, *Dimensions of Soviet Economic Power*, 1962), net, 1955 weights, excludes arms.   It is definitely unclear over what boundaries the 1940 figure extends (the annexed territories may have contained about 11 per cent of Soviet industrial capacity at that date, to judge by the number of workers as a whole: see note on (11) to (14)).   Apart from Shimkin and Leedy, the most serious indices are those of Kaplan and Moorsteen (*A.E.R.* June 1960), Seton (*Manchester Statistical Society*, Jan. 1957), and Nutter (*The Growth of Industrial Production in the Soviet Union*, Princeton, 1962).   The former get a 1 per cent slower rate of growth throughout.   Seton agrees with Shimkin and Leedy post-war, and is probably inaccurate pre-war.   Nutter (pp. 326, 525) does not differ widely from Kaplan and Moorsteen.

(2)   Shimkin, op. cit.   All machinery and equipment other than consumers' durables and military end-items.

(4)   Wiles, unpublished MS.   1937 weights except for the 3 in 1928, which is based on 1928 weights.

(5)   *Nar. Khoz.* 1958, p. 350 (gross); except for 1940 old territory (Wiles unpublished), and 1950-61 which is a net index on 1958 weights from Willett (in Joint Economic Committee of Congress, *Dimensions of Soviet Economic Power*, 1962).

(6)   Index of the volume of materials and labour *inputs*, from Raymond Powell, RAND-RM 2454, p. 9.   I have arbitrarily increased the figures for 1940 and 1950 to allow for the omitted input of forced labour.   The weights are of 1937; 1928 weights would make little difference (ibid., p. 3).

(7)   1897-1926, and Jan. 1929: F. Lorimer, *The Population of the Soviet Union*, Geneva, 1946.   1959: Eason, *Foreign Affairs*, July 1959.   1940 old territory: Nove and Newth, *Bulletin* of the Oxford University Institute of Statistics, Feb. 1957, subtracting 1·5 million because of exaggerations in the 1939 census: cf. P. Galin, *Kak Proizkhodilis Perepisi Naselenia SSSR*, Munich 1951.   Remainder: Bergson as in (28), p. 442.

(9)   *Nar. Khoz.* 1956.   The figure of 61·8 is 1·2 greater than the official one, on the assumption that the increase in the Soviet (as opposed to newly annexed) towns was omitted, as demonstrated to be the case for the whole population by Nove and Newth, op. cit.

(10)   1928: N. Jasny, *The Socialised Agriculture of the USSR*, Stanford, 1949, p. 788.   Rest from *Nar. Khoz.* 1959, p. 423.   In all cases I applied percentages of collectivised households from *Nar. Khoz.* 1958, p. 9.   Figures are for end of year, exclude sovkhozy and MTS—see (11).

(11)   *Nar. Khoz.* 1959, p. 588.

(11) to (14)   These figures definitely include the annexed territories in 1940.   There were about 2 million non-agricultural employees in the territories annexed in 1940 and 1945, before annexation (Harold Wool, *Statistics of Population, Labor Force, and Employment in the Soviet Union*, National Bureau of Economic Research, April 1959, III/10) About a half of these probably fled.

(12)   As for (11), except that 1913 is from Lorimer, op. cit. p. 22.

(13)   Hours actually worked per year, except for figures in brackets, which give the official work week (M. Dewar, *Labour Policy in the USSR*, London, 1956, p. 15. S. Schwarz, *Labor in the Soviet Union*, London, 1953, Chap. 6).   Other figures from Nutter, op. cit., p. 348.   Nutter simply multiplies official figures for hours per day by official figures for days per year.   The official 48 hour week established in 1956, and even the 41 hour week established in 1960, yield larger numbers of hours per year than the 1955 figure; this is because such figures omit sick leave and other authorised and unauthorised absences actually taken.

(14)   As for (11).

(15)   *Nar. Khoz.* 1959, pp. 786-87.

(16)   N. DeWitt, *Education and Professional Employment in the USSR*, Washington, 1961, p. 444.

(17)   1913-28: S. N. Prokopovich, *Russlands Volkswirtschaft unter den Sowjets*, Zurich, 1944, Chap. II/4: idem, *Histoire Economique de l'USSR*, Paris, 1952, p. 398.   From 1928 J. Chapman, *Review of Economics and Statistics*, 1954, with interpolations based on Wiles, same *Bulletin* as in (7), Nov. 1954; includes kolkhoz market and all services.

(18)   1913-28: Prokopovich, loc. cit.: income-tax being negligible and state loans non-existent, no deductions are made from the wage.   From 1928 Chapman, op. cit., with interpolations from Wiles, same *Bulletin* as in (7) Sept. 1953, and Kaser, *Soviet Studies*, July 1955; accepting Wiles' figure for 1948, and deducting income taxes and state loans.   Throughout the series no allowance for miscellaneous and social service incomes: see (20).

(19)   (18) ÷ (17).   The figure 28 is for 1920-21; account is taken of heavy distributions in kind, amounting to 74 per cent of the real wage.   Otherwise no account is taken of free social services.   No account is taken of subsidiary earned or private incomes, or changes in the working week.

(20)   Personal and communal consumption at market prices, excluding education, from Bergson as in (27), p. 48, divided by (7).   Differs from (19) by including peasants, especially their consumption in kind, and state health and recreation expenditures. Is also sensitive to the rate of participation in the labour force.   1937 weights, except for first figure in 1928, which is based on 1928 weights.   1961 figure from Golden in ' Dimensions ', as in (26), pp. 354, 360, 366.

(21)   *Nar. Khoz.* 1956, p. 163; *Nar. Khoz.* 1960, p. 613.   ' General space ', i.e. incl. kitchens and passage-ways.   This is about 135 per cent of living space (N. Jasny, *Essays on the Soviet Economy*, New York, 1962, p. 50).   The official figures exaggerate the improvement in housing; cf. T. Sosnovy, *The Housing Problem in the Soviet Union*, New York, 1954.

(24)   J. Karcz, R M 1930, Rand Corporation, Santa Monica, pp. 229, 340, 354.   Average of all prices except kolkhoz market and MTS fees.

(25)   R. Moorsteen, *Prices and Production of Machinery in the Soviet Union*, Rand Corporation, 1962, p. 72.   1937 weights throughout, except that the 70 in 1928 is based on 1928 weights.

(26)   For years before 1929 inclusive I use the following figures in md. rubles of 1926/7: 1913—20·35; 1921—7·96; 1925—18·33; 1928—26·24 (national income, Marxist concept; *Kontrolnye Tsifry* 1928/9, p. 398; S. N. Prokopovich, *Narodnoe Khozyaistvo SSSR*, New York, 1952, p. 321).   The figure 7·5 rests on my own unpublished estimate of national income, Western concept, 1926/7 weights (mainly from *Kontrolnye Tsifry* 1928/9, pp. 398 ff. 435 ff.); it is for 1926/7 to 1928/9.   For 1928-37: Bergson as in (28), p. 226; the first figure in a pair uses 1928 weights, the second 1937 weights.   1932 is interpolated according to these weights (Wiles, unpublished).   1937-50: Bergson, loc. cit., 1937 weights.   1950-61: Cohn in Joint Economic Committee of Congress, *Dimensions of Soviet Power*, Washington, 1962, pp. 74-5 (mixed weights, mainly of 1955).

(27)   The official volume index: cf. Holzman in ed. A. Bergson and S. Kuznets, *Economic Trends in the Soviet Union*, Harvard, 1963, p. 288.   The underlying figures in current foreign trade rubles check well if deflated by foreign wholesale prices, and there seems to be no serious weighting problem (Wiles, unpublished).

(28)[1]

Gross National Product by Expenditure
(md. current rubles, market prices)
(Figures in parentheses denote volume index, 1937 = 100:
first such figure in 1928 is on 1928 weights, all others are on 1937 weights)

	1928	1937	1940	1944	1948	1950	1953	1955	1958[6]
Personal consumption[3]	21·84	170·9	260·8	211·8	—	500·5	—	660·9	866·2
Communal consumption[2]	0·68	8·6	12·6	13·3	—	26·5	—	35·7	45·2
Education	0·87	17·0	23·8	20·9	—	59·0	—	69·3	83·7
Gross investment	7·32	59·4	67·6	53·6	—	208·0	—	285·0	424·4
	(22·4/32·4)		(75·9)	(58·0)		(142)		(197)	
Government administration	0·73	4·4	6·8	7·4	—	13·9	—	12·6	12·0
	(-/61·5)		(120)	(102)		(127)		(109)	
Police	0·09	3·0	7·1	6·6	—	23[8]	—	15	15·0
	(-/11)		(183)	(133)		(307)		(190)	
Defence (as in budget)[4]	0·76	17·4	56·5	135·7	—	80·8	—	105·4	90·6
	(7·6/10·9)		(225)	(640)		(225)		(302)	
[Science (budgetary & enterprise allocations)]	—	—	—	—	—	[0·9][5]	—	[1·5][5]	[3·3][5]
GNP	32·29	280·7	435·2	449·3	—	911·7	—	1183·9	1537·1
	(39·7/67·2)		(103)	(114)		(137)		(182)	

(29)[7]

Net National Income by Origin
(% of factor cost)

	1928	1937	1940	1944	1948	1950	1953	1955	1958
Industry	} 33·2	37·9 { 31	—	—	} 36	—	} 46	—	—
Construction		39[9]							
Agriculture	36·2	31·2/36	—	—	28	—	23	—	—
Transport & communications	4·8	5·3/7	—	—	8	—	10	—	—
Trade	5·7	4·9 } 23	—	—	} 28	—	} 21	—	—
Services	20·1	20·7							

[1] Bergson, op. cit., pp. 46, 64, 66, 225, 361, 395, unless otherwise stated.
[2] Mainly health, includes a small 'other' item. The volume index is for health alone.
[3] Incl. house rents, imputed rents of owner-occupied houses, military subsistence, farm consumption in kind.
[4] Excl. military subsistence.
[5] J. G. Godaire, in *Dimensions of Soviet Economic Power*, Joint Economic Committee of Congress, 1962, p. 37. Is spread among other items for purposes of addition.
[6] Nancy Nimitz, RAND RM-3112-PR, June 1962, p. 11. Stands in continuity with Bergson, op. cit.
[7] 1937-53 from Herbert Block in *Trends in Economic Growth*, Joint Committee on the Economic Report, Washington, 1958, p. 284. 1928-37 from:
   Oleg Hoeffding, *Soviet National Income and Product in 1928* (New York, 1954);
   Abram Bergson, *Soviet National Income and Product in 1937* (New York, 1953).
   These two sources are in continuity with each other and not with Block.
[8] The detailed succession is interesting here. In 1951-54 the figures run: 23, 22, 16, 16.
[9] I have split Block's figure for industry and construction in accordance with the proportion allocated to each by the Gosplan, in 1926-27 rubles; cf. Kaser, *Economic Journal*, 1957, p. 102.

THE STUDY OF THE SOVIET ECONOMY IN THE USA

Alexander Gerschenkron

TWENTY-FIVE years ago, on the eve of the last war, our knowledge of Soviet economic development was small indeed. There was, of course, no scarcity of writings on the subject. The shelves of the Slavic Division in the Library of Congress in Washington and of other great libraries in the country were crowded with books, fat and lean, on the New Economic Policy of the 1920s and the Five-Year Plans that followed it. But the scholarly content of that literature was low. With a few notable exceptions, they contained superficial descriptions of current events. As a rule, depending on the bias of the individual author, statistical data published by the Soviet government were either accepted with childlike faith or rejected *in toto* with an equally naive scepticism. Moreover, there were few attempts to address even the most obvious economic questions to the material. Cost structure, methods of price formation, relative prices, determinants of investment decisions, role of fiscal and monetary policies—to give just a few signal instances—received hardly more than passing mention. Neither interest in those problems, nor competence in treating them, was in evidence. In many cases, good knowledge of the Russian language was the only legitimation which the writers concerned could offer in order to justify their posing as specialists on the Soviet economy; and at times even that qualification was wanting.

This unsatisfactory state of affairs began to change during the Second World War when a number of Soviet economic studies was prepared at the instance of the U.S. government. In those studies independent approaches were for the first time applied to calculations of Soviet national income. In addition, much effort was devoted to the investigation of Soviet capabilities in the individual branches of the economy. The bulk of that work has remained unpublished. Nevertheless, the critical methods for the treatment of Soviet statistical data, as developed at the time, strongly influenced the direction and the character of later studies, when sustained scholarly research on the Soviet Union began at several American universities, first and foremost at the Russian Institute at Columbia University and at the Russian Research Center at Harvard University. Because of the present writer's close connection (particularly between 1948 and 1956) with the latter institution, it is convenient to describe the problems that had to be confronted and the decisions that were reached in terms of the experience gleaned at Harvard.

The first and most important question referred to the nature of the work to be performed. In the last years of the war, the belief was variously expressed that after its termination the Soviet Union would be willing to abandon its autarkic policies and engage in large-scale commercial and financial transactions with foreign countries. Hence, in the mid-forties, great interest was attached to problems connected with Soviet state trading, such as the possibilities of discrimination and/or dumping on the part of the foreign trade monopoly. A good deal was written on the methods of financing a large and growing volume of trade, its probable composition, and related questions. But within a few months after the fall of Japan the first Soviet acts of cold war as well as the adoption, early in 1946, of the fourth Five-Year Plan, showed clearly that the Soviet dictatorship was determined to continue its pre-war policy of giving absolute priority to heavy industry and of keeping the volume of foreign trade at a very low level. Accordingly, problems of Russia's international economic relations, and in particular those of Russo-American trade, receded far into the background. By the same token, it became obvious that Russia's domestic economy was to be the main object of study. There, however, lay real alternatives.

IT was tempting to devote attention primarily to the current economic scene in Russia, and to organise and direct research accordingly. This was an attractive possibility for more than one reason. First of all, it promised easy and early accomplishments. Pursuing this course, it would have been natural to engage a number of readily available men, who possessed a thorough knowledge of Russian, had in the past published books and articles on various aspects of the Soviet economy, and could be expected to continue to do so under the auspices of a university research centre. Much of the job could be done as teamwork, and publication of a monthly or quarterly bulletin, registering and interpreting important economic events in Russia, would have fitted well into such an arrangement. In addition to yielding very certain results, this way of doing things would have appealed both to government agencies and to broad sections of the public, whose interests quite naturally concentrated on current affairs and the processes of day-to-day change.

These were real advantages. Outweighing them was the consideration that this course would have left the field of Soviet economic studies in the charge of journalistic superficiality and analytical incompetence. If serious scholarly work on the Soviet economy was to be done, another road, much longer and more arduous, had to be chosen. Preoccupation with current problems had to be eschewed, at least for a considerable time. Instead, basic research involving painstaking statistical work and generous use of tools of economic analysis was to be the primary objective. This perforce meant concentrating on the period beginning in the late 1920s and continuing throughout the 1930s. The form which this research had to assume was a series of monographs devoted to individual significant aspects of the Soviet economy and prepared by well-trained economists.

The next problem, of course, was to find the men qualified to do the work. In the past, American economists had shown an almost complete lack of interest in Soviet economic problems, the two or three exceptions serving to confirm the general neglect. No one could expect seasoned scholars to abandon their research and to spend much time and effort on mastering what is after all a rather difficult language as well as a great deal of background information that is necessary for any intelligent ' area study '. Clearly, a new field had to be built up by new people, and graduate students in economics were the obvious source.

The years immediately following the war were particularly propitious for the purpose. The G.I. Bill was attracting large numbers of unusually mature students to the universities. Some of them had acquired some knowledge of Russian during their years of service thanks to the Army Special Training Program which had used very modern and effective methods of language instruction. Nevertheless, in order to induce a graduate student in economics to convert himself into an ' expert on the Soviet economy ' special incentives had to be offered. In some cases, the Russian Research Center at Harvard would start financing a prospective research fellow at the time of his or her graduation from the so-called Soviet Area Program in which a degree of Master of Arts in Regional Studies was obtained after two years of work. Thereupon, the student, with the generous aid of the Center, would spend up to two years preparing for his General Examination for the Ph.D. in Economics. The quid-pro-quo was the student's obligation to undertake thereafter to write a Ph.D. dissertation in the field of Soviet economy, and, upon completion of the dissertation, to spend another year in converting it into a publishable book. This meant that the student's connection with the Center at times lasted as long as six years.

This was a protracted business, but the arrangement appeared fully justified by the results. For the first time, a group of well-trained economists was attracted to Soviet economic studies. Since the Center underwrote their period of research for years ahead, they were able to engage in projects which required long and painstaking efforts. A great deal had to be learned. In particular, the art of separating the meal from the bran in Soviet statistics had to be mastered, the learning processes in this respect not being helped much by a sham debate as to whether or not the Soviet government falsified its statistics deliberately. But the problem was not merely to assess the degree of reliability of the individual series, to test them for internal consistency, and to discover the true meaning of a statistical figure which was often presented in a deliberately misleading fashion. Even more important was to learn how to combine statistical data so as to obtain information which never was intended to be divulged by the compilers and publishers of Soviet statistics. And statistical analysis was closely connected with economic analysis, producing gradually a fuller understanding of the basic elements of the Soviet economy, its processes of change, and its mode of operation.

This work was guided by still another important decision. The nature of the effort and its scale presupposed an effective research organisation.

But organised research has its own hazards. There is the frequent desire to organise too much; to foist a research director's favourite topic upon a hesitant, if not unwilling, research worker; to press for teamwork, particularly for inter-disciplinary research, which was, and still is, an 'O.K. word' with so many organisation men in research. These temptations, too, had to be resisted. The prospect of joint research would have appealed to lesser talents, but would have been scorned by independent and creative minds. Nor would an excellent student accept work on a subject unless it genuinely excited his curiosity and aroused his research instincts. The ultimate selection of a topic had to come from the student himself. Care had to be exercised lest a relatively insignificant topic were chosen. But in a virgin field there was no dearth of highly important subjects.

Decisions of this sort did not remain peculiar to the Russian Research Center at Harvard. In particular, the RAND Corporation in Santa Monica, California, pursued a very similar policy, making a signal contribution to research on the Soviet economy. Today, as one looks back and reviews the results of those efforts, they appear impressive indeed. Some three hundred years ago a Dutch scholar, now almost forgotten, chose a proud device for his coat-of-arms: *Quantum est quod scimus*. While it is true that there are still many things which we do not know about the Soviet economy, the increase in knowledge that has occurred during the past decade and a half is truly stupendous. At least in these relative terms, the American students of Soviet economic development may well feel justified in appropriating old Boxhorn's self-confident motto.

IT would far exceed the scope of this note to give a complete listing of the important studies that appeared in print during that period, while a partial listing would do injustice to the works omitted. But at least a brief survey of some of the areas in which significant work has been done should be in order. In the field of national income and output an original and effective method was devised for calculating the national income of the Soviet Union within a conceptual framework employed in Western presentations of national accounts; in a series of successive studies the computations were first made at current Russian prices and the magnificent work was crowned by a volume in which the previously computed data were expressed in constant prices, thus offering for the first time a reliable and detailed picture of the rate of the aggregate growth of the Soviet economy. In various other studies, special attention was devoted to the rate of growth of industrial output, to productivity of labour in Soviet industry, and to Soviet capital formation. In reference to the entire period since 1928, it is probably no exaggeration to say that as a result of these studies our information on the rate of Soviet economic growth is superior even to that available to Soviet planners, who for the earlier parts of the period still operate with patently inadequate yardsticks. Studies of Soviet prices threw light on the peculiarities of the price structure in Soviet Russia and the degree of meaningfulness inherent in the Soviet price system.

No less important was a thorough investigation of the evolution of real wages, revealing an astonishing lag of the latter behind the growth of output. A monograph on Soviet taxation presented the relevant material as a problem of eliminating the gap between the purchasing power in the hands of the population and the available supply of consumers' goods at the existing prices. The role of the interest rate, and of its substitutes, in determining investment decisions was investigated. The policies of Soviet industrial enterprises were the subject of at least two important studies, showing curious and wide discrepancies between the idealised picture usually presented in Soviet literature and the actual behaviour of managers of industrial enterprises. Those studies were illuminatingly supplemented by an investigation of Soviet methods of accounting. A *magnum opus* written by a productive scholar, unconnected with the main research organisations in the field, offered a thorough examination in quantitative terms of the collectivised agriculture of the Soviet Union. The Soviet iron and steel industry and the Soviet railroads became the subject-matter of two studies which in their mastery of the respective materials and in analytical sophistication were fully comparable to monographs on industrial organisation in the United States. Soviet economic writings under Stalin were reduced to a jejune regurgitation of the pronouncements of the dictator, but the lively debates in the twenties dealt with real and important alternatives of Soviet economic development. In a significant study, the arguments and counter-arguments of those days were translated into the language of modern economics and served to illuminate the complex situation which existed in Russia in the second half of the twenties, out of which emerged Stalin's policy of collectivisation of agriculture and superindustrialisation.

This enumeration naturally conveys no idea of the depth of analysis reached in the individual studies. But it should give at least some impression of the range of the problems that were treated and of the vigour and concentration with which the field of Soviet economic studies was attacked. There can be no doubt that the results attained amply testify to the soundness of the basic decisions made. The roundabout way proved a highly productive one. Thanks to the long series of fundamental investigations, it has become possible to deal with current economic problems of the Soviet Union in a competent and sophisticated fashion, and at the same time to hazard intelligent guesses—conditional predictions—about the path the Soviet economy is likely to travel in the future. One has only to refer to the reports submitted by the community of American students of the Soviet economy to the Joint Committee of the U.S. Congress, or to study the papers and the discussions of some scholarly conferences in which past research and current analysis were deliberately connected, to find plentiful evidence for the progress achieved through first withdrawing into basic research and then returning to the examination of current problems.

THE success is obvious. The study of the Soviet economy has been effectively transformed into an integral part of the discipline of economics. In fact, at least in some respects, the preoccupation with the Soviet economy has had effects transcending the limits of a mere area study. In trying to gauge the rate of growth of an economy which grew fast and whose structure was rapidly changing; and in attempting comparisons between the Soviet levels of income and output and those of other countries, the students were forced to face up squarely to the problem of the nature of the yardsticks used. It would not have done simply to shrug the index number problem away by merely referring to its annoying existence, as had been done so often before. Accordingly, there appeared both historical and theoretical interpretations of the index number problem in industrialising economies, which already have found many an echo in areas quite unconnected with Soviet studies. In addition, the economists working on the Soviet economy had to be particularly conscious of the ways in which results of statistical computations should be published. The Soviet statistical material was often uncertain and most of the time fragmentary. To transform it into usable statistical data it was necessary to make a great many arbitrary assumptions and estimates of varying degrees of plausibility. It is not surprising, therefore, that it became the practice to call for publication of most detailed statistical appendices to the texts of the studies. This is something that could and should be imitated in many a field of historical statistics for countries other than the Soviet Union, where the shortcomings of the original data and the problems of treating them are not very different. A full view into the statistician's kitchen, for instance, would be most desirable in any presentation of long-term income and output series for many Western countries in the nineteenth century.

While many an important aspect of Soviet economic development has been treated in the studies alluded to here, there is, of course, a good deal of room for further basic research. The number of monographs devoted to the individual Soviet industries could be considerably increased. An area which so far has remained almost entirely outside the purview of scholarly attention is Soviet technology. A series of studies investigating the economic problems involved would be eminently desirable and would take several years to accomplish. In particular, a study of obsolescence in the Soviet economy—of ' moral depreciation ' as the Soviet economists call it, following Marx—would be enlightening indeed, particularly if it could be presented in comparative terms, using for the purpose the relevant developments in the American or in some other Western economy. While we know a good deal about the way in which industrial enterprises are run in Russia, the management of collective farms has not yet been studied in any comparable fashion, and an investigation would certainly prove very rewarding.

THESE few examples probably do not begin to exhaust the variety of further significant research projects. But one additional point may be in order. In the past, when the large backlog of purely economic problems pressed for urgent investigation, inter-disciplinary research had to be looked upon with misgivings and attempts in that direction discouraged. Today, after much of the basic economic work has been done, this is no longer true to the same extent. Sociological, political, perhaps psychological themes may be profitably conjoined with economic analysis. Most notably, it is to be recognised that in Soviet Russia economic decisions most frequently are a function of political necessities or desirabilities of the Soviet government. The mechanics of the exercise of dictatorial power make for the primacy of politics over economics, the tenets of the materialistic conception of history to the contrary notwithstanding. A serious and detailed study of politics as a determinant of economics, and of the resulting deviations from optimal economic solutions, would be extremely useful. Nevertheless, it probably would be illusory to expect that a study of this kind could be successfully carried out as the joint enterprise of an economist and a political scientist. If the focus of such work is to remain economic, a project conducted in its entirety by an economist who has managed to acquire the necessary grasp of Soviet politics would be much more likely to yield significant results.

For the moment, however, the chances that a great deal of interesting and original economic research will be done are less than excellent. In the last few years, the influx of young and promising talent into the field has been slow. There are many reasons to account for this. For one, research on the Soviet economy no longer offers the wide open spaces which invited students fifteen years ago. Moreover, a great change has occurred in the American labour market for young economists; it has become a pronounced sellers' market. Universities and colleges throughout the country have been expanding rapidly, and academic demand for economists seems to have been growing, if anything, at a still higher rate. In contrast to the previous practice, leading universities have been offering assistant professorships to graduate students who have not yet completed the requirements for the doctor's degree. Finally, able graduate students find it very easy today to obtain generous individual grants from various foundations. In these conditions, Ph.D. theses can be prepared without the individual having to submit to the rhythm of work and the responsibilities which are inevitably imposed even by the most liberal research organisation. A bright graduate student of economics can proceed much faster along the conventional road of academic advancement by choosing a thesis topic in economic theory or related areas which does not require the long years of arduous work necessary for successful empirical research in the Soviet field. Obviously, the problem is not an easy one. Much will depend on the imaginativeness and resourcefulness of the men in charge of the larger research organisations; on their ability, that is, to suggest new themes and to find ways and means to compensate outstanding students for the unavoidable retardation in their careers, thus once more making the area of Soviet economic study attractive to them.

To discover appropriate solutions would seem most important for more than one reason. The scholars working in the field of Soviet economic research have come to constitute a closely-knit group, even formally organised in a miniature professional organisation of their own. This has advantages and disadvantages. The spirit of comradeship and the friendships formed in the years of common apprenticeship in the research centres create many opportunities for consultation and stimulation. At the same time, however, they have produced somewhat excessive loyalties and reticences. It is, for instance, not easy to find reviewers in the United States willing to comment in professional journals frankly and bluntly on books published by their colleagues in the field. There has been much mutual admiration and a curious absence or near-absence of public disagreement in what, after all, is an uncertain and controversial subject. An infusion of young talent would blow whiffs of fresher air over the field; it would also generate new stimuli and open up promising vistas for further original work, thus serving to continue what was once a daring venture into the unknown and has proved a successful and highly significant operation in research.

SOVIET STUDIES IN WESTERN EUROPE

BRITAIN

Victor S. Frank

' THE POLITICAL CENTRE OF GRAVITY of the world, which up to the time of the second world war was in western Europe, has now moved outwards, east, west and south. But the British educational system has taken little account of these developments. So far as it considers any area outside the United Kingdom it still seems able only to see western Europe, with an occasional bow to north America and the Commonwealth. Western European languages, civilisations and history dominate the arts faculties of British universities.'

That is how an authoritative Government survey summed up the situation two years ago.[1] It echoed a similar criticism made in another Government report fourteen years earlier: 'Our culture is at present provincial in the sense that it is purely Western.'[2] The 1961 report went on: 'It is the Sub-Committee's belief that the world has changed so much in the last ten to fifteen years, and the importance of the non-western world has grown so fast, that the universities need to recognise this in the balance of their studies.' And in an unintentionally funny sentence the august body promoted this world to a respectable status: 'It is satisfied—the Sub-Committee stated (p. 42)—that these regions and their civilisations are, generally speaking, appropriate for university study.'

Both the Scarbrough and the Hayter Reports covered a much wider field than does the present article, which merely offers some reflections on the genesis, the state, and the purposes of Russian studies in this country, as they appear to a man of continental antecedents without the benefit of personal first-hand experience of academic life in Britain either as a student or as a teacher.[3]

THE REPROACH LEVELLED by the Hayter Committee against the universities ('. . . this state of affairs is anachronistic and shows an inadequate

---

1 University Grants Committee, *Report of the Sub-Committee on Oriental, Slavonic and African Studies*, London, H.M. Stationery Office, 1961, p. 41. Subsequently quoted as *Hayter Report*.

2 Foreign Office, *Report of the Interdepartmental Commission of Enquiry on Oriental, East European and African Studies*, London, H.M. Stationery Office, 1947 (reprinted 1959), p. 31. Subsequently quoted as *Scarbrough Report*.

3 My thanks are due to a number of scholars whom I was privileged to question and, in particular, to Mr David Footman, Fellow of St. Antony's College, Oxford, who very generously placed at my disposal a report on *United Kingdom Training and Research in the Russian and Asian Fields*, delivered by him and Col. G. E. Wheeler at the Soviet-Asian Relations Conference at Los Angeles in 1959. Needless to say, the conclusions reached in the present article are mine alone.

response to the changes now occurring in the world ', p. 41) appears to have been too sweeping. To a certain extent, the Sub-Committee was preaching to the converted, or rather, was reflecting the views of those academic bodies and individual scholars who had recognised the need of reorienting the study of the non-western world and, in particular, of the Russian world, long before the Hayter Committee was called into being. In fact, one of the members of the Committee was Mr F. W. D. Deakin, Warden of the new St. Antony's College at Oxford which had been called into being by a generous donation from a private benefactor, and which had set itself the specific task of research in the modern history of that non-western world which, in the Hayter Committee's view, had now become a subject ' appropriate for university study '. The same applied, on a smaller scale, to the initiative of the London School of Economics and Political Science, where Soviet government and institutions, as well as Soviet economy, have been taught since the early 1950s. Soviet economic institutions were also being studied, from the 1940s on, at the universities of Birmingham and Glasgow.

These institutions, however, were honourable exceptions. On the whole, despite the impetus given to Russian studies by the 1947 Scarbrough Report, most governing bodies of British universities, both old and new, were still organising their arts curricula on nineteenth-century lines, both as to the volume and the character of Russian studies.

It was the war and the immediate post-war developments which first revealed the woeful inadequacy of Russian studies in this country. While British universities could rightly boast of a number of outstanding scholars in this field, they did not and could not produce enough graduates with an adequate knowledge of the Russian language and of Soviet affairs. The immediate need from 1941 on was simply for people capable of reading and speaking Russian to act as interpreters and as intelligence and liaison officers. To a certain extent the gap was filled by members of two groups—the Anglo-Russians and the Russian emigrés. Both, by their very nature, were transient phenomena and offered no long-term solution.

The first group consisted of members of those vigorous prerevolutionary British business communities in St. Petersburg and Moscow most of whom had found their way to Britain after 1917. Major Birse, the immaculate interpreter for Mr Winston Churchill and Mr Clement Attlee at the wartime and post-war summit meetings, was an outstanding member of this group. He, like many other Anglo-Russians, possessed not only the ideal language qualifications, but also that intuitive understanding of the Russian mentality which comes naturally only to people who have once been truly at home in Russia.

The Russian emigrés who formed the second group had either settled in Britain immediately after the end of the Civil War in Russia, or had reached the safety of British shores as refugees from Hitler-dominated Europe—from Germany, Czechoslovakia, France, or Yugoslavia. True, the Russian colony in Britain was never so strong or so intellectually active as the Russian colonies in Paris, Berlin, or Prague. But there were enough of them and of their children to provide a sizeable number of Russian-speaking recruits to the services and government departments.

Both these groups, however, were rapidly dwindling, with the older generation dying off and most of the younger merging into the surrounding milieu and losing their language and their interest in things Russian. In the long run, as far as language was concerned, the solution lay obviously in teaching Russian to English students. The University Extension Courses run for the benefit of officers and national servicemen by the Universities of London and Cambridge in the war and early post-war years, did much to solve this short-range problem.

The need for interpreters, translators, and liaison officers, however, was but part of a much wider need—the need for an indigenous academic tradition such as has existed for many generations in the field of classical, French, or German studies. What Britain lacked was a pool of qualified native experts in Russian and Soviet affairs—not so much in the field of language and philology (that was being taken care of by the crash programmes, and by existing language departments), as in modern history, political institutions, economy, geography, and so on.

This want was exacerbated by a characteristic, apparently common to academic institutions all over the world. The 1947 Scarbrough Report had noted the innate tendency of all universities, British and continental alike, to concentrate their interest in regional studies on their purely philological aspect. The report had some acid comment to offer on this count: ' Where languages, and especially the more difficult languages, enter into the work of a department, there is a natural tendency for pure linguistics to dominate the outlook ' (p. 29). And the report went on to quote the words of a distinguished scholar whose observations, though primarily referring to Far Eastern studies, appear to have been relevant to Russian studies in this country until fairly recently: ' An institute which gets into the hands of a philologist runs the risk of becoming a machine for turning out doctoral theses on obscure grammatical matters. These are no doubt interesting in one aspect of a national culture. But students [engaged in these pursuits] tend to become like a man who is always taking his car to pieces and never goes for a drive. . . . I speak with some conviction on this point because I once wrote an Historical Grammar myself, but abandoned linguistic studies because I found that I was sinking into a philological trance and was becoming unconscious of the realities which words described ' (p. 30).

So far the 1947 Scarbrough Report. But even though the report induced the Treasury to give substantially larger grants to universities for the specific purpose of bolstering modern, non-linguistic studies, many departments and institutes, particularly in Oxford and Cambridge, were not shaken out of their ' philological trance '. In fact, as one scholar put it to me, the Scarbrough money went largely into existing institutions and was spent, as he put it, ' on useless research '; ' Oxford and Cambridge were still dominated by philology '.

These remarks touch on one aspect of Russian studies which sets it apart from most other academic fields. It is this: unless you are a pure philologist, you cannot be politically neutral as a scholar of Russian, or Soviet, things. Whether this is a good or a bad thing is irrelevant. When dealing with, say, Russian twentieth-century history, or with post-1917 literature, you cannot, by the very nature of things, avoid taking sides. The simple fact is that since the ' target area ' (to use a radio expression) is dominated by politics, since most Soviet historians, economists, and literary critics are first of all committed politicians or propagandists, foreign scholars are bound to take into account, and react to, interpretations provided by their Soviet colleagues. They can either accept them, wholly or in part; or they can reject them, wholly or in part, and replace them by their own interpretations. In either case they take up a political attitude, explicitly or implicitly.

I suppose it is the frightening realisation of the inevitable political involvement which has driven so many gifted scholars in the field of Russian and Slavonic studies into the ivory tower of philology. For if you are engaged on working out ' The Pitch of Serbo-Croatian Word Accents in Statements and Questions ', or ' The Trochaic Metres in Early Russian Syllabo-Tonic Poetry ', or if you are interested in ' Antioch Kantemir and his German Translators ',⁴ you are in effect seeking refuge in the philological trance, in a state, that is, which protects you from the realities which words describe. Linguistics is the opium of the scholars.

WHAT IS THE PRIME PURPOSE of Russian studies in Britain and, indeed, in any major western country? Several answers to this question are legitimate. To begin with, these studies must evidently satisfy certain utilitarian purposes. The country needs, to an ever rising degree, teachers, translators, intelligence officers, journalists, commercial correspondents, and librarians well versed in one of the major languages of the world.

This requirement presupposes a well-organised process of teaching Russian—on the secondary and on the higher levels of education; it also presupposes the existence of a sufficient number of teachers on both levels and the provision of openings for graduates. And although things are far from perfect, there are encouraging signs of positive developments in all these fields.⁵ Supply appears to be keeping pace with demand, and the Hayter Report, while suggesting that Russian teaching in the schools

---

⁴ Titles of articles published in 1960 and 1961 in the main scholarly journal in the field of Slavonic studies in this country, *The Slavonic and East European Review* (University of London). It ought to be pointed out, however, that in the last few years the *Review* has maintained a far better balance between philology and more topical subjects.

⁵ See the Report of the Committee appointed by the Minister of Education and the Secretary of State for Scotland in September 1960, *The Teaching of Russian* (London, H.M. Stationery Office, 1962, *Annan Report*). Russian in secondary education is still, however, lagging far behind other languages. In 1961 at Ordinary level 154,000 took French, 55,000 took Latin, and 25,000 took German. Only 1,027 took Russian. In the same year at Advanced level some 16,900 took French, 6,300 Latin and 4,900 German. Only 236 took Russian (*Annan Report*, p. 3).

be enlarged, said it was ' not possible to argue that the language departments should be producing many more linguists to meet the demand from
employers ' (p. 51).

The second purpose of Russian studies has nothing to do with utilitarian considerations. It consists in the furtherance of pure disinterested
research, of the pursuit of truth for truth's sake, which, after all, is what
scholarship and university tradition are all about. Serbo-Croatian word
accents and trochaic metres in early Russian syllabo-tonic poetry are, and
deserve to be, investigated in the course of this pursuit with the same
intensity and ingenuity as modern Russian nuclear terminology or communist penetration into Africa.

But there is a third—and a more challenging—purpose of Russian
studies in this country, indeed in any country outside the orbit of the
USSR. It partly overlaps with the second purpose, but has a character
all its own, linked as it is with the all-pervasive presence of politics in
Russian studies. It is simply this: So long as genuine research and true
scholarship in the USSR, the natural fountainhead of Russian studies,
are vitiated by the control and guidance of a political organisation, the
Communist Party of the Soviet Union, so long as Russian scholars themselves are forbidden or unable to interpret evidence about their native
history and civilisation in a genuinely scholarly way, the task must be
taken over by scholars outside the Soviet Union.

It may be argued that it is no business of British (or American, or
French, or Italian) scholars to do a job which rightly belongs to Russian
scholars; that it is both an impertinence on their part and an unnecessary
burden on them, to try to take the place of Russian scholars in the field of
Russian research. But, the world being what it is nowadays, these objections are not valid. Russia's business is the world's business. When a
history of the CPSU is written by a British scholar, he is doing a job
which in normal circumstances would, no doubt, have been done by a
Moscow or Leningrad historian. Things being what they are, however, no
history of the CPSU deserving that name can be written in the Soviet
Union. When an Oxford scholar attempts to interpret the current literary
scene in the Soviet Union, he too is performing a task which, in normal
circumstances, would and should have been done by a Russian critic or
historian of literature.

In fact, the work being done by scholars in this country helps to fill
the gap opened in the history of Russian civilisation by the existence of a
regime which in fact denies that there can be any objective truth apart
from ' class truth '. If this country had been governed for half a century
by a totalitarian regime bent on perpetuating itself, and, with this aim in
mind, making the genuine dispassionate study of its history, civilisation,
and contemporary institutions impossible; if the efforts of British scholars
over the last 45 or 50 years in history, sociology, and other humanistic
studies had been diverted into channels profiting not the truth, but the
political ends of the dictatorship, would this not be considered a cata-
strophe by other nations? And would it be a matter for surprise or

resentment if American or Russian scholars were to continue research into British history or English literature?

This is precisely what has happened to Russia. And the rescue operation conducted by the small group of British experts on Russian affairs is, to my mind, a highly important, if not *the* most important, facet of Russian studies in this country.

SEEN FROM THIS ANGLE, the political factor comes in with a vengeance. For if political sentiments outweigh scholarly standards, they can endanger the great rescue operation. There have been several instances of this, although fortunately they occur less and less frequently now. In its early years the quarterly review *Soviet Studies* (published on behalf of the Department for the study of Social and Economic Institutions of the USSR of the University of Glasgow) startled and shocked a good many of its readers. Two examples may suffice: In 1954 one of the most significant events in the USSR was the publication of an article by the literary critic Pomerantsev in which he put forward a passionate plea for ' sincerity '. It was widely interpreted as one of the first protests against the regime-enforced lie. The comment in *Soviet Studies* ran: ' In the literary field Pomerantsev has offered his critics an easy line of attack by failing to make it quite clear whether the writer's sincerity advocated by him as the highest standard would govern, say, a revival of Zoshchenko's auto-psychoanalysis or of Akhmatova's interest in religious mysticism.'

Now, whose definitions are these? Surely not those of any contemporary Soviet critic arguing against Pomerantsev's plea. I don't know where the term ' Zoshchenko's auto-psychoanalysis ' comes from, nor what it means. But the words ' Akhmatova's interest in religious mysticism ' come straight from Zhdanov's denunciation of the great poet in 1946. Why gratuitously revive this nonsensical accusation in 1954, at a time, that is, when Soviet critics and readers had begun to discard the vicious and mendacious Zhdanov jargon and to talk like human beings again?

Again, the reviewer in *Soviet Studies* of Andrey Olkhovsky's book, *Music Under the Soviets* (New York, 1955), wrote:

> ' In a socialist society the artist is regarded as a social being and treated as such. He has an earning capacity beyond one's dreams of avarice, but by the nature of his artistic ancestry [?] still needs to bolster up his artistic ego with the satisfaction of material success. This fact, together with the very close relationship existing between musicians in Moscow . . . tends towards a kind of artistic inbreeding and a consequent separation from the people. This can only lead to a reversion towards bourgeois principles which, whether we like it or not, have no validity in the USSR, where service to the people is the only criterion.'

Whatever meaning may be discerned in this curious passage is clearly a communist-oriented meaning, arguing the case of the Party against the artists.

To my mind, these passages (many more might have been quoted) illustrate an attitude unworthy of the critical scholar, and one which impedes the great rescue operation.

THE HAYTER REPORT and the financial support to the universities made by the University Grants Committee on its recommendations, have done much to place Russian studies in this country on a firmer and more permanent basis. Opinion varies among experts as to whether these measures have gone far enough. One of them called the Report ' a definite breakthrough ' and pointed to the development in Oxford University where five new appointments in non-language disciplines are due to be made shortly. They are concerned with Soviet economics, Russian history and geography, and a subject new in English university curricula—' international communism '. Similar advances are due, or have already taken place, in a number of the new universities, most of the posts going to non-language departments.

Others are less glowing in their appraisal of the Hayter Report. They point to the main weakness in the structure of Russian studies in this country, the lack of postgraduate students, and complain that the Hayter Report has failed to provide a proper remedy. The present State studentships are very few in number and financially inadequate. There is, according to these critics, a vicious circle as far as the development of Russian studies is concerned: there are not enough jobs at universities to induce young men to go in for the lean years of postgraduate work; and since there are not enough postgraduates, no new posts are being created.

The other main weakness, the traditional divorce between philology and history and cognate fields of study is being gradually overcome. The idea of comprehensive regional studies is gaining ground—not only in London where the facilities are unique owing to the co-existence of the well-endowed School of Slavonic and East European Studies and the London School of Economics; not only in the redbrick universities, but also in Oxford, where strict departmentalisation (either history *or* language) was the rule until fairly recently.

It is in this field that expansion of Russian teaching at secondary school level acquires its importance. Undergraduates with a solid groundwork in Russian attained before they reach the university waste less time at graduate level later on in learning the language, and are therefore able to span a wider field of study, taking in not only the non-language disciplines, but also literature.

A great many problems remain unsolved. The general impression is that at the top excellent work is being done by teachers and scholars; that things are improving at grass root level, but that there are dangerous weaknesses in the intervening area. All the teachers I spoke to complained bitterly about the shortage of post-graduate students, about the thinness of that *Nachwuchs* without which continuity of work in the academic field is impossible. Here urgent measures are required.

FRANCE

Basile Kerblay

R EADERS familiar with the abundance of English-language literature on the USSR are sometimes surprised that French authors occupy such an insignificant place in bibliographic references. Should this lacuna be attributed to a certain recession in the knowledge of the French language abroad, to the mediocre nature of some works, to delay in completing research, or more simply, to lack of interest in the Soviet Union on the part of the French?

The latter explanation would appear surprising indeed to anyone familiar with the attraction exerted on generations of Frenchmen by the Russians, from the Marquis de Custine's celebrated *Lettres*, written in the spirit of an eighteenth-century humanist visiting ' *la Barbarie* ', to the more substantial works of Melchoir de Vogué (*Le Roman Russe*, 1886) and A. Leroy-Beaulieu (*l'Empire des Tsars*, 1899). Bearing in mind, too, the contributions made to Slavonic studies by Frenchmen like A. Boyer, R. Labry, L. Leger, J. Legras, A. Mazon, L. Reau and others, one might be forgiven for thinking that the French should be better equipped than most to understand the new Russia which has emerged from the Revolution.

The October Revolution did not leave French public opinion unmoved. A large number of intellectuals, among them Victor Serge, Boris Souvarine [1] and Jacques Sadoul, were passionately involved in this heroic period. Each has left a record, often cruel but always moving, of his experiences. To such men, the USSR is either an article of faith or an impediment, rarely an object of study.

The wave of emigrés which during the twenties took the place of the old-regime exiles who had returned home included in its ranks an elite of philosophers, writers and artists such as Berdyaev, Bulgakov, Merezhkovsky, Diaghilev, Chaliapin, and Chagall. On French soil, they became heirs to great trends in Russian thought and art just when all independent cultural centres were being extinguished in the USSR. However, this generation of Russians was too preoccupied with events to take a sufficiently detached view of developments in the Soviet Union or to found any study centres of the sort which were established by some emigrés after the Second World War. Essays in this direction were rare but of exceptionally high quality. No one can forget Berdyaev's *Les sources et le sens du communisme russe* (1938), Vladimir Weidlé's *La Russie présente et absente* (1949), or N. S. Prokopovicz's *l'Histoire économique de l'URSS* (1952).

It was not until the end of the Second World War that research into

---

[1] Boris Souvarine's *Stalin* (Plon, 1935, new edition 1940, 677 pp.) is a penetrating study of the dictator's ideas and policies between 1917 and 1939.

the Soviet Union became organised. What lent it an initial impetus in the years 1945-50 was the upsurge of interest in the USSR that succeeded the Allied victory. Several study centres or groups came into being at this period. The Institut d'Etude de l'Economie soviétique brought out *Cahiers de l'économie soviétique* (1945–49); the Centre d'Etudes de l'URSS published a number of monographs, and the Centre Culturel de l'Association France-URSS sponsored a review entitled *Connaissance de l'URSS*. These ventures proved to be short-lived, and fortunately so, since the publications of this period were not only biased but of a generally mediocre standard. The only items worthy of note are the memoirs or personal accounts written by French diplomats and military personnel on assignment to the USSR (e.g. R. Coulondre, G. Catroux, General Guillaume and Admiral Peltier). See also textbooks published by the Marxist university teachers P. George and Ch. Bettelheim on Soviet geography and economics respectively.[2]

A second impetus, more productive and lasting than the first, stemmed from the discovery of post-Stalinist Russia. French tourists, government officials, and research workers were now able to visit Russia under the auspices of organised tours and missions. A group of post-graduate students of Russia, most of them trainee teachers, did a one-year course at Soviet universities. Thanks to these new classes of post-graduates, Russian studies are not so concentrated in Paris as they used to be, and professorial chairs have been founded at Clermont Ferrand, Dijon, Rennes, and Toulouse in addition to those that already existed at Aix, Bordeaux, Lille, and Lyons. Their youthful incumbents are quite as interested in the Russia of today as in that of yesterday. At the Law Faculty in Strasbourg, Professor Mouskhely has organised a study centre devoted to the USSR and the countries of the East which has, since 1960, been publishing a periodical with abstracts from the principal Soviet periodicals dealing with the social sciences, together with an annual review devoted to the Soviet Union and containing a digest of legal, economic, and political studies, mainly by Parisian authors.

In Paris, too, long-established nurseries for future experts such as the Sorbonne and the Ecole Nationale de Langues Orientales are redoubling their activities. In the latter establishment, on the initiative of Jean Train and with the participation of G. Blanc, M. Laran and G. Philippot, Soviet geography and history are in future to be objects of intensive instruction. On the research side, new centres are being organised and have started to yield results, notably the Centre d'Etudes sur l'URSS et les Pays slaves, attached to the Division des Aires culturelles of Department VI of the Ecole des Hautes Etudes (Sorbonne), directed by

[2] R. Coulondre, *de Staline à Hitler: souvenirs de deux ambassades 1936/1939* (1950); G. Catroux, *J'ai vu tomber le rideau de fer* (1952); General Guillaume, *Pourquoi l'armée rouge a vaincu* (1948, English edition 1949); Admiral Peltier, *Attaché naval à Moscou* (1953); P. George, *l'URSS, Haute Asie, Iran* (1947, since revised); Ch. Bettelheim, *La planification soviétique* (1945); *l'Economie soviétique* (1950, this work has not been revised and is now out of date).

F. Braudel, the USSR-China Department of the Centre d'Etudes des Relations internationales at the Fondation Nationale des Sciences politiques, directed by MM. Duroselle and Meyriat, and the Planned Economy Department of the Institut des Sciences économiques appliquées, directed by MM. Chambre and Perroux.[3]

THREE types of work can be distinguished in the flood of books on the USSR that has appeared in France in the past ten years: (i) books of an academic nature; (ii) books giving an account of journeys or missions to the USSR; and (iii) books less concerned with the USSR itself than framed within the context of philosophical or political reflections on Marxism or communism in general.

Numerically, the academic research category is dominated by studies devoted to the Soviet economy, in which pride of place goes to the works of Henri Chambre, director of studies at the Ecole des Hautes Etudes. These are focussed upon three main fields:

(a) Soviet theory and practice in economic regionalisation, which are analysed in the only work [4] on the subject in Western literature and in a series of exhaustive regional studies on the Kuzbas and Kazakhstan (in preparation);

(b) the various trends in Marxist thought ' de Karl Marx à Mao Tsé Toung' (an English translation is in preparation), which also covers the most recent controversies between Soviet economists [5];

(c) economic growth in the USSR and its principal factors (intellectual investment, foreign trade, etc.).

The young economists Jean M. Collette and Jean P. Saltiel, who work under the supervision of Henri Chambre, have provided excellent studies on the latter subject. An equally brilliant team is working under André Piatier's direction, also at the Ecole des Hautes Etudes. Their work concerns the basic concepts of Soviet economics (national income, capital), agricultural problems, and planning.[6] An extremely valuable study of economic history published by Eugène Zaleski (*La planification de la croissance en URSS et les fluctuations économiques 1918/1932*, 1962) is shortly to be supplemented by a second volume dealing with the period following the first Five-Year Plan. In the same category, though not by the same team, is the excellent little essay entitled *La Formation du*

3 This department's studies are published in Series G of *Cahiers de l'ISEA*. Cf. Bernard Cazes, *L'apport des Cahiers de l'ISEA à la soviétologie*, in *Cahiers du Monde russe et soviétique*, Nos. 1–2, 1963.
4 H. Chambre, *L'aménagement du Territoire en URSS* (1959); *Le Développement du bassin de Kuznetsk*, ISEA, Series G, No. 8, 1960.
5 ' Prix, Valeur et Rationalité économique ', in *l'URSS*, 1962.
6 J. M. Collette, *Le taux de croissance du Revenu soviétique*, ISEA, Series G, 1961; by the same author, *Recherche, Développement et progrès économique en URSS*, ISEA, Series G, 1962; J. P. Saltiel, *Le commerce extérieur de la France et de l'URSS, Problèmes de compétition*, ISEA, Series G, 1963; H. Wronski, *Le Trudoden* (1957); M. Lavigne, *Le Capital dans l'économie soviétique* (1962); Wronski's book is the most comprehensive study to date on methods of remuneration in the *kolkhozy*.

système soviétique de planification (1956), published by the Polish economist Czeslaw Bobrowski during his years of exile in France.

Although legal, literary, and historical studies have always, by tradition, been vigorously pursued in France, it must be conceded that the experts have not hitherto been greatly attracted by the Soviet period. While the works of Jacques Bellon, J. Yves Calvez, René David, Louis Greyfié de Bellecombe, and Michel Mouskhely all bear witness to the vitality of the French school of comparative law,[7] historical studies are, by contrast, extremely few and far between, and rarely amount to more than good popularisations.[8] In the literary field, only the Soviet poets have attracted attention, though studies of greater scope are in preparation. François de Liencourt's pieces on the sociology of the Soviet theatre[9] and Georges Nivat's essays on Alexis Tolstoy[10] hint at the probable quality of future publications. Also worthy of mention is the special number devoted by the French review *La Table Ronde* (June 1963) to intellectual life in the USSR (the articles by I. Esmein, G. Nivat, H. Zamoiska, and J. M. Collete merit special attention).

A special place must be accorded to French works on the Moslem peoples of the Soviet Union, since they are probably unrivalled by any other country. The driving force behind this research is Alexandre Bennigsen of the Ecole des Hautes Etudes, who has collaborated with Ch. Quelquejay-Lemercier in producing the first volume of a history of national movements among the Moslem peoples of Russia. A bibliography of the Moslem press in Russia is in preparation. Included in this group are studies by Chantal Quelquejay-Lemercier and Hélène Carrere d'Encausse.[11]

Mme Carrere d'Encausse also directs the USSR-China Department of the Centre d'Etudes des Relations internationales, which is currently engaged on an important history of Franco-Russian relations between 1917 and 1940 (to be published by A. Colin) under the supervision of J. B. Duroselle. Stuart Schram has already published one chapter

[7] J. Bellon, *Droit pénal soviétique et droit pénal occidental* (1961); J.-Y. Calvez, *Droit international et souveraineté en URSS* (1953); R. David, *Les données fondamentales du droit soviétique* (1954); L. Greyfié de Bellecombe, *Les conventions collectives de travail en Union soviétique* (1958); Mouskhely and Jedryka, *Le gouvernement de l'URSS* (1961).
[8] François Xavier Coquin, *La Révolution russe (1917–1918)* (1962); Nina Gourfinkel, *Lénine* (1959); Pierre Naville, *Trotsky vivant* (1962); Pierre and Irène Sorlin, *Lénine, Trotsky et Staline 1921–1927* (1961), a study of the Soviet and Western press of the period.
[9] Nina Berberova, *Alexandre Blok et son temps*; Claude Frioux, *Maiakovski par lui-même* (1961); Sophie Lafite, *Essenine* (1959), a selection of texts and portraits. François de Liencourt, ' Le théâtre, le pouvoir et le spectateur soviétique ', in *Cahiers du Monde russe et soviétique*, Nos. 2–3, 1961. Readers of *Survey* will recall ' Repertory of the Fifties ' by the same author (January 1963, No. 46).
[10] ' La genèse d'un roman historique: Pierre le Grand d'Alexis Tolstoi ', in *Cahiers du Monde russe et soviétique*, No. 1, 1961.
[11] A. Bennigsen and Ch.Quelquejay, *Le sultangalievisme au Tatarstan* (national movements among the Moslems of Russia) (1960); readers will recall Bennigsen's article ' The Moslem intelligentsia in the USSR ', in *Survey*, No. 28, April 1959; A. Bennigsen and H. Carrere d'Encausse, ' Le Daghestan ', in *Revue des Etudes islamiques*, 1955, No. 23.

of this work, 'Christian Rakovskij et le premier rapprochement franco-soviétique ',[12] based on research into hitherto unpublished archives and documents. Worthy of equal mention is Georges Haupt's work on the relationship between Lenin and Huysmans, produced in the course of research into the history of the Second and Third Internationals carried out at the Ecole des Hautes Etudes.[13]

In 1959, all this academic activity gave birth to a quarterly review published by the Division des Aires culturelles of the Ecole des Hautes Etudes and entitled *Cahiers du Monde russe et soviétique*. Its editorial board comprises most of the university staff whose names have just been quoted. Its originality as compared with other foreign reviews devoted to the USSR derives, as its name suggests, from its refusal to divorce the study of recent developments from that of the past history, not only of the Russian people but of the various races which make up the Soviet Union today. This also accounts for its very wide range of contributors. In addition, the review concentrates upon thematic bibliography and descriptions of archives. It publishes a bibliography of books and articles devoted to the USSR, which aims to become a French-language equivalent of *The American Bibliography of Russian and East European Studies*, edited by the University of Indiana.

OCCUPYING a position intermediate between travel books and research of an academic nature are studies or reports made as a result of missions to the USSR, works whose serious content rates comparison with the best academic publications. For instance, Jean Benard, Claude Gruson, and Simon Nora, Finance Ministry officials who had exchanged views with Gosplan economists in Moscow, published their conclusions in *Les méthodes actuelles de planification en URSS*.[14] This testified to a broad spirit of comprehension coupled with constructive criticism of the functioning of Soviet economic mechanisms since the establishment of the *sovnarkhozy*. Jean Bernard of the Commissariat au Plan français studied regional planning in the course of a study tour of the USSR, while Jean Chombart de Lauwe, professor of agronomy at Grignon and a leading expert on rural economy, returned from his two visits to the USSR full of the impressions of a man who is anxious to know what answer Soviet experience can supply to the problem of industrialising agriculture.[15] René Dumont, professor at the Institute of Agronomy in Paris, who had an opportunity of visiting some fifteen *kolkhozy* and *sovkhozy* in 1962, will very shortly be publishing the results of his inquiries in a book which will range over the whole structure of Soviet agriculture.

[12] *Cahiers du Monde russe et soviétique*, 1960, Nos. 2 and 4.
[13] ' La correspondance inédite de Lénine et Huysmans (1905–1914) ', *ibid*. 1962, No. 4, and 1963, Nos. 1–2.
[14] *Cahiers de l'ISEA*, Series G, No. 7, 1959, to be completed by Series G, No. 10, 1963; *Le receuil des données comptables pour l'établissement du plan septennal 1959/1965* (with an introduction by H. Chambre and B. Kerblay).
[15] Jean Chombart de Lauwe, *Les paysans soviétiques* (1961).

French pieces of reporting on the USSR—even the best of them, like those by M. Gordey—are far too topical to survive for long. However, testimony by political figures such as Jules Moch, Emmanuel d'Astier, or Héron de Villefosse preserves its historical value because we are as interested in the author's personal reflections as in what he can tell us about the country and the men he met there.[16]

Finally, it would be impossible to conclude this list of works without mentioning those which have made the reputation of certain French philosophers and sociologists, among them Raymond Aron (*Entretiens de Rheinfelden, Dix-huit leçons sur la société industrielle,* 1962, *La Paix et la Guerre entre les nations,* 1962); Merleau Ponty (*Humanisme et Terreur,* 1947, *Les aventures de la dialectique,* 1955, *Signes,* 1960); and, from the Marxist angle, Henri Lefebvre (*Les problèmes actuels du marxisme,* 1958). In these, the Soviet phenomenon is seen in the more general context of reflections on contemporary society, personal liberty or culture,[17] thus revealing how difficult it is to define the exact boundaries of the Soviet domain proper.

It only remains to attempt to assess all these studies by distinguishing the weak and strong points of the French contribution, a task which is not rendered easier by the fact that virtues and vices which are ascertainable in general terms are not necessarily to be found in each separate work under review.

W HAT will probably strike the foreign observer most forcibly about the list of inadequacies is the makeshift nature of French research and its obsolete equipment. Anyone who has worked in the Bibliothèque de Documentation internationale contemporaine, which boasts the largest collection of Soviet books and publications in Paris, will know the physical conditions under which these are kept. Lack of specialising bibliographers, insufficient funds, and administrative departmentalism all help to account for the dearth of coordination which has sometimes prevailed among various libraries in regard to purchasing policy. This is yet another manifestation of the traditional individualism which sometimes goes hand in hand with brilliant personal triumphs but is incompatible with team-work.

More serious than these traditions or material difficulties are the keen prejudices felt in some intellectual circles, prejudices which sometimes affect the orientation of research. In order to understand the situation, one has to remember that in France, perhaps more than elsewhere, everything that involves the Soviet Union acquires—due to the electoral importance of the French Communist Party—special significance in the realm of domestic politics. Some left-wing intellectuals, as Raymond Aron has

---

[16] Jules Moch, *URSS les yeux ouverts* (1956); Emmanuel d'Astier, *Sur Staline* (1963); Héron de Villefosse, *L'oeuf de Wyasma* (1962).

[17] The periodicals *Preuves* and *Contrat social* are associating themselves with this quest for a new form of humanism and, at the same time, encouraging critical appraisal of the communist world, past and present.

demonstrated, take refuge in the ' opium ' of radicalism out of a sense of impotence, while others (a widespread attitude among university teachers) are so anxious to appear objective that they refuse to regard the USSR as an object of serious study.

The political implications attributed, rightly or wrongly, to these studies bring in their train a number of consequences which are, in our view, unfortunate:

(a) the unwillingness or reluctance of some people to undertake or initiate research into the USSR if it covers the past thirty years—which partly accounts for the paucity of literary or historical works dealing with that period;

(b) the difficulty of recruiting homogeneous research teams and the risk of skirting the fringes of certain subjects by avoiding full discussion of them;

(c) the fact that, in the absence of a ' consensus ' of values, a work can be assessed only by its external criteria—a distortion which is not, unfortunately, peculiar to studies of the USSR but common to a large number of university projects. The reason why such a large proportion of ' erudite ' works induce boredom is that their quality has to be assessed by their formal guarantees, by whether or not the author has familiarised himself with the techniques of his special subject, by whether or not his bibliographic references are adequate. In short, erudition has stifled thought;

(d) that contact between university staff and those whose professions lead them to take an interest in the USSR (e.g., journalists, trade unionists, public servants, diplomats, business men, and technical experts) is far from as common or productive as it could be. Although the French government employs experts of the greatest merit, their names are not those that appear at the foot of articles. Disregarding a few exceptions,[18] such as Michel Tatu's remarkable reports in *Le Monde,* the public at large remains largely unenlightened by a sensation-hungry press.

In contrast to the narrowness of mediocre works, the qualities which in our opinion characterise the best French contributions to knowledge and understanding of the USSR are an extremely broad horizon coupled with the detachment needed in order to assess the development of one form of social order and define its relationship with another. To these authors, the USSR is a member of the great family of industrial societies which have, thanks to economic techniques and particular policies, accomplished rapid though extremely varied changes since leaving the stage of underdevelopment. In Raymond Aron's view, the prime task is to investigate the common rather than the distinguishing features of this evolution by reference to other industrial societies. François

---

[18] E.g. the special numbers devoted to the USSR by *Réalités, La Nef, La Table Ronde, Les Temps modernes,* and *Economie et Humanisme,* and the systematic work of *Documentation française,* which regularly publishes French translations of the major organs of the Soviet press.

Perroux [19] stresses the need to analyse the constituents of a 'generalised economy' of which the Soviet planned economy, like the capitalist, is only one application, while Chombart de Lauwe attempts to derive useful though mainly 'negative' lessons in regard to Western industrialisation of agriculture from the Russians' experience of agricultural difficulties. The danger of such generalisations lies in their occasional disregard of the history and special characteristics of Russian civilisation or the Soviet regime.

By contrast, knowledge of the past and an ability to relate it to the present invests the works of a French expert like Pierre Pascal with memorable profundity, especially when he seeks to analyse the various trends in Russian and Soviet thought or to present a picture of the history of the Russian peasant.[20] Similarly, by carefully stressing the interdependence of ideology and economic and social structures (see *Le marxisme en Union Soviétique*, 1955), Henri Chambre opened the doors to French research into that territory. The same determination not to separate Soviet studies from Russian studies and to enlist all forms of social science in acquiring a knowledge of the Soviet world has inspired the endeavours of *Cahiers du Monde russe et soviétique* since its inception.

TO anyone contemplating the future of Soviet studies in France, the prospects appear far more favourable than the number of works hitherto published would at first suggest. Not only are technical aids improving rapidly thanks to the impetus given by Clemens Heller, and by H. Lelièvre, of the Direction des Bibliothèques de France, towards co-ordinating the work of libraries and record offices (an important centre for research and bibliographic publications on Russia is currently being formed at the Maison des Sciences de l'Homme in Paris); but younger generations of teachers and research students whose traditional training has been supplemented by first-hand experience of the Soviet Union, thanks to grants enabling them to study there, will, in the years ahead, come to occupy an increasingly significant place in French education and French research. Let us hope that universities will fling wide their doors to them by creating, apart from the existing chairs of Russian language and literature, more chairs of history, economics, etc. This will enable Russian civilisation to be studied in the requisite depth, and ensure that the rigidity of university structure ceases to present an obstacle to the recruitment of first-class brains.

---

[19] François Perroux, *La coexistance pacifique*, 3 vols., 1960.
[20] 'Les grands courants de la pensée russe contemporaine 1855–1950 ', in *Cahiers du Monde russe et soviétique*, Jan.–Mar. 1962; 'Le paysan dans l'histoire russe ', in *Revue historique*, Jan.–Feb. 1934. Inspired by this, the author of the present article seeks to analyse, in the rural life of modern Russia, the surviving traces of traditional peasant culture and its transformation: B. Kerblay, 'L'évolution de l'alimentation rurale en Russie 1896–1960 ', in *Annales*, Sept.–Oct. 1962; *Les marchés paysans et Kolkhoziens en Russie* (to be published by Mouton); *L'évolution de l'isba russe au XIX°–XX° siècle* (in preparation).

Nevertheless, the foregoing requirements are not sufficient in themselves. Three other conditions strike us as indispensable if research into the Soviet Union is to yield fruitful results.

(i) *The USSR of today cannot be studied with the methods customarily applied to ancient civilisations.* Only living contact can capture the spirit of a country in the throes of rapid evolution. This is why meetings between Russian and Western experts, historians, economists, jurists, technicians, etc. (encounters which some conferences have already brought about), study tours, and opportunities to work in Russian institutes and libraries afford exceptional chances of augmenting our knowledge of the Soviet Union. We must hope that such facilities will be granted without discrimination against person or object of study and that there will be some relaxation in the regulations governing visits, travel, and access to archives by foreigners in the USSR, so that the reciprocal conditions envisaged in cultural agreements do not remain an empty figure of speech. The mutual understanding which is so desirable will never spring from mutual suspicion.

(ii) *Individual, piecemeal research is an anachronism in a world where team-work and international cooperation are meeting with growing success.* If we have omitted to speak of the lacunae in the French contribution to the study of the USSR it is because the areas to be prospected can be appreciated only in the general context of international research. This need for organised research and for an international division of labour is better understood in France today thanks to the work of various groups that have been set up there. In the sphere of documentation and bibliography, the current growth of coordination between German, American, British, French, and Italian libraries and institutes should soon result in joint publications.

(iii) *Study of the USSR does not constitute an isolated branch of learning, and can only be fructified by advances in the social sciences which sustain it.* Thus, it is principally in the fields in which French research has progressed furthest, via original methods and hypotheses, that we may expect developments of benefit to our subject. We shall confine ourselves here to pointing out a few of the major trends without claiming that our list is a comprehensive one.[21]

(a) In the domestic field, the advances recorded by French economic programming methods, together with the Russians' utilisation of certain Western econometric techniques, ought logically, in France, to encourage comparative study of planning problems and further the exchange of views that has already been initiated by both sides, even though

---

[21] One cannot, for instance, ignore the healthy state of religious studies, a field in which the French occupy a leading position. *Cf.* Maklakov, *L'Eglise orthodoxe et le pouvoir civil en URSS* (1946); Rouët de Journel, *Le monachisme russe* (1952); Nikita Struve, *Les Chrétiens en URSS* (1963); the oecumenical activities of the *Istina* Dominican centre in Paris, directed by Mgr Dumont; also Léon Leneman, *La Tragédie des Juifs en URSS* (1959).

ideological, that is to say, political factors entail that there must still be an appreciable gulf between basic concepts.

(b) In the field of historical research, the blows dealt at 'histoire événementielle' by the *Annales* school should produce equal repercussions in the Russian domain. The young French historians who are beginning to take an interest in the Soviet period should soon be turning out works of a high standard. They have a vast enough field to explore in this respect, including diplomatic archives, the Ministry of the Interior's files on emigrés, banks' records of movements in capital, and, last but not least, the French press, always a barometer of varying currents of opinion.

(c) In the field of sociology, French research into the USSR is orientated in two fundamental directions. The first concerns the sociology of Soviet art and literature and was prompted by the revival which the analysis of the relationship between ideology, culture, and society has occasioned in traditional literary studies. The second, inspired by the work of French Islamologists and Turcologists, is centred upon the culture and history of the Moslem peoples of the Soviet Union. There is no doubt that the systematic work which has been going on in these two fields for a number of years will soon bear fruit.

(d) In the field of international studies, the problem of the relations between the communist bloc and the underdeveloped countries is attracting more and more attention.[22]   France and the Soviet Union, whom geography has always kept apart, now find themselves in contact, if not in competition, in Africa. This implies that French students of the USSR will have to take more account of the curiosity about the Soviet 'model' shown by intellectual elites in the young independent States. Let us hope that their reflections on this subject will soon give birth to some original literature. In this way, new and still virgin territory could open up for French-speaking students of the USSR.

---

[22] *Cf.* J. B. Duroselle and Jean Meyriat, *Les nouveaux états dans les relations internationales* (1962), especially the chapter entitled 'Les nouveaux états faces aux modèles soviétiques et chinois'.

GERMANY

Jens Hacker

EASTERN European studies in Germany can look back on a decades-old tradition. Although they were sustained by professorial chairs and seminars at the Universities of Vienna and Berlin before the First World War, Breslau, Königsberg, and Leipzig emerged as the new centres in this field after 1918. The earlier school of *Osteuropa Forschung* concerned itself principally with the scientific investigation of the language, literature, and history of the East European peoples. Law and economics took second place, while other spheres of knowledge and activity received scarcely any systematic attention. For all that, Germany occupied a leading position in this field after the First World War. Not only were there a large number of excellently filled professorial chairs, but several important institutes performed exemplary work during this period and won great repute both at home and abroad. Valuable specialised periodicals also made an authoritative contribution to the international standing of German research on Eastern Europe.[1]

This fruitful phase was largely vitiated by the Hitler regime. Hitler's attitude, not only towards the Jews but towards Russia and the countries of Eastern Europe as well, coupled with his attempts to make *Ostkunde* serve his own political ends, imperilled the continued existence of objective German research into Eastern Europe. Some scholars emigrated, others had their activities curtailed or were removed from their posts, and still others abandoned research projects in favour of branches of learning less afflicted by the political pressures of the national-socialist regime. It is gratifying to note, however, that only a small number of specialists actively supported the totalitarian national-socialist ideology.

In the course of war-time and post-war developments, all the universities, institutes, and libraries which constituted centres of scientific East European research east of the Oder-Neisse line were lost. Research centres in the Soviet-occupied zone, too, largely ceased to function because, once again, their staff had to submit to the principle of scientific

---

[1] On the development of Eastern research in Germany up to 1945, cf. K. Mehnert, 'Abriss der slawistischen Osteuropa-Forschung in Deutschland seit 1945', in *Wissenschaftliche Beiträge zur Geschichte und Landeskunde Ostmitteleuropas* (Herder Institut, Marburg, No. 1, 1951); G. Stökl, 'Deutsche Ostforschung', in *Wort und Wahrheit—Monatsschrift für Religion und Kultur* (Freiburg), November 1957; W. Markert, 'Geschichte Osteuropas', in *Geschichte in Wissenschaft und Unterricht* (Stuttgart), No. 1, 1957; G. Kennert, 'Zur Lage der deutschen Osteuropa-Forschung', in *Osteuropa-Wirtschaft* (Stuttgart), No. 1, 1960. Useful material on the history of South-East European research can be found in: J. Matl, 'Die kulturellen Beziehungen zwischen dem deutschsprachigen Mitteleuropa und dem Südosten in der Gegenwart', in *Südosteuropa-Jahrbuch* (Munich), Vol. 4, 1960; id., 'Zukunftspläne der Südostarbeit', ibid. Vol. 6, 1962; F. Ronneberger, 'Vorschläge zur Einordnung der Südosteuropa-Forschung in die Aufbaupläne der deutschen Hochschulen', in *Südosteuropa-Studien* (Munich), Vol. 1, 1962.

partiality. The leading publishing houses specialising in East European literature, notably those at Königsberg and Leipzig, were either destroyed or seriously damaged, and all the specialised periodicals—with one exception—ceased publication. Many research centres and libraries at universities situated in the West sustained considerable damage from bombing raids or were depleted by evacuation, and many of the younger research workers were killed in the war.

Finally, in the years following 1945, East European studies ground to a complete standstill in Germany. It was not until five years later that they began to gather momentum again, this time confronted by the new problems posed by a radically changed domestic and international situation, and it was 1950 before full reconstruction could begin in earnest. A good decade having elapsed since then, it is now possible to summarise some of the experience gained in the interval and to form a few provisional conclusions.[2]

THE initial period of reconstruction was governed by the need to procure staff and material facilities. New institutes were founded, existing centres enlarged, professorial chairs and seminars established at universities. The *Deutsche Forschungsgemeinschaft* helped with reconstruction work, assisted libraries to expand their stocks, made grants for research and travel, and promoted scientific publications. Its contribution at this stage was vital. In addition, other German organisations and internationally active American promotional associations played an important part in the reconstruction and development of East European studies in Germany by making research facilities available, if only for a limited period in most cases.

The outcome of institutional reconstruction after the débâcle of 1945 may be summarised by saying that from 1950 onwards German research on Eastern Europe was largely pursued at research centres operating independently of the universities. This was because at this period staff problems tended to outweigh material considerations, and because the supervision and furtherance of scholarly activities came largely under the autonomous control of the various *Länder*. On the basis of library facilities, for instance, the brunt of the work should, from the outset, have devolved upon Munich, Kiel, and Marburg.[3] Despite this trend, however, the bulk of scholarly work is now carried out by institutes

---

2 In view of the limited space available, what follows is only a rough survey with no claim to completeness. It is confined solely to East European research and does not touch on educational problems. Sovietology is the only field to receive closer scrutiny. Bibliographic references are limited to publications which have won international recognition.

3 The Bavarian State Library in Munich owns the largest collection of East European literature in the Federal Republic, and currently houses more than 150,000 volumes. At Kiel the library of the University's Institute of World Economy has survived intact. The valuable ' Osteuropa-Sammlung ' of the former Prussian State Library, transferred from Berlin to Marburg (and now called the West German Library), has more than 100,000 volumes.

which either operate within the framework of universities or maintain close ties with them. It is incorrect to suggest, as some people do, that East European research in the Federal Republic has run riot. There are, admittedly, a multitude of institutes devoted to these questions, but they lay no claim to scientific method and thus have no connection with East European *research* in the Federal Republic.

A general review of teaching and research work at the universities reveals that, now as previously, eight specialists out of ten devote themselves to Slavonic languages and East European history, while other branches of learning—religion, philosophy, law, political science, economics, sociology, and the geographical study of national customs—claim the attention of only two out of ten. This unequal distribution of weight affords no grounds for self-satisfaction.

The adequacy of existing developments in *Ostforschung* extends only to the two 'classical' schools of Slavonic languages and literature and East European history. The first is currently represented by professorial chairs at all German universities, and several centres, e.g. Munich, Hamburg, Berlin, Tübingen, and Mainz, are staffed twice over. Chairs of East European history exist at fourteen universities, that is, at all except Freiburg, Heidelberg, Würzburg, and Saarbrücken. In contrast to the twenty-one chairs of Slavonic languages and literature and the fourteen devoted to East European history, there is only one chair of East European Law, Politics, and Sociology (Kiel), one chair of East European Law (Berlin), and two chairs of East European regional studies (Berlin and Tübingen), of which the one at Berlin has not been occupied since its foundation in 1956. To these must be added the chairs of East European economics and sociology and of South-East European economics and sociology founded at Munich in 1962. The work being done in other branches of study is of a very limited nature.

The main centres of research in Germany today are Berlin, Munich, and Kiel, although progress at Kiel has stopped short and great opportunities are being neglected. At all three places, Eastern European studies form an extension of the two 'classical' schools. The study of law in Eastern and South-East Europe is pursued at institutes in all three cities. Berlin, Kiel, and Munich also represent centres of economic and sociological research, while Munich occupies a prominent position in the field of economic geography and Kiel in that of geographical studies. One vital factor is that research centres in these cities have excellent libraries at their disposal. A new centre for East European research is now being established at Cologne.

ALTHOUGH it was not easy to co-ordinate the efforts of newly established scientific institutes, a useful division of labour was quickly evolved at the larger research centres. The Johann Gottfried Herder Institut of Marburg is responsible for East-Central Europe (the Baltic States, Poland, Czechoslovakia, and German territories in the East), while the Südost-Institut at Munich concentrates on the Danubian and Balkan States (Hungary, Rumania, and Yugoslavia). The principal concern of the two Osteuropa Institutes—at the Free University, Berlin, and in Munich—remains 'Eastern Europe proper'; i.e. Russia or the Soviet Union.[4] A glance at the research work carried out by all the centres under review discloses that regional emphasis rests, as it always has done, on Russia (and the Soviet Union) and on Germany's Eastern territories, whereas the East-Central and South-East European States, notably Poland and Czechoslovakia, together with other countries of the South-East European area, are not accorded the attention they merit. In recent times somewhat more intensive research has been undertaken only in the case of Poland.

Examination of scholarly achievements in individual fields produces very varied results. Slavonic studies are, by tradition, directed more towards language and literature, even today, than towards the history of ideas. Those who pursue them are confronted by the same problems that preoccupy other modern students of language: a crisis in philological methods on the one hand, and methodological controversy among students of literature on the other. Dimitry Tchizevsky has perceptively defined the chief task of Slavonic studies in Germany today as ' to reconcile the scientific theories currently espoused in the East and West and to combat the still prevalent " intuitive " approach to the Slav world, especially in so far as such an approach threatens to invade scholarly circles. Without a knowledge of modern trends in the study of language and literature we run the risk of losing contact with international scholarship and also with colleagues who are working on other aspects of modern philology. By failing to combat the widespread dilettantism that still exists, we could easily lose the ground which Slavonic studies have gained since the Second World War.'[5]

Quite apart from this, Slavonic studies have to contend with two external difficulties: lack of lecturers and lack of instructional works and text-books suitable for study at university level. While the dearth of qualified instructors in the Russian language is least marked, since it is by far the most commonly learnt Slav tongue, the shortage of teachers proficient in the Western and Southern Slav languages makes itself very keenly felt. Many universities have failed to establish enough lectureships in this field and frequently make do with teachers who perform their duties as a side-line. Not until these institutional prerequisites are fulfilled and more professional openings exist will language students take a livelier interest in the Western and Southern Slav tongues.

The situation in regard to text-books and manuals is absolutely grotesque. For instance, although a number of text-books devoted to

---

[4] Stökl. loc. cit. On the work of this and other individual institutes, cf. J. Hacker, ' Osteuropa-Forschung in der Bundesrepublik ', in the Supplement of the weekly *Das Parlament* (Hamburg), 14 September 1960.

[5] Dimitry Tchizevsky, ' Die Lage und die Aufgaben der Slavistik in der Bundesrepublik Deutschland ', in *Archiv für das Studium der neueren Sprachen und Literaturen* (Braunschweig), April 1963, p. 40.

Church Slavonic exist in West European languages, there is neither a proper German-language grammar of modern literary Russian nor a Russian historical grammar. The historical grammar published in the Soviet zone, a German translation from the Russian, is characterised by wholly false statements derived from Stalin's writings. The German histories of Russian literature written hitherto represent no more than a useful first step towards the production of a text-book proper. The position in regard to text-books for other Slavonic languages is even worse. German specialists appear to feel largely absolved from the need to create for themselves the tools of their trade by the publication of text-books in the various Slav countries—and that at a time when more and more universities are allowing students to take Russian as the first or second main subject in their examinations.

Since instruction in Russian has become widespread in secondary schools in the Federal Republic during the past few years and is to be placed on a substantially broader footing in the future, and since pupils are showing an increasing interest in learning Russian, the experts should also make it their business to write text-books suitable for use in schools. No one has yet compiled either a Russian grammar or a history of Russian literature on sound scholarly lines.[6]

BY contrast, the position in regard to East European history is considerably better. For a good decade now, Germany has boasted a school of research into East European history that is not only vigorous but diverse in its range and lines of inquiry. This is all the more important because in the Third Reich its terms of reference were politically coloured and consequently distorted, so that a radically new conception of its methods and objectives was required from the outset. What is noteworthy is not only the high degree of co-operation in this field, but also the fact that general historians regard it as a school in its own right.[7] Moreover, fruitful contacts with American specialists in East European history have been strengthened in recent years.[8]

This branch of research has focussed its attention on one central problem. Until a very short time ago, the whole of modern Western historical thinking was dominated by the conception of the Latin-Germanic family of peoples as the keystone of European and, indeed, world history. The obsolete notion that Eastern, East-Central, and Southern Europe are not integral parts of Europe proper has not yet been entirely dispelled. It goes hand in hand with the picture of history formed in the last century, which placed the entire East European area outside

6 Ibid. p. 48 et seq.
7 Thus, East European history did not constitute an independent section at the last *Historikertag* at Duisburg in 1962. Questions relating to East European history were incorporated in the general debates.
8 Cf. W. Kirchner, *Probleme amerikanischer Osteuropa Forschung*, a lecture delivered at Hamburg on 28 June 1963 and published by the Hamburg branch of the Deutsche Gesellschaft für Osteuropakunde.

the pale of European history. 'This is no accident, but a consequence
of the political configuration in the 19th century, when this picture of
history received its accepted shape at the hands of modern historical
study—a consequence, too, of the limitation of European history to the
Latin and Germanic peoples, which gained almost unquestioning
acceptance after Leopold von Ranke.'[9]

It will always be an astonishing fact that even perceptive historians of
wide interests—Dawson, Toynbee, and Freyer, to mention only a few
names from the immediate past—have either arbitrarily dismissed or
given only the scantiest attention to the historical evolution of peoples and
States on the eastern borders of the Latin-Germanic world.[10]

German research into East European history during recent years has
been expressly concerned with removing this historical misapprehension
and with contributing to the necessary revision of an outmoded conception of history.[11] It is certainly no accident, therefore, that a whole
series of German specialists in East European history are now devoting
themselves to historical transitions and border areas and are thereby
breaking new ground, often in the face of outdated national-cum-political
prejudices. Although the question of Europe's eastern frontiers looms in
the background, that question is here stated in a wholly responsible way
which avoids all over-simplification: ' Forms of government, political
structures, intellectual movements and social changes are regarded as an
indissoluble complex of causal factors. In their full acceptance of
Russian, Polish, and Baltic research, these studies are not only the foundation of a new scholarly dialogue but, despite the limitations of the
subject, important components in a future history of Eastern Europe
regarded as a special generating area of European history.'[12] In fact,
these studies are playing a special part in helping to fit the area into the
total picture of European history. If the history of Eastern Europe is
now—as opposed to the superseded view—becoming more and more a
part of world history in the contemporary mind, German research in
that province may count this as one of its prime achievements.

Among the most neglected aspects of German historical research is
Germany's Eastern policy during the First World War, under the Weimar
Republic, and in the years between 1933 and 1945. Nor have there been
more than a few special investigations of Russo-German (and German-
Polish) relations during the Weimar and National-Socialist periods.
German scholars have largely left it to their British and American
colleagues to examine the nature and extent of the National-Socialist
system of rule, and have so far recovered lost ground only in the realm

9 Cf. G. Stökl's instructive preface to Oskar Halecki's book *Grenzraum des Abend-
landes—Eine Geschichte Ostmitteleuropas* (Salzburg, 1958), p. 13.
10 H. Ludat, *Der europäische Osten in abendländischer und sowjetischer Sicht* (Cologne/
Braunsfeld, 1954), p. 9.
11 Ludat, op. cit.; Stökl, op. cit.; G. Stadtmüller, ' Geschichte Europas als Problem ', in
the Supplement of *Das Parlament*, 18 November 1959.
12 Markert, op. cit., p. 55.

of purely military history.[13] Now that such abundant documentary material relating to Hitler's Eastern policy has become available and been partially evaluated, this deficiency can be made good. So far, only one work of any magnitude has dealt with Russo-German relations in the post-war period.[14]

Surveying German publications on research into East European history, one is struck by the number of important monographs.[15] However, the road from specialised treatises to general works of universal interest must be paved by even better co-ordination. The only general surveys of import so far produced are those by Günther Stökl and Georg von Rauch.[16]

IT is regrettable that post-war research into East European history has had so little effect on the composition of history books for German schools. Examination of eighty-six books published since 1945 has revealed that none of the works under scrutiny gives a useful view of Russian history. They are, like their predecessors, overwhelmingly Westward-orientated, betraying the lingering influence of Ranke's picture of history.[17]

The remaining fields of German East European research which have hitherto lacked institutional support—East European economics and law—are easy enough to survey. Since both are represented by a comparatively small circle of specialists, excellent co-operation and careful division of labour have prevailed until now. For the moment, however, both schools are incapable of doing justice to their manifold tasks, namely, the continuous observation and analysis of economic and legal developments in the countries of the Eastern bloc.[18]

German research into East European economics concentrates principally on the Soviet economic system, its peculiarities, mode of operation, planning methods, and theoretical foundations. To a minor extent, attention is also paid to the economic development of the other countries in the Eastern bloc, mainly Poland and Czechoslovakia. Since the

[13] F. T. Epstein, ' Das " Dritte Reich " und die Sowjetunion 1939 bis 1944 ', in *Neue politische Literatur—Berichte über das internationale Schrifttum* (Villingen), No. 4, 1963; H.-A. Jacobsen, ' Zur Konzeption einer Geschichte des Zweiten Weltkrieges ', in the Supplement of *Das Parlament*, 26 September 1962.

[14] B. Meissner, *Russland, die Westmächte und Deutschland. Die sowjetische Deutschlandpolitik 1943–1953* (Hamburg, 1953).

[15] Among them: O. Anweiler, *Die Rätebewegungen in Russland 1905–1921* (Leiden, 1958); D. Geyer, *Lenin in der russischen Sozialdemokratie* (Cologne/Graz, 1962); P. Scheibert, *Von Bakunin zu Lenin—Geschichte der russischen revolutionären Ideologien 1840–1895*, Vol. I (Leiden, 1956).

[16] G. Stökl, *Russische Geschichte—Von den Anfängen bis zur Gegenwart* (Stuttgart, 1962); G. von Rauch, *Geschichte des bolschewistischen Russland* (Frankfurt, 1963) 2nd (revised) ed.

[17] H.-J. Torke, *Die russische Geschichte in den Lehrbüchern der Höheren Schulen der Bundesrepublik Deutschland* (Braunschweig, 1962).

[18] Kennert, op. cit., p. 135; G. Geilke, ' Inhalt und Aufgaben der Ostrechtskunde ', in *WGO—Die wichtigsten Gesetzgebungsakte in den Ländern Ost—, Südeuropas und in den ostasiatischen Volksdemokratien* (Hamburg), February 1961.

Soviet economic system has also been exerting an increasing hold on
East Germany in recent years, research into the East European economies has accordingly embraced this area as well.[19] A series of basic
studies on East European economic research has been published in
recent years.[20]

German research into East European law is unequivocally focussed
on the fields of constitutional and international law, with administrative
and criminal law taking second place. Too little attention has hitherto
been paid to the study of civil law, court procedures, labour laws,
kolkhoz law, international civil law, and foreign trade regulations.
Comparative analysis is equally deficient, the first question on the agenda
being to what extent Soviet law has to be adopted by other countries in
the Eastern bloc and how far autonomous legal development was and is
still possible in these States. It is worth noting that German students of
East European law have undertaken the first documentation of the
Warsaw Pact system and the first juristic analyses of the two major
organs of international law in the Eastern bloc.[21]

Many of the other fields of German research into Eastern Europe are
still on the threshold of development, though one must not overlook the
fact that a number of notable works have been published on the subject
of East European political science,[22] philosophy, and ideology.[23] The
most obviously neglected field is that of sociology, which few researchers
have troubled about hitherto.[24]

The superiority of American research is particularly noticeable in

---

[19] K. C. Thalheim, ' Das Osteuropa-Institut an der Freien Universität Berlin ', in
Osteuropa-Wirtschaft (Stuttgart), June 1959.

[20] W. Hofmann, *Die Arbeitsverfassung der Sowjetunion* (Berlin, 1956); E. Boettcher,
Die sowjetische Wirtschafts-politik am Scheidewege (Tübingen, 1959); P. Knirsch,
Die ökonomischen Anschauungen Nikolaj I. Bucharins (Berlin, 1959); O. Schiller,
Das Agrarsystem der Sowjetunion (Cologne/Graz, 1960); E. Klinkmüller and M. E.
Ruban, *Die wirtschaftliche Zusammenarbeit der Ostblockstaaten* (Berlin, 1960).

[21] B. Meissner, *Das Ostpakt-System* (Frankfurt, 1955); (ed. by the same author) *Der
Warschauer Pakt—Dokumentensammlung* (Cologne, 1962); A. Ushakov, *Der Rat für
gegenseitige Wirtschaftshilfe (Comecon)* (Cologne, 1962). Further standard works
include: R. Maurach, *Handbuch der Sowjetverfassung* (Munich, 1955); B. Meissner,
Die Sowjetunion, die baltischen Staaten und das Völkerrecht (Cologne, 1956); id.,
Sowjetunion und Selbstbestimmungsrecht (Cologne, 1962); H. Fiedler, *Der sowjetische
Neutralitätsbegriff in Theorie und Praxis* (Cologne, 1959); K. Westen, *Die rechts-
theoretischen und rechtspolitischen Ansichten Josef Stalins* (Lindau/Constance, 1959).

[22] B. Meissner, *Russland unter Chruschtschow* (Munich, 1960); id., *Das Parteiprogramm
der KPdSU* (Cologne, 1961); W. Leonhard, *Kreml ohne Stalin* (Cologne, 1959);
W. Grottian, *Lenins Anleitung zum Handeln—Theorie und Praxis sowjetischer
Aussenpolitik* (Cologne, 1962). Foremost among those who have dealt with the
communist world movement, hitherto a particularly neglected subject, is R. Lowenthal,
Chruschtschow und der Weltkommunismus (Stuttgart, 1963). Standard work on
Russo-Chinese relations: K. Mehnert, *Peking und Moskau* (Stuttgart), 1962.

[23] H.-J. Lieber, *Die Philosophie des Bolschewismus in den Grundzügen ihrer Entwicklung*
(Frankfurt, 1961), 3rd ed.; I. Fetscher, *Von Marx zur Sowjetideologie* (Frankfurt,
1960), 5th ed.; M. G. Lange, *Marxismus-Leninismus-Stalinismus* (Stuttgart, 1955);
K. Marko, *Sic et non. Kritisches Wörterbuch des sowjetrussischen Marxismus-
Leninismus der Gegenwart* (Wiesbaden, 1962).

[24] B. Meissner, *Russland im Umbruch* (Frankfurt, 1951). The well-known book by
Klaus Mehnert, *Der Sowjetmensch* (Stuttgart, 1958), also deals with important
sociological aspects.

the realm of Sovietology, a controversial and frequently abused term which requires precise definition. Hans Koch, who was the first to attempt to systematise Sovietology for the German-speaking area, defined '*Sowjetkunde*' as a universalist science from the formal and material aspect—formal because it is not a primary science but embraces and categorises several separate branches of knowledge—e.g. Soviet history, philosophy, law, economics, geography, sociology, and ideology—whose number is variable. From the material standpoint, therefore, Sovietology is universalist in character because the cognitional-theoretical basis of the phenomena which it handles lays claim to general validity.[25] This clear and convincing conceptual definition effectively shuts the door on all the pseudo-scientific, popularised works which gladly sail under the flag of ' Sovietology ' and help to discredit the young science.

Sovietology is primarily a topical science. Its institutionalisation in Germany is bound to run into difficulties, first, because German research into Eastern Europe has a traditional bias towards the study of language and history, and second, because it is not yet in a position, from the point of view of personnel, to take on the manifold tasks of Sovietology. For the moment, therefore, it must remain a highly controversial question whether this field of study should be institutionally welded on to the universities at all. Their conservatism, which was shown when chairs were being founded for ' non-classical ' branches of East European studies, will doubtless make itself felt even more strongly in this instance. There may also be a fear that universities will be courting the risk of ' politicisation ' if they establish professorial chairs for special branches of topical study.

Meanwhile, the first step toward institutionalising Sovietology has already been taken outside the university domain. It was primarily due to the initiative of Boris Meissner that the Bundesinstitut zur Erforschung des Marxismus-Leninismus (Institute of Sovietology) was founded at Cologne in April 1961. Thanks to generous financial assistance from the Federal government, the work of the Institute could be planned on a broad basis, and it has already become one of the major centres devoted to East European research. Its official task is to analyse the worldwide phenomenon of communism in all its variety of outward manifestations, and to investigate it from the standpoint of various branches of learning (history, philosophy, law, politics, sociology, economics, culture, etc.). The Institute's list of publications already includes a number of valuable studies, and more are in preparation. The main opportunities for Sovietological research in Germany lie in supplementing American research in that field—which concentrates more on political, sociological, and economic aspects—by means of historical, philosophical, and juristic analyses. This applies particularly to ' Eastern bloc research ', Sovietology's most important component.

[25] H. Koch, ' Sowjetkunde als Aufgabe ', in *Jahrbücher für Geschichte Osteuropas* (Munich), 1957.

THIS survey would be highly incomplete without some reference to three of the positive aspects of German research into Eastern Europe. No other Western country produces such a wealth of publications on this subject as the Federal Republic. Particular mention should here be made of scholarly journals, which play a most essential part in this field of research, though more in regard to Slavonic studies and East European history and law than to East European economics. These periodicals are, without exception, of a high standard.[26] In addition, a whole series of non-specialised regional journals make very frequent contributions. In the book field, however, many publications do not measure up to the required—and attainable—standard, and the number of really important monographs is still very limited. The list of well-edited compilations is equally small. Many collected works exhibit special weaknesses in that their lack of formal consistency often fails to do justice to their scientific pretensions.[27]

On the other hand, one must not overlook all the work that has been done in recent years in assembling and collating available material. Although it seemed at first, after 1945, as though lack of sources would permanently preclude the resumption of systematic research into Eastern Europe, examination of the library stocks still in existence disclosed that a substantial proportion of the literature on the subject had, in fact, survived. Not only were extensive collections built up, but considerable progress was made in compiling comprehensive catalogues.

Finally, reference must be made to the Deutsche Gesellschaft für Osteuropakunde. This body has performed a great service by co-ordinating the work of the various fields of East European study and setting up sections devoted to history, law, political science, economics and sociology, in which East European specialists can consult together. Research programmes are discussed and future projects aligned at the special sessions convened at longish intervals by the Association's various groups.

In conclusion, let us point out a few more shortcomings of a particularly glaring nature. This survey has shown that, despite all endeavours to the contrary, East European research in Germany still falls short of the stage of development warranted by the international situation and the changed status of East-Central Europe. It will depend primarily on the recruitment problem whether or not German research in this field proves equal to its manifold tasks in the future. Young qualified men will

[26] Principal among these are: *Jahrbücher für Geschichte Osteuropas* (Munich), quarterly; *Zeitschrift für Ostforschung—Länder und Völker im östlichen Mitteleuropa* (Marburg/Lahn), quarterly; *Forschungen zur osteuropäischen Geschichte*, being the publications of the Osteuropa-Institut and the Freie Universität, Berlin (Wiesbaden). In addition there are, of course, the well-known periodical *Osteuropa*, and its three offshoots.
[27] A few reputable exceptions: *Osteuropa-Handbuch*, ed. by W. Markert, Vol. I, *Jugoslawien* (Cologne, 1954); Vol. II, *Polen* (Cologne, 1959); also *Die Sowjetunion in Europa—Vorträge* (Papers of Münster University's Arbeitsgemeinschaft für Osteuropaforschung), (Wiesbaden, 1962).

only take an interest in East European studies if they are offered favour-able openings for professional advancement. Universities ought therefore to resolve to supplement professorial chairs and lectureships by the crea-tion of more assistant lectureships. Potential candidates for doctorates and diplomas ought also to be offered scholarships at the student stage to enable them to embark on a university career. The perseverance with which institutes have for years tried to establish permanent assistant posts should at last be rewarded. In the long run, it will be possible to employ assistants in research work only if sufficient pensionable posts of adequate status are created. Similarly, the advisability of creating research fellowships in the field of Sovietology—a domain in which the Americans have gained such valuable experience—should also be examined.

Exchanges of information between German and other Western specialists, particularly from the United States, should be more strongly encouraged. Moreover, German students should be afforded greater opportunities than heretofore to visit American research centres, some of which have at their disposal considerably more material than the German institutes, especially in the field of political science, economics, and sociology. Even though much has already been done by a number of German publishers to produce adequate translations of standard works resulting from Anglo-American research, these activities should be stepped up still further.

If German research into Eastern Europe is currently regarded as a fairly uninfluential branch of learning, this is not its own fault alone. The German press, in particular, has failed in its duty by giving too little prominence to the positive achievements of East European research in Germany. The requisite contact between the press and East European research groups, especially those devoted to Sovietology, is largely lacking. Similarly, the press ought to give far more prominence to works of East European research with a genuinely scholarly basis and draw a clear distinction between them and pseudo-scientific or popularised publications on the subject. There is also an absence in Germany of any effective mutual permeation of East European research and national policy. While the U.S. State Department and Britain's Foreign Office enlist the advice of East European experts on an extensive scale, precisely the opposite is observable in the Federal Republic. Indeed, it is regret-table how few experts on the East are employed within the framework of the West German foreign service; nor does the Bonn Foreign Office maintain any research department.

Lastly, it should also be stated that the resumption of East European research in Germany since 1950 has been subjected to a barrage of accusations from East European quarters. Ever since the Berlin crisis, attacks by Russian, Polish, and Czech journalists, based mainly on obscure effusions by East German propagandists, have increased. Their polemical style, which betrays private uncertainty, is obviously aimed at

evading a genuine scholarly debate on fundamental questions, and at
impairing the cultural relations between Germany and her Eastern neigh-
bours. Their intensity reveals, too, how much importance the Russian
communists attach to East European research in Germany. These mono-
tonously reiterated attacks, crude historical falsifications, distortions, and
misrepresentations, are part of Moscow's defamatory campaign against
the Federal Republic. Although ludicrous assertions of this type should
not exercise any effect on the future development of East European
research in Germany, it is clear that the propaganda offensive has not
been entirely ineffectual outside Germany. This makes it all the more
essential that German experts on Eastern Europe should produce a self-
portrait of this branch of teaching and research, and one which contains,
apart from the history and development of research in this field in
Germany, an objective and balanced account of the caesura symbolised
by the year 1945.

WESTERN MARXIST LITERATURE 1953-1963

George Lichtheim

A BRIEF survey of West European and American literature on Marxism during the past decade may usefully begin with an even briefer account of recent developments in what is sometimes described as Marxology. The relevant distinction is not always quite clear-cut, for the discovery of neglected source material may give rise to theoretical reinterpretations. The publication in 1932 of the so called *Paris Manuscripts* of 1844 is a case in point. In this case it took several decades before translation from German into other languages had familiarised West European and American readers with a hitherto unknown chapter in Marx's intellectual development. A more recent point concerns the publication in 1953 of a one-volume edition of the first draft of *Capital* (*Grundrisse der Kritik der politischen Oekonomie 1857-1858*, Dietz Verlag, Berlin, 1953; originally published in Moscow, 1939-41). This important work has not so far been translated into any other Western language, and only a few specialists have made use of it, notably Professor Wittfogel in his well-known study of Asiatic society (*Oriental Despotism*, Yale, 1957). Similarly it is too early as yet to express an opinion about the long-range usefulness of the edition of Marx's and Engels's works now nearing completion in East Germany (*Karl Marx-Friedrich Engels : Werke*, Dietz Verlag, Berlin). In any case East Germany, like the remainder of Eastern Europe, is not included in this survey.

West of what it is now perhaps no longer fashionable to describe as the Iron Curtain, the study of Marxism properly so called may be said to have been institutionalised in at least two important centres: the Amsterdam *Internationaal Instituut voor Sociale Geschiedenis* and the *Istituto Giangiacomo Feltrinelli* in Milan. Both have in recent years published original manuscripts, as well as historical and critical studies too numerous to mention. Feltrinelli's *Annali*, and the Amsterdam *International Review of Social History*, are now indispensable to the student of socialist history. Since 1961 their West German pendant, the *Archiv für Sozialgeschichte* in Hanover, has once more resumed the tradition of German Social-Democratic interest in the study of socialist origins in general, and Marxism in particular. With the SPD's official dissociation from its own past, this literature has come to wear an academic look, but a certain continuity of thought with the older Social-Democratic tradition is maintained in the publications of the *Archiv*, which for the rest are distinguished by the scholarly tone to be expected from an enterprise of this character. For the wider public there is the

eight-volume edition of Marx's writings and letters edited by Professor
Lieber for the great West German publishing house of Cotta in Stuttgart.
This combines solidity with elegance, but is plainly designed for the
general reader, and hence does not employ the customary scholarly
apparatus. The same might be said of the *Marxismusstudien* published
at irregular intervals, on behalf of the West German Evangelical Academy, by J. C. Mohr in Tübingen. These are collections of critical and
historical essays on various aspects of Marxism, from a predominantly
Christian-Socialist standpoint. They testify to the interest now taken in
the subject by German academics in general, and Protestant theologians
in particular, but are somewhat removed from the traditional hard-core
Marx studies based on textual analysis. With the *Tübinger Vorträge
über Marxismus und Sowjetstaat*—a series of lectures also published by
Mohr, under the auspices of Tübingen University—the work of this
school makes contact with the broad stream of 'Sovietology' not
specially devoted to the study of Marxian origins.

NOTHING remotely resembling this literature exists anywhere in the
English-speaking world. Outside Germany, Holland, and Switzerland
(where some interesting philosophical essays on Marxism have appeared),
systematic study is limited to France and Italy. In the latter country, in
addition to Feltrinelli's *Annali*, mention must be made of the *Istituto
Antonio Gramsci* in Rome, which continues the intellectual tradition of
one of the Italian Communist Party's founders in a spirit not always easy
to distinguish from outright 'revisionism'. Gramsci's complete works
have now been published by Einaudi. Their subversive character, notably
in the domain of philosophy, cannot fail to strike the orthodox Leninist
(not to mention the followers of Mao Tse-tung). Yet left-wing, as well
as right-wing, critics of the Italian Communist 'establishment' may find
spiritual nourishment in the writings of this gifted and original thinker
who never quite renounced his intellectual descent from Hegel and Croce.
Gramsci's notion that political hegemony (a term he preferred to
'dictatorship') is linked to theoretical superiority, and hence entails a
claim to leadership in all fields of culture, makes an evident appeal to
intellectuals in an environment where it is common form on the Left to
affirm that Marxism must be able to rival the Catholic church. There is
a link between Italian 'revisionism' and the Polish variant represented
by Kolakowski, but the theme cannot be pursued in this space.

   Work of this kind has no exact counterpart beyond the Alps, for
German Marxism is now a shadow of its former self. Its surviving
representatives are immersed in traditional philosophy, having abandoned politics in despair. Professor Bloch is a case in point. Since his
departure from East Germany, in 1961, this veteran exponent of a somewhat romanticised Hegelian Marxism has steadily retreated into traditional metaphysics (cf. Ernst Bloch, *Naturrecht und menschliche Würde*,
Frankfurt a.M., 1961; see also *Das Prinzip Hoffnung*, two vols., Frankfurt, 1959: Bloch's *magnum opus*, written during the war and originally

published during the 1950s in an East German edition which reflected the atmosphere of the Stalin era). For all his Marxism, Bloch is a very Germanic thinker: a learned epigone of the Romantics, with his roots in Goethe, Schelling, and the ' philosophy of nature '. Outside Germany this kind of thinking is hardly comprehensible. Bloch's current popularity in West Germany, like the interest in the young Marx, may be regarded as evidence that romanticism is still alive, at least in the universities; it clearly has little to offer the workers or the new technological intelligentsia. Significantly, this particular fashion accommodates itself quite well to the more traditional interest in Nietzsche, Kierkegaard, Heidegger, and the ' philosophy of existence '. Indeed, the best study of the young Marx and his philosophical origins has been written by a pupil of Jaspers: Heinrich Popitz (*Der Entfremdete Mensch: Zeitkritik und Geschichtsphilosophie des jungen Marx*, Basle, 1953). In these writings, Marx appears as the link between German Idealism (with its roots in Kant, Schiller, and Herder), and the ' realistic ' post-1848 age, when the industrial revolution had begun to impinge upon the older bourgeois society; in other words he is seen as a utopian reluctantly converted to positivism. His original aims having remained unfulfilled, it is now legitimate, in the eyes of his latter-day admirers, to revert to philosophy. Bloch's *Philosophische Grundfragen: Zur Ontologie des Noch-Nicht-Seins* (Frankfurt, 1961) is pure Heidegger, though refracted through the idiosyncratic prism of a mind not really attuned to the tedious business of logical analysis.

A more traditional (and more disciplined) form of Hegelian Marxism is represented by Theodor W. Adorno, whose *Aspekte der Hegelschen Philosophie* (Frankfurt, 1957) can be studied with profit, not least by readers initially confused by Georg Lukacs' writings on the same subject, which cannot enter into consideration here. For the rest, Adorno carries on his shoulders almost unaided the weight of the only Marxist tradition in unbroken contact with the pre-Hitler period: that of the Frankfurt *Institut für Sozialforschung*, whose main surviving representative he is (cf. his critical study of Husserl, *Zur Metakritik der Erkenntnistheorie*, Stuttgart, 1956; also his lectures on the sociology of music, *Einleitung in die Musiksoziologie*, Frankfurt, 1962). It is no great exaggeration to say that, with Professor Herbert Marcuse (whose *Reason and Revolution: Hegel and the Rise of Social Theory* saw a second edition in 1955), Adorno represents what is left of the philosophical Marxism of the Weimar period. Unlike Marcuse he has returned from the USA to Germany. Unlike Lukacs, who at one time in the early thirties could be reckoned as a member of the ' School of Frankfurt ', he has never made the slightest concession to Stalinism. The Frankfurt group has remained what it was in exile: the theoretical inspiration of what in Germany is now known as ' the homeless Left '. It may be more than a matter of passing interest that while its original members had to leave Germany in 1933 for ' racial ' as well as political reasons, its current following could easily pass any racial test—not to mention the group around the *Marxis-musstudien*, which is largely drawn from the Evangelical milieu. But this is a post-war development. Marxism has finally been acclimatised in West Germany, and even been accepted as part of the national tradition; in the process it has, however, ceased to be politically relevant.

TO cross the Rhine is to re-enter politics. France, like Italy, is a country where Marxism co-exists with an intellectually viable Catholicism, as well as with the official liberalism of Western society. All three elements are curiously combined in a recent enterprise of considerable distinction: the *Pléiade* edition of Marx edited by M. Maximilien Rubel, a noted exegete of Central European extraction. With an impressive combination of scholarship and elegance, this edition of the *Oeuvres* (*Bibliothèque de la Pléiade*, Paris) blandly ranges Marx among the classics of European literature. It also brings together two intellectual traditions hitherto regarded as mutually exclusive, for the Preface to vol. I (1963)—the only one issued so far, and containing inter alia the whole of the first volume of *Capital*—has been contributed by M. Francois Perroux, who may fairly be described as a left-wing Christian Democrat: his employment of the term ' socialisation ' clearly owes something to the 1961 Papal Encyclical, *Mater et Magistra*. The event was duly noted by M. Jean-Yves Calvez—best known for his massive study, *La Pensée de Karl Marx* (Paris, 1956)—in an appreciative review in the liberal daily *Le Monde*. M. Calvez, a critical student of Marx's philosophy, is a prominent Jesuit theologian with a solid knowledge of the German language. M. Rubel for his part can lay claim to being not only an outstanding Marx scholar (and, it should be added, an excellent translator and editor), but an orthodox Marxist, though several light-years removed from what is regarded as orthodoxy in Moscow. *His* Marx is not only the greatest of Socialists, but an authentic democrat as well, and moreover a philosopher in the central tradition of Western thought since the Renaissance: in his political philosophy indeed a direct descendant of Spinoza. Enshrined in the splendours of the *Pléiade* edition, these unconventional Social-Democratic and Christian-Socialist interpretations bring to the surface of French intellectual life a question which has long agitated its depths: what will ultimately become of Marxism in a predominantly Roman Catholic country? Or, to put it differently, how can Catholics with socialist sympathies, like MM. Calvez and Perroux, employ their recently gained freedom to promote ' socialisation '? How far indeed can they make use of Marx without falling into heresy?

Perhaps one ought not to expect an unambiguous reply to this delicate question. M. Perroux, in the Preface just mentioned, gets around the difficulty by expressing the hope that it may become possible to work for ' une socialisation humaine plénière, c'est-à-dire qui embrasse tous les hommes et soit propice à l'épanouissement de chacun '. Meanwhile one notes that he treats the USA and the USSR as polarised, yet parallel, examples of an industrial society wherein the producers are controlled by dominant minorities in actual possession of power—' masters and servants of the machine '. These systems have a similar structure, but different aims, and are thus rivals for global hegemony. General de Gaulle would doubtless agree; so (from a different viewpoint) might those left-wingers in France whose periodical literature has recently struck a judicious balance between traditional Trotskyist, and modish ' Chinese ', themes: for them too there is no basic difference between Western capitalism and Eastern state-ownership. (Where they depart from the ' revisionist ' or Christian-Socialist analysis, is in affirming that the Vatican and the Kremlin are about to conclude an alliance against the revolutionary proletariat.)

THESE clearly are political issues not in evidence some years ago, when virtually every French writer on Marxism introduced the subject with a lengthy analysis of ' human alienation '. (In M. Calvez' work, which inaugurated the fashion, some 560 out of a total 630 pages were devoted to various aspects of this theme.) Yet there is a link, for does the alienation of man not arise from the split of society into a minority of controllers and a majority of machine-minders? The crucial point here is that for the modern sociologist this dissociation is inherent not just in capitalism, but in industrial society as such. This is the point rammed home by M. Perroux, who challenges the Marxists to show how the power of the technocrats can be overcome. Can the workers in fact emancipate themselves, if emancipation is taken to signify the overcoming of those functional (class) differences which have their roots in the division of labour? The question has been asked before by liberals like M. Raymond Aron (*Dix-huit leçons sur la société industrielle*, Paris 1962); by ' New Left ' socialists like M. Kostas Axelos (*Marx—Penseur de la technique*, Paris, 1961); by former Leninists who are still orthodox Marxists, such as M. Henri Lefebvre (*Problèmes actuels du Marxisme*, Paris, 1958). It has now been given an additional twist by M. Perroux, for whom ' the power of the technicians ' negates ' the power of the proletariat ', the ' negation of this negation ' perhaps taking the form of the ' rise of a new political elite, neither exclusively proletarian nor exclusively technocratic '. This at least has the merit of posing the problem in concrete terms; readers of the recent English translation of Professor Stanislaw Ossowski's *Class Structure in the Social Consciousness* (London, 1963) will discover that this eminent Polish sociologist had by 1957 come to similar conclusions.

If there is a solution, we are for the present denied it. M. Lefebvre in 1958 (cf. supra) was content to register the crisis of Marxism produced by the Stalinist experience: not simply by the revelations about Stalin's personal rule (which did not really impinge upon the theoretical issue), but by the discovery that the Soviet Union had become a hierarchical society. This most distinguished of French Marxists—a far better interpreter of Marx than Sartre, whose recent writings he has subjected to trenchant criticism—is too honest to obscure the cleavage between Marx's original libertarian impulse, and the actual outcome of the revolution directed by Lenin. Yet for him this does not mean the end of Marxism, but rather ' renewed contact with the initial élan ' which drove the young Marx to inscribe the liberation of man upon his banner. ' This contradiction must be sharpened, not mollified, even if its acuity were to become more and more painful. . . .' The reader is reminded that Marx wanted total freedom, while at the same time, in the name of science, he demanded recognition of ' objective necessity '. The resulting tension must be affirmed, not denied. If the resolution of the conflict (which Marx had sought in history) cannot at present be realistically envisaged, that to Lefebvre is no reason for despair, or for relapse into the renunciation inherent in theology : the philosopher is called upon to struggle against ' every *alienation* which restricts the growing participation of the individual in the ensemble of powers possessed by man as a social being '. This conclusion restores both the spirit of the 1844 *Manuscripts* and the critical function of philosophy, which latter (contrary to Marx's optimistic prediction in the *Theses on Feuerbach*) is not ' overcome ' but preserved. In brief, the struggle is unending. The ageing Marx of the third volume of *Capital* had terminated his life-work on a similar resigned note, which to an adult socialist movement should perhaps be more appealing than the youthful romanticism of the 1844 *Manuscripts*. Though Lefebvre fails to say so, his own conclusions amount to a similar stoical determination to ' soldier on '.

Lefebvre is in a tradition which for good reason has no precise counterpart outside France : that of an 18th century rationalism which shades off imperceptibly into Marxism, via the ' socialist humanism ' of Marx's ' utopian ' predecessors. In reading him—as indeed in reading Sartre, whose highly idiosyncratic version of the dialectic he has subjected to polite but deadly criticism—one is reminded of the unbroken link between present-day French Marxists of all shades, and their 18th century ancestors. A periodical like *La Pensée : Revue du rationalisme moderne*, which for decades has tried to combine scientific positivism with Marxism, is hardly possible elsewhere. Yet Lefebvre, like Sartre and Merleau-Ponty, also represents the post-war wave of German-inspired existentialism and Hegelianism (cf. his *Le Matérialisme dialectique*, Paris, 1962). Since his break with the Communist Party he has increasingly turned to those aspects of philosophy which have a bearing upon the human situation as such. Here is a link with the young Marx, whose writings have been so important to the existentialist neo-Marxians in France and elsewhere. With Lefebvre the party lost the only major intellectual figure it possessed, outside the neo-positivist group around *La Pensée* whose old-fashioned rationalism no longer satisfies a generation which has imbibed German metaphysics. The party indeed can still point to a serious historian, Auguste Cornu, the author of a solidly constructed and heavily documented three-volume biography of Marx and Engels (Paris, 1955-62); but in the philosophical field it has had to content itself with the rigid Stalinist Roger Garaudy, whose *Dieu est mort :*

Etude sur Hegel (Paris, 1962) achieves the almost impossible by rendering dull and lifeless the fascinating subject of Hegel's philosophy of religion. Seven years after Jean Hyppolite had introduced the serious study of the subject in France (cf. *Etudes sur Marx et Hegel*, Paris, 1955), Garaudy's laborious compilation furnished proof that the French Communist Party's licensed philosopher had literally nothing to say that could not be found in any Soviet textbook. By comparison with this tedious performance, the Thomist critique of Hegel and Marx advanced by Georges M.-M. Cottier (*L'Athéisme du jeune Marx : ses origines hégéliennes*, Paris, 1959; cf. also the same author's *Du romantisme au Marxisme*, Paris, 1961) had at least the merit of raising the debate to its proper level.

THE major element in the French situation since 1945 has been the assimilation of German philosophy. With Sartre and Merleau-Ponty, whose ' revolutionary humanism ' represented the philosophical counterpart of their political fellow-travelling (terminated in Merleau-Ponty's case some years before his untimely death in 1961), this was primarily a matter of translating existentialism into political terms. With Jean Hyppolite and A. Kojève (who stems from an earlier phase), it was a matter of absorbing the Hegelian tradition. With Raymond Aron and Georges Gurvitch—whose *Dialectique et Sociologie* (Paris, 1962) performs the interesting feat of turning positivism into a critical weapon against both Hegel and Marx—one may say that liberalism and empiricism have at last recovered some of the intellectual relevance they lost in the 1930s. Among the minor figures, who strictly speaking represent Marx-scholarship rather than theorising *about* Marx, one may mention two post-war immigrants from Central Europe: Maximilien Rubel (cf. his *Karl Marx : essai de biographie intellectuelle*, Paris, 1957) and Lucien Goldmann; the latter a follower of Lukacs and the author of, among others, a collection of essays and polemics (*Recherches dialectiques*, Paris, 1959) which in some degree revive the tradition of Central European Marxism : both in their lively sense of continuity with the great age of German-Austrian theorising before 1933, and in their somewhat doctrinaire treatment of literary and metaphysical themes. One consequence of all this passionate involvement is that the French are now familiar with the intellectual background of Marxism and no longer surprised when a scholar like Gurvitch links the critique of Marx to that of Fichte and Hegel. Compared to the easy familiarity with this tradition which has remained the prerogative of the Germans (as witness the Tübingen *Marxismusstudien*), there is indeed something academic about all this learning; but from the confident manner in which it is being handled one gets the impression that the French have now become thoroughly European in their assumptions, and are no longer content to stay at home and rehash their own inherited concepts. Something like a fusion of French and German thinking has occurred at any rate in this sphere. When one remembers the pre-war ambiance it is no trifling matter that so many

French writers are now able to read German, and to meet philosophical challenges from across the Rhine on equal terms. Whatever else Marxism may have done or failed to do, it has changed the atmosphere and terminated the cosy self-sufficiency characteristic of Parisian intellectual life before the war. France is now, for the first time, a centre not only of Marxist studies, but of an important and original literature based on thorough assimilation of Hegelian and post-Hegelian philosophy. The somewhat inflated international reputation of Sartre (whose voluminous *Critique de la raison dialectique* (1961) cannot be considered in this space) is only the best known, and not necessarily the most significant, index to this situation.

NO mention has so far been made of economics, but here too the barriers have begun to fall. It is doubtless more than a coincidence that in the pre-1945 period France made no important contribution to either Keynesian or Marxian economics. The former has continued to be dominated by Anglo-American writers, with the French still trailing some way behind. But in the field of Marxian theorising there is now, for the first time, a major French contribution: M. Ernest Mandel's two-volume *Traité d'Economie Marxiste* (Paris, 1962): significantly, the work of a writer who, though domiciled in Belgium, has assimilated the whole corpus of German-Austrian and Anglo-American literature, and is thus equipped to meet the academic economists on equal terms. There is nothing very original about his exposition of doctrine from Marx to Hilferding, or about his treatment of the standard themes: capitalist development, crises, imperialism, planning, etc. But this massive work really does achieve what it sets out to do: it brings Marxist theory up to date, takes due account of the 'Keynesian revolution' (whose 'positive elements' are welcomed as 'a return to classical conceptions', even though Keynes' dependence on neo-classical marginalism is stressed), and sketches out a theory of socialist planning plainly inspired by the Western post-war literature on the subject. If the tone is somewhat doctrinaire, the spirit is scholarly and analytical. Soviet apologetics are rejected as a 'pragmatic transformation' of theory in the service of politics, and the official thesis that the economy of the USSR, with its reliance on monetary and commodity relations, represents socialism, is dismissed as a revision of Marxism. 'The apologetic character of these conceptions is manifest,' remarks the author (op. cit., vol. II, p. 427), with a side-glance at 'the persistence of social inequality and the alienation of labour': both evidence that the USSR has not—or at any rate not yet—emerged from the transitional stage anterior to socialism.

The practical relevance of these conclusions at the present time needs no stressing. While not specifically 'Trotskyist', this critique (plainly inspired by the tradition of the various Soviet anti-Stalin opposition groups) merges with the general stream of left-wing thought in France and Belgium, and it does so at a level of theorising which official communist publications cannot hope to match. There is here a parallel to the ' pro-Chinese ' current, but also to the pre-war literature of Austro-Marxism and left-wing socialism in general. It is noteworthy that this tradition, whose representatives once dominated the discussion in Central Europe, should now have found a refuge in France. Are Paris and Brussels becoming homes of lost causes? At any rate M. Mandel has shown that it is possible to write a major treatise on economics without departing either from Marxist fundamentals or from academic standards. His bibliography alone is a guide to the entire modern literature on the subject.

Economics being traditionally an Anglo-American speciality, one may ask why this kind of work has no counterpart in the English-speaking world. Perhaps the explanation has to do with the absence of a Marxist tradition not dependent on the Soviet Union. At any rate it is a fact that such economic theorising as has emerged in recent years (cf. Mr Paul Sweezy's *Theory of Capitalist Development,* London, 1949) is in the Leninist tradition. Professor Sweezy is of course a noted American scholar. Possibly the USA is not a suitable field for the growth of independent Marxist theorising. Britain has proved somewhat more fertile, but not much. Mr Strachey's post-war writings hardly qualified as Marxist theorising, though their author retained some elements of his earlier allegiance. Communist literature, as represented e.g. by Mr Maurice Dobb, remains heavily centred on the USSR, and almost totally uncritical. For the rest, independent Anglo-Marxism has produced one professional economist, Mr Ronald Meek (see his *Studies in the Labour Theory of Value,* London, 1956) and a number of historians, sociologists, and literary critics whom it would be invidious to single out for separate treatment, the more so since they are well known to the English-speaking public. Historians do not need to be told about Mr Christopher Hill or Mr Hobsbawm, while readers of the *New Left Review* are familiar with the neo-Marxist sociology and anthropology prominent in that journal. If a general remark is in order, it is to the effect that Britain has hitherto been spared the tedious disputations between Marxians and Freudians which for a while threatened to monopolise the attention of American socialist intellectuals. It has not, indeed, escaped the ravages of existentialism. Yet in this traditionalist country even left-wing socialists have for the most part remained true to the native empiricist tradition. For proof one need only consult Mr Gordon Leff's critique of Marxism in *The Tyranny of Concepts* (London, 1961).

No survey of Anglo-American literature on and around Marx is proposed in these concluding remarks. So far as official communist writing goes, the reason is simple: we are here concerned with Marxist theory, and one cannot discuss a non-existent subject. There are a number of communist writers in Britain, and a few in the United States, but none of them qualifies as a theorist in any meaningful sense of that much abused term. Neo-Marxism and the literature of the New Left, on the other hand, form a subject that calls for treatment which cannot be undertaken here. For different reasons it is not proposed to discuss at length a work such as Professor Robert Tucker's critical study, *Philosophy and Myth in Karl Marx* (Cambridge, 1961). This plainly is part of an American debate whose assumptions are not generally shared in Europe, and must be seen against its own national background. For the rest it may be described as an attempt to familiarise the American academic world with the philosophical origins of Marx, and specifically with the anthropology of the *Paris Manuscripts*. These, like the whole of German pre- and post-Hegelian philosophy, are considered by Professor Tucker from a standpoint which fuses Christian ethics and individualism in what may fairly be called a peculiarly American manner: a sort of intellectual counterpart to the late Mr Dulles's weekly sermon on the evils of communism. The originality of this performance has excited some concern among critics, not all of whom appear to share the author's conviction that German philosophy since Kant can be treated as a 'neurosis'; elsewhere it is likely to be regarded as a sign that a discussion with which Europeans have long been familiar has finally reached the other shore of the Atlantic.

Nor is America the only continent of European settlement to experience such visitations. Australia too has lately come into the picture, with an interesting and provocative study by a political scientist connected with the Australian National University, Dr Eugene Kamenka's *Ethical Foundations of Marxism* (London, 1962). Dr Kamenka, a young scholar of Russian extraction displaced to Australia (where he underwent the influence of Professor John Anderson), is an original writer and—unlike Professor Tucker—a critic of Marx who is yet in the central tradition of European thought. His book, which combines some traditional socialist themes with the philosophical concerns of the Andersonian school (perhaps best described as a kind of naturalism akin to that of Dewey), belongs to a libertarian tradition not far removed from anarchism. For the adherents of this school, Marx in some sense is not radical enough, notably in his failure to dispense altogether with the legacy of Hegel. At this point radical empiricism and anti-historicism seem to issue in a new idealism, for which the future is truly open and undetermined. There are, we are told, no historical laws, only free and unfree movements struggling for predominance. It may be questioned whether this libertarian socialism can make contact with the actual labour movement, failing which it runs the risk of turning into a new romanticism. But at this point our brief survey has to stop. Having circumnavigated the globe we are brought back to the sobering conclusion that the current dilemma of socialist theory looks pretty much the same from every geographical angle.

SOVIET PHILOSOPHY THROUGH WESTERN EYES

Eugene Kamenka

IN 1955, the theoretical and political journal of the Central Committee of the CPSU, *Kommunist*, turned its attention to the laziness and depravity of Soviet philosophers. Of the 1,000 or more graduate philosophers supposedly active in the Soviet Union, it said, only about 100 published with any degree of regularity; the remaining 900 preferred to rest on their laurels. 'Their philosophical swords are covered with rust . . . bleak " quotology " has become their stock in trade. . . . They are capable of making a deal with their conscience, they praise a book to the skies today and readily tear it to pieces tomorrow. . . . We must put an end to such depravity.' [1]

On this occasion, at least, *Kommunist* sounded sensible to Western philosophical ears. Soviet mathematics and physics have the highest reputation in the Western world; Soviet astronomy, chemistry, geology, geomorphology, and, to a lesser extent, certain areas of Soviet archaeological and historical studies, play a more modest but still distinguished role in the international progress of knowledge. Soviet philosophy has no such reputation and plays no such role. Soviet philosophers have not succeeded in gaining the respect, or even the interest, of their Western professional counterparts; their ' studies ' in dialectical materialism have so far made no significant contribution to the advance of philosophical knowledge or to the sharpening of philosophical issues. A technical, non-sociological history of serious philosophical thinking between 1900 and 1963 will contain no Soviet names.

Lenin, no doubt, occupies a somewhat special and more ambiguous position. He, like Marx, had a mind of the first order. Though his energies were bent largely upon practical issues and the struggle for power, though philosophy was to him only of incidental interest, the force of a first-class mind can be discerned through the frequent naïveté and dilettantism of his philosophical writings and notes. But the main twentieth-century developments in philosophy, especially those in the English-speaking world, have led to reformulations of the classical philosophical disputes that rob Lenin's insights of most of their immediate impact and relevance. When that able Oxford philosopher, the late Mr George Paul, devoted a serious professional article to Lenin's theory of perception, he was generally taken to have made a slightly odd foray into the jungles of pseudo-philosophy.

The possible ambiguity surrounding the position of Lenin does not extend to his Soviet disciples, even to the admittedly more ' professional '

---

[1] *Kommunist*, No. 5, 1955, p. 22.

and 'academic' teachers of philosophy in the Soviet Academy of Sciences
and the growing number of Soviet universities. The textbooks on Marxist
philosophy and dialectical materialism written by Marxists in the West—
by such men as the veteran Maurice Cornford—cite dutifully from the
sacred texts of Marx, Engels, Lenin, and (until recently) Stalin; rarely, if
ever, do they mention a professional Soviet philosopher by name. The
220 pages of John Lewis' *Marxism and the Open Mind* (1957) mention
precisely three Soviet philosophers [2] in one perfunctory paragraph
explaining Soviet views on ethics; their names do not reappear in the
index of authors referred to. The American compilation, *Philosophy for
the Future—The Quest of Modern Materialism* (1949), edited by the
materialist Roy Wood Sellars, V. J. McGill, and Marvin Farber, contains no single Soviet philosopher in its lengthy index of over 500 authors
cited by the contributors.

If Soviet philosophers have virtually no standing among dialectical
materialists outside the Soviet Union (including the far abler philosophers
of Poland), and among serious Western writers sympathetic to Marx
and materialism, they have even less standing among those working
within the main trends of modern philosophical thought. The English
journal *Philosophy*, which publishes regular 'philosophical surveys' of
contemporary philosophy of other countries, contained no reference to
any Soviet philosophers or to Soviet philosophy as such from the year
1944, when it published a propagandist address forwarded to it by the
Soviet Ambassador in London, until 1963, when it published my article
on 'Philosophy in the Soviet Union'. The general reaction of a Western
professional philosopher asked to read a Soviet production *as philosophy*
finds excellent expression in these comments by the Scottish philosopher
C. A. Campbell on I. I. Osmakov's article 'On the Logic of Thinking
and the Science of Logic':

> With every desire to be just, and making every allowance [for Camp-
> bell's lack of Russian and the fact that Osmakov is addressing a
> Soviet audience that shares his assumptions] . . . it must be remarked
> that Osmakov's use of language falls very far short of the standard
> of precision now demanded of Western philosophers. Russian philo-
> sophy has been virtually untouched by twentieth century trends
> outside their borders and it is clear that the influence of the analytical
> philosophers from Moore and Russell onwards, so powerful in the
> West, has had little or no effect upon the linguistic practices of
> philosophers in the Soviet Union. . . .
>   It is perhaps unnecessary to say of Osmakov's article that, if
> considered as a contribution to a philosophical understanding of the
> nature of Logic, it is without serious significance. The theory he
> propounds is arrived at, and defended, not on the basis of a thorough
> analysis of Logic's subject-matter (the forms of valid argument, or
> of reasoned discourse), but as a deduction from the general Marxist-

---

[2] A. F. Shishkin, mentioned only as author of a note on the decay of Anglo-American
ethics, and Rosental and Yudin as authors of the *Short Philosophical Dictionary*

Leninist philosophy. . . . The real significance of Osmakov's article is, for Western readers, ' sociological '.[3]

THE admirers of the Soviet Union who contributed much of the Western writing on the USSR between the two world wars and for some years after, were generally neither particularly interested nor even remotely competent in the field of philosophy; those who were interested and competent, like Sidney Hook and Max Eastman, seem to have found adulation of Soviet progress and Soviet thought considerably more difficult. Most of the admirers, to be sure, were also writing in the long ' philosophically null ' period that settled upon the Soviet Union between 1931 and 1948. The *Twelve Studies in Soviet Russia* edited for the New Fabian Research Bureau by Margaret Cole in 1933 contained studies on the economy, on finance, on power and industrial development, the Russian worker, agriculture, the political system, the legal system, women and children, architecture and town planning, radio, press and publishing, archaeology, on the intellectual worker (written, of course, by Naomi Mitchison), and on the film. There was no reference to philosophy. Beatrice and Sidney Webb, in the 973 pages of their *Soviet Communism: A New Civilisation* (1935 and subsequent revisions), turned serious attention to philosophy once (and then in a footnote):

> There is, similarly, no formal teaching of philosophy, and (except in the Communist Academy for the higher education of Party members and then only for the purpose of refuting criticisms of Marxism) next to no exposition or criticism of the works on philosophy, theology or metaphysics, by either mediaeval or modern authors. There is, in fact, a positive discouragement of any purely ' bookish ' culture. We do not presume to estimate how much may not be lost by this all-pervading ' positivism '.[4]

In 1946, it is true, Dr John Somerville, now Professor of Philosophy in Hunter College of the City University of New York, published his *Soviet Philosophy—A Study of Theory and Practice* and boasted in the Preface of ' the vast importance of the subject, both in the practical terms of international relations, and the scholarly terms of exploration at the foundations of a new culture.' The book received a preposterously enthusiastic, if brief, review in the journal *Philosophy of Science* and became the occasion for an interchange between Somerville and Sidney Hook which Somerville ended by a complaint of academic impropriety against *The Nation*: in retrospect, one can only say that the book seems just as disgraceful (as the first English study of Soviet philosophy) now as it seemed to Sidney Hook then. Claiming to be an exposition and not a

[3] C. A. Campbell, ' The Soviet Concept of Logic ', in *Soviet Studies*, vol. 3 (1951–52), pp. 279, 285, 286. Osmakov's article, on which Campbell's is a solicited commentary, was published in *Voprosy Filosofii*, No. 3 (March), 1950.

[4] Sidney and Beatrice Webb, *op. cit.*, 3rd ed., p. 745, note. Their index, which contains the delightful entry ' torture, physical, not used ', might have said so with more accuracy about academic philosophy.

criticism, it quickly degenerates into unintelligent and adulatory propaganda. Unintentionally no doubt, the book must have proved to many Western philosophers that Soviet philosophy and its admirers were just as bad as Western philosophers had always thought. For the main view, both among Western philosophers not especially interested in the Soviet Union and among the serious experts studying Soviet culture as a whole, remained that which we still find being put in 1960 in the careful and competent volume on the USSR published in the *Survey of World Culture:*

> ... the study of philosophy in the USSR is probably more stultified than any other branch of learning. . . . The Institute of Philosophy of the Soviet Academy of Sciences is made up largely of *diamatchiki* (purveyors of dialectical materialism), while the journal *Voprosy Filosofii* (Questions of Philosophy) is given over largely to such non-philosophical questions as the existence of vegetation on Mars or ' Military Questions in the Works of N. G. Chernyshevski '.

While conceding that the study of foreign, non-Marxist philosophy, even if only for purposes for refutation, has recently been promoted in the Soviet Union, the authors conclude:

> Up to the present, however, it can be said that theoretical physicists and mathematicians in the USSR have come nearer to making philosophical contributions than have the ' philosophers ' themselves.[5]

At the XIIth International Congress of Philosophy in Venice in 1958, and at the XIIIth Congress in Mexico in 1963, the delegation of Soviet philosophers said and did nothing whatever that might help to invalidate these conclusions.

THE post-war development of Russian and ' Sovietological ' studies, coupled with the revival of academic interest in Marxian and Marxist thought, and the undoubted expansion of comparatively serious philosophical work in the USSR since 1948, has nevertheless produced a growing number of dissenting voices, even among serious and able Western philosophers. The University of Glasgow has formed an institute for Soviet studies and has published, since 1949, the serious academic journal *Soviet Studies,* which includes Soviet philosophy in its purview; the Russian study projects at Columbia and Harvard have produced a number of first-rate volumes bearing directly or indirectly on the study of Soviet philosophy; the Free University in Berlin and the Evangelical Academy at Tübingen have promoted serious studies in Marxism and Soviet thought; in most universities of the free world a resultant quickening of interest in such studies has taken place. Professor I. M. Bochenski, Professor of the History of Contemporary Philosophy in the University of Fribourg in Switzerland, has focused the attention of his Institute of East European Studies on the sustained and systematic

5 *USSR: Its People, Its Society, Its Culture,* Thomas Fitzsimmons, Peter Malof, John C. Fiske and staff (New Haven, 1960), pp. 161–62.

examination of philosophical thinking in the communist world; the journal *Studies in Soviet Thought* and the *Sovietica* series of books published by his institute since 1958 make up the largest corpus of Western work in the field. Not unnaturally, the men engaged in these enterprises have gradually become more and more convinced of the significance of Soviet philosophy, *even as philosophy*. Dr George L. Kline published in 1952 his *Spinoza in Soviet Philosophy*, a translation of seven essays on Spinoza by Soviet philosophers, with a lengthy and detailed introduction; the Jesuit Professor Gustav A. Wetter issued in the same year the extensively revised German version of his monumental study of Soviet philosophy (translated into English in 1958 as *Dialectical Materialism: A Historical and Systematic Survey of Philosophy in the Soviet Union*), in which Soviet philosophy is treated as a vulnerable but significant system confronting neo-Thomism. Professor Bochenski, whose smaller book *Diamat* had appeared in German in 1950, wrote in 1959 [6]:

> Since A. A. Zhdanov's intervention on 24 June 1947, Soviet philosophy has undergone a remarkable development. A period justifiably called ' silent ', which began with the condemnation of A. M. Deborin on 31 January 1931, and came to an end only through the above-mentioned intervention, was followed by expansion, both quantitative and qualitative. First, far more philosophical writing has appeared since then; second, Soviet philosophy has once again become the battleground of different tendencies, and genuine philosophical investigations have come more and more to relieve the hitherto massive quotology. Some of these works are not without interest even for philosophers in the free world—especially those of them who, like the publisher of this series [Bochenski], share with Soviet philosophy objectivism, epistomological realism, the recognition of ontology and formal logic, and a belief in the integrity of the concept of man. But even philosophers who think otherwise will find themselves able to take a growing interest in Soviet philosophy in its onward development.

It is true that Professor H. B. Acton, in his careful study of Marxist philosophy from the standpoint of what Continentals would call ' English empiricism ', concluded that Marxism ' is a philosophical farrago ' [7]; but the Cambridge philosopher of science, Mr Gerd Buchdahl, reviewing the excellent book *Einstein und die Sowjetphilosophie* by Professor Bochenski's colleague, Dr S. Müller-Markus, ended on a more hopeful note:

> It is a sobering experience to find many of the usual problems of Western philosophy of science coming up one by one, though transformed and remodelled in order to bring them into line with the ceremonial ruling language of the day. Is it too much to hope that this most serious of impediments (the ceremonial)—so contrary to the

---

[6] *Bibliographie der sowjetischen Philosophie*, I (Dordrecht, 1959), p. 1 (Vorwort).
[7] H. B. Acton, *Illusion of the Epoch* (London, 1955), p. 271.

avowed spirit of the whole thing, with its proclaimed opposition to clericalism!—may not one day give way to a more self-conscious awareness of the true meaning of intellectual adventure, and thus lead to the much hoped-for rapprochement between the intellectuals of East and West? [8]

THE study of Soviet philosophy, like the study of the philosophical controversies that have surrounded extra-sensory perception, requires an unlimited capacity for not being bored. The group associated with Professor Bochenski, which places the greatest emphasis on the careful and detailed scrutiny of all the available original sources, and often acts as though it were compiling a comprehensive card index of all Soviet philosophers, displays this capacity in the highest degree. Associated with it is an incredible overvaluation of the philosophical importance and interest of purely methodological and quantitative phenomena (such as bibliographies, number of writers and number of words written) which simply could not move into the forefront of consciousness in men grappling with genuinely exciting philosophical material.[9] The growth of formal logic in the Soviet Union, for instance, is illustrated not by the exciting ideas that Soviet philosophers have produced on the subject, but by the number of books and articles devoted to it. The 'achievements' for which Soviet philosophers are praised are achievements that have become commonplaces in competent Western philosophical thought.

Part of the trouble seems a certain blurring of aims, as noticeable in Professor Kline's *Spinoza in Soviet Philosophy* as it is in most of the contributions to *Studies in Soviet Thought*, and absent from such intellectually more interesting studies as Professor Marcuse's *Soviet Marxism*. The Sovietologists who have trained their lenses on Soviet philosophy have done so initially, and quite properly, as part of a wider interest in Russian or communist culture, or both. Their enquiries are partly

---

8 *Soviet Studies*, vol. 13 (1961–62), p. 446.
9 Consider, e.g., the paragraph with which Dr T. Blakeley opens his article, ' A Bibliography of Soviet Philosophy ' (*Studies in Soviet Thought*, vol. 1, p. 12): ' The revivification which brought Soviet philosophy out of its pre-1947 " quiet " period was marked by a very significant increase in both the quantity and quality of Soviet philosophic literature. It would have been only natural [*sic!*] that this renaissance be accompanied by, and recorded in, bibliographies which would aid researchers to avoid repetition and duplication of effort. Contrary to all expectations, Soviet philosophers, who form a school which is one of the few in contemporary philosophy which is " scientific " in this respect, have failed to produce a bibliography which would reflect the development since the " discussion " of 1947.' Dr Kline approaches his infinitely more interesting subject in a significantly similar, if less obviously philistine, way. By the second sentence, his Introduction to *Spinoza in Soviet Philosophy* has focused on considerations of *quantity*: ' In the period from 1917 to 1938, 55,200 copies of Spinoza's works were published in the Soviet Union . . . [in the past thirty years] Nine books on Spinoza have been published, totalling some thousand pages; forty-six articles in philosophical and literary journals, totalling over 600 pages; nineteen chapters or sections of books (histories of philosophy, collections of philosophical essays, etc.) totalling about 450 pages.' Would anyone, surveying the philosophical achievements of any country, count the number of pages published unless he believed that the achievements were to be judged on standards not even applicable to countries like Ghana and Malaya?

sociological and partly ideological; the 'philosophical' productions they find most interesting are those which mark a reversal in attitude, a new approach, or those dealing with a hitherto neglected field of study. Because a significant number of these shifts in Soviet philosophy in recent years have been in the direction of establishing the preconditions of better philosophy in a non-Marxist sense, there is a temptation illegitimately to transfer the interest that these shifts have in terms of the study of Soviet ideology to their (almost without exception negligible) significance for the study of philosophy in general. If Western philosophers are to be persuaded of the *philosophical* importance of Soviet work, they will have to be persuaded not by such journals as *Studies in Soviet Thought*, but by the actual translation of the best Soviet articles in such books as Kline's and in the new journal of translations, *Soviet Studies in Philosophy*, issued by the International Arts and Sciences Press of New York under the editorship of Professor Somerville since the summer of 1962. The most interesting of these contributions, so far, alas, is the article 'Philosophy and Science' which Professor A. J. Ayer of Oxford contributed to *Voprosy Filosofii* (January 1962), and even the simplicity of its argument will disappoint his Western admirers while no doubt indicating quite accurately the level of audience he took himself to be addressing.

ALL this is not to deny that there have been considerable improvements in the standards and attitudes of academic philosophers in the Soviet Union, and that the 'Sovietologists' have done useful if modest work in drawing these improvements to the attention of a wider public in the West. Fundamentally, these improvements are to be explained, assessed, and made part of the premises for prediction not in philosophic terms, but in the context of political, economic, and sociological studies of the USSR. The current story of Soviet philosophy finds its natural place in the sociology of knowledge, in which philosophers—such as myself—may take an interest; it does not yet form part of the infinitely more valuable and restricted story of philosophy proper.

The prospects of dialogue between any two nations or even two schools in the field of philosophy are never easy to assess: philosophical gulfs yawn even more deeply than political gulfs, 'existentialists' and Oxford analysts, neo-Kantians and logical positivists, Hegelians and British empiricists, have often felt that they lack even a common language in which to dispute. Hume had no impact on philosophy in Great Britain throughout the first half of the nineteenth century, while Germans regarded him as a great philosopher because he had woken Kant from his dogmatic slumbers. The professionalisation of philosophy and the phenomenon of ever-increasing specialisation have, no doubt, resulted in philosophers finding inspiration from far smaller men than Leibniz, Spinoza, Descartes, Hume, and Kant, but there is as yet on the horizon no Soviet philosopher who could conceivably excite interest and admiration in a foreign land. The dialogue between Western and Soviet philosophers can only begin when Soviet philosophers acquire something of the integrity and sophistication of genuine philosophical argument either from the West, or from a future generation of Soviet philosophers that has progressed far beyond present standards. At present, as the imprisoned Soviet mathematician A. Yesenin-Volpin notes in the philosophical manuscript he smuggled to the West, ' every student in Russia who has arrived at philosophical scepticism by his own thinking can consider himself a new Columbus. (Actually, Columbus was not a great man.) ' [10] That these considerations do not apply equally to the perimeters of philosophy, where Soviet philosophers are parasitic upon the knowledge or achievements of Soviet scientists, is only another indication of the lack of independent force and achievement in Soviet philosophical thinking itself.

[10] A. Yesenin-Volpin, *A Leaf of Spring* (London, 1961), p. 171.

WESTERN WRITING ON SOVIET LITERATURE

Gleb Struve

WHETHER there is such a thing as Soviet literature (in the sense of Soviet Russian or Soviet Ukrainian literature, etc., as distinct from all the multinational literatures of the Soviet Union in their totality), or whether one should rather speak of the Soviet period in the history of each of those national literatures, a period which has many specific characteristics of its own, is a controversial matter which need not be discussed here. What follows is based on the acceptance of this widely used conventional term and on its application to Russian-language literature produced in the Soviet Union.

Like some other branches of Sovietology, the study of Soviet literature does not have a very long history. There was little general interest in it shown before the second world war, when the Soviet Union, a land of mystery or a potential source of subversion to most ordinary people in the West, suddenly became a co-belligerent or even an ally. But, though it did not attract widespread interest, the study of Soviet literature had begun, of course, much earlier. The first attempt to present a more or less unified general picture of literary developments in Russia since the Bolshevik Revolution (the division of Russian literature, after 1920, into two branches—one inside the country, the other in self-imposed exile—was a fact which had, and has, to be borne in mind, but the emigré literature attracted even less attention in the outside world), was made in 1933, when Marc Slonim and George Reavey published their book *Soviet Literature: An Anthology* (American and French editions appeared later). As the subtitle indicates, the book was designed primarily as an anthology of representative writings of the Soviet period (though some untypical works by such pre-Soviet writers as Andrey Bely and Gumilev were included in it), but it contained also a general introduction by Marc Slonim, recording the main developments in Soviet literature through 1932.

By that time there existed also a considerable body of translations of Soviet fiction into Western languages, both in anthologies and as books by individual authors. The work of several writers who had almost immediately attracted the attention of the outside world—such as Pilnyak, Babel, Sholokhov, Gladkov (not to speak of Alexander Blok's poem 'The Twelve')—was thus made available to non-Russian readers; but upon a closer examination of what was being translated in those days one cannot help seeing how arbitrary and haphazard the selection was. To cite but a couple of striking examples: such an interesting work as Konstantin Fedin's *Goroda i gody* (Cities and Years), which was also an important landmark in the development of the Soviet novel, was not translated into English until 1962 (it is true that French and Spanish versions of it had appeared much earlier); nor was Leonov's *Barsuki* (The Badgers), another book that marked the emergence of the novel as a literary form in post-revolutionary literature, made available to English readers until after the second world war, and to this day there is no American edition of it. Zamyatin's *My* (We), a prophetic vision of the totalitarian state, though published in the United States (in a very unsatisfactory translation) and in some other countries, could apparently find no publisher in Britain, and no copy of the American edition was available in the British Museum Library, so that when George Orwell, in 1945, having read about it was anxious to read the novel itself, I had to lend him a copy of the French version. The influence which this work of Zamyatin's had on Orwell's own *1984* was attested by himself.

The Slonim-Reavey anthology was followed in 1934 by Max Eastman's *Artists in Uniform*, and a year later by the present writer's *Soviet Russian Literature*. The former, one of the first books—if not the first— to come from the pen of a disillusioned Western communist, an adherent and admirer of Trotsky, was based largely on first-hand knowledge and impressions gleaned during a prolonged stay in Moscow, and contained a great deal of valuable material on the Soviet literary scene; it gave the Western reader his first glimpse into Stalinist cultural policies, and this at a time when large sections of the Western intelligentsia were inclined to see Soviet communism through rose-coloured spectacles. As for my own book, it was the first attempt to give a systematic account of what happened to and in literature in Russia after 1917. For many years it remained the only comprehensive survey of Soviet literature in any language, including Russian. It seems to me worth putting on record that the initiative did not come from me, the book being suggested and then commissioned by Mr Frederick Warburg (then one of the directors of Routledges), and was thus clear evidence of an interest in Soviet literature on the part of Western publishers: until then—that is, until 1933—the Soviet period of Russian literature had been given only a small place in such general surveys of modern Russian literature as those of D. S. Mirsky, Vladimir Pozner, and N. Arseniev.[1] It is also worth mentioning perhaps that in 1932 the present writer, who had just replaced D. S. Mirsky as Lecturer in Russian Literature in the School of Slavonic and East European Studies, University of London, gave a course on contemporary Russian literature which included along with Bunin and some other emigré writers, a survey of the work of several Soviet writers, such as Zamyatin, Leonov, Pilnyak, Fedin, and others. This was probably the first such course to be given in a European university (in the United States, as far as I know, the University of

---

[1] *Contemporary Russian Literature* (London, 1926); *Panorama de la littérature russe* (Paris, 1929); *Die russische Literatur der Neuzeit und Gegenwart in ihren geistigen Zusammenhängen* (Mainz, 1929).

California was the only institution in which contemporary Russian literature was taught regularly in those days by the late Alexander Kaun, and he did include Soviet writers in his courses).

While my *Soviet Russian Literature*, produced in conditions that were far from propitious to serious research in depth (the library resources in England at that time were quite inadequate), had, despite all its omissions and shortcomings, a fairly good reception from Western reviewers,[2] one could hardly speak of it as a great success with the public; the interest in things Russian, including literature, was confined in those days to a very small minority, represented for the most part, in England especially, by ' parlour pinks ', to whom a book like mine could have little appeal. Typical of its reception on the Left was a review by Alec Brown, a well-known translator of Russian writers, both Soviet and non-Soviet. Entitled ' Criticism as Propaganda ', it was published in *Left Review* (October 1935). Perhaps it is worth rescuing from oblivion one very original critical judgment passed by Mr Brown himself. In defending Panferov and his novel *Bruski* against my strictures, Mr Brown wrote: ' Panferov . . . stands out a head and shoulders above Sholokhov exactly by the broadness of his writing and his deep concern with the individual '.

A quarter of a century later, namely in 1960, another well-known translator of Russian fiction, Bernard Guilbert Guerney, made the following intriguing and enigmatic statement about my book in the Foreword to his paperback *Anthology of Russian Literature in the Soviet Period:* ' I also commend, and that most warmly, Professor Gleb Struve's *Soviet Literature: 1917–1950*—but only to those who happen to share my taste for the macabre, the grand-guignolish. I strongly doubt if, in all the galactic range of literary scholarship, there is to be found a more delectably spine-tingling phantasmagoria ' (p. xxiv). At the same time, I cannot refrain from noting here that Mr Guerney has just proclaimed Valery Tarsis non-existent and his *Bluebottle* ' one of those hoax-parodies the British are so jolly clever at ' (*Saturday Review*, 28 September 1963).

---

[2] The London *Times Literary Supplement* devoted a front-page article to it, which displayed both a good knowledge of the subject and considerable insight. Part of the passage on Boris Pasternak in this anonymous review article is worth recalling at an interval of nearly thirty years: ' Even more illuminating was the unsparing attack upon the poet whose genius stands out today as Blok's did at an earlier period— Boris Pasternak. Of wide culture, disciplined in thought and highly personal in his emotional appeal, Pasternak has adapted the Futurists' destructive way with conventional poetic usage to a form of lyrical expression that is entirely his own. His remarkable originality became apparent with the publication, in 1922, of a volume of lyrics written years earlier, *My Sister Life*, whose freshness and intensity of vision are fused with the unexpected rhythms of colloquial speech. Since then his verse and prose alike are charged with the same extremely personal feeling, the same individual sensibilities. He is necessarily what is called a difficult writer; indeed, as the result of his continuous movement on the plane of metaphor, he is frequently obscure. But there is nothing in Pasternak's poetry that provides a shadow of excuse for the onslaughts upon him delivered by the philistines of the left. The chorus of denunciation of his antisocial tendencies boded no good ' (*TLS*, 20 June 1935).

In the Soviet Union itself my book was simply ignored.[3] Soviet scholars, even if they had entertained the idea of producing their own record of Soviet literature, must have given it up because of the sharp ideological struggle and the continuing reappraisal of the past; the latest such record was Georgy Gorbachov's *Sovremennaya russkaya literatura* (Contemporary Russian Literature, 1929). But Gorbachov, who represented the extreme left wing of the 'On Guard' group and refused to toe the line, had by the beginning of the 1930s become an enemy of the people and disappeared into limbo. The violent purges that followed involved a great number of writers, including several well-known ones, who were either banned from literature or even physically liquidated. In the circumstances, there could be no question of compiling an historical record of Soviet literature: such a record would have had to be rewritten several times before it was completed. All subsequent plans of producing a history of Soviet literature were invariably shelved. When they at last materialised—soon after Stalin's death—the two-volume *Outline History of Soviet Literature* [4] was found almost immediately wanting when the past of Soviet literature came to be further reappraised and a number of Stalin's literary victims were restored to literary life.

THE post-Stalin situation in Soviet letters, determined as it was, in part at least, by the policy of 'cultural coexistence', made it impossible for Soviet literary scholars and critics to ignore any longer various negative reactions to Soviet literature in the outside world, and in particular to socialist realism. They began to accuse me and a number of other Western scholars, especially the American ones (the names particularly often mentioned in this connection were those of Victor Erlich, Marc Slonim, Ernest J. Simmons, and William E. Harkins, among the Americans, and W. Lettenbauer, among the Europeans; more recently those of Avrahm Yarmolinsky, George Gibian, and Maurice Friedberg were added to them),[5] of falsifying and distorting the picture

3 To the best of my knowledge, the first Soviet references to my book belong to the post-second world war period, and were made in connection with the campaign against 'cosmopolitanism' and 'servility before the West', launched by Zhdanov in the autumn of 1946. See Alexander Anikst, 'Slander in the Guise of Scholarship', in *Soviet Literature* (1947, No. 10, pp. 62–65) and L. Timofeyev, 'Pismo v redaktsiyu', in *Kultura i Zhizn* (9 March 1947). Anikst's article was not meant for the home market and appeared in the English edition of the magazine only. Both Anikst and Timofeyev made much of my inclusion among Soviet writers of such 'renegades' as Zamyatin and Zoshchenko. A thoroughly revised and considerably enlarged edition of my book was published in 1951 in the United States (*Soviet Russian Literature: 1917–1950*).
4 *Ocherk istorii russkoy sovetskoy literatury*, published in 1954–55 by the Soviet Academy of Sciences.
5 V. Erlich, *Russian Formalism: History and Doctrine* (1955); Marc Slonim, *Modern Russian Literature: From Chekhov to the Present Day* (1953); E. J. Simmons, *Russian Fiction and Soviet Ideology* (1958); E. J. Simmons, editor, *Through the Glass of Soviet Literature* (1953); W. E. Harkins, *Dictionary of Russian Literature* (1956); W. Lettenbauer, *Russische Literaturgeschichte* (1955); A. Yarmolinsky, *Interval of Freedom: Soviet Literature during the Thaw, 1954–1957* (1960); G. Gibian, *Literature under Communism* (1960); for M. Friedberg's book, see below.

of Soviet literature, of presenting the 1920s as the period of florescence, of diversified richness, and of speaking of the 1930s as marking the beginning of the decline of Soviet literature. In thus attacking independent Western students of Soviet literature, Soviet literary scholars inevitably get entangled in a maze of contradictions. The reappraisal of the past of Soviet literature, which began during the so-called thaw—and acquired increasing momentum after 1956—involved the rehabilitation and revival (at times, it is true, a rather half-hearted one) of a number of writers of the 1920s, in other words, it went along the lines which are still represented as 'falsification' and 'distortion' perpetrated by students of Soviet literature in the West.[6]

If Soviet scholars and critics today could afford to be quite frank and truthful, they would have to admit that many of the things which have now become the commonplace of their own literary scholarship (such as the cult of Stalin and its reflection in, and impact on, literature; the ruthless purges of men of letters in the late 1930s; the rabid anti-Western witch-hunt of the Zhdanov period; the award of Stalin literary prizes to mediocrities and nonentities; the rewriting of literary works to suit the current Party line, and so forth), were for the first time told fully and truthfully precisely in those Western works which they still denounce as false and distorted, while they themselves still prefer to use such hypocritical euphemisms as 'the cult of personality', to gloss over many things, to conceal many facts (this is particularly true of the so-called 'rehabilitation' of previously ostracised writers, which is never accompanied by a full disclosure of the circumstances of their literary and/or physical demise; this, of course, in striking contrast to the continuous accumulation of all sorts of details about the 'atrocities' of the *ancien régime*).[7]

The latest (and in fact the first more or less to deserve its name) Soviet history of Russian literature of the Soviet period, the three-volume *Istoriya russkoy sovetskoy literatury*, published between 1958 and 1961 under the auspices of the Soviet Academy of Sciences, is still quite unsatisfactory in many respects. It is full of omissions (in part determined by the principle of monographic treatment of certain selected

6 All this was part of a preparation for the Fourth International Congress of Slavists in Moscow, in the autumn of 1958, at which Soviet literary scholars for the first time confronted as a body their Western colleagues. Realism and its fortunes through the ages was the main theme of the congress. A fairly thorough examination, with chapter and verse, of various American contributions to the study of Soviet literature was made by A. Brukhansky in an article entitled ' Izuchenie ili falsifikatsiya? ' (*Russkaya Literatura*, 1958, 1). Considerable attention to Western studies of Soviet literature was paid by East German Slavists; see ' *Ostforschung* ' *und Slawistik. Kritische Auseinandersetzungen* (Berlin, 1960). Nearly the whole of this volume, which contains papers read at a conference of the Slavic Institute of the East German Academy of Sciences, is polemically oriented against the study and interpretation of Russian (primarily Soviet) literature in the West.

7 This concealment is true both of the introductions to various reissues of ' rehabilitated ' writers and of the entries in the first volume of the *Kratkaya Literaturnaya Entsiklopediya*, even though the general trend of this new literary encyclopaedia could be described as ' liberal ' (in the sense in which this word has come to be used with reference to the Soviet cultural scene).

individual writers, with relatively short general surveys of periods at the beginning of each volume [8]; and in part due to the fact that some writers are still under a taboo), and of hypocritical glossing over of certain unpleasant facts. It is nevertheless a great improvement on the 1954–55 *Outline*. Its various small-type appendices ('Chronicle of literary events', etc.) contain a great deal of factual information, not otherwise easily accessible to Western students of Soviet literature, and are valuable despite their incompleteness and selective bias. Yet what was true ten and twenty years ago still holds true today: a Soviet reader can still learn much about the past of his own literature from works written by independent scholars outside the USSR, works to which not even all Soviet scholars, let alone the average Soviet reader, have ready access.

Western writing about Soviet literature has grown enormously in the last ten years. To the few pioneer works of the pre-war period, or even of the early 1950s, have now been added a number of others, both general and more specialised. Several of them represent genuine contributions to knowledge. This is particularly true of some of the more specialised works, dealing either with certain aspects or certain periods of Soviet literature. Among them one may single out Edward J. Brown's *The Proletarian Episode in Russian Literature, 1928–1932* (New York, 1953), Harold Swayze's *Political Control of Literature in the USSR, 1946–1959* (Cambridge, Mass., 1962), Herman Ermolaev's *Soviet Literary Theories, 1917–1934: The Genesis of Socialist Realism* (University of California Press, 1963). All three are based on a close study of first-hand materials and deal with subjects which still cannot be tackled without constraint by Soviet scholars. Of outstanding interest and value is Victor Erlich's book on Russian Formalism, another topic on which one can hardly expect at present an impartial study to be produced in the Soviet Union. Rufus W. Mathewson's stimulating investigation of *The Positive Hero in Russian Literature* (New York, 1958) ties up certain aspects of Soviet literature with some important trends in the literature and literary criticism of the nineteenth century. V. Seduro's *Dostoevsky in Russian Literary Criticism* (New York, 1957) is a useful analysis of Dostoevsky criticism in the Soviet period, even if not always satisfactory on the earlier phases. Maurice Friedberg's *Russian Classics in Soviet Jackets* (New York, 1962) sheds light on the problem of the Russian literary heritage and its handling in the Soviet period. All these works are products of the expansion of academic study in the USA of the Soviet period. This is certainly something to be welcomed, although the medal has also a reverse side—a relative neglect of the prerevolutionary period and of Russian literature in exile. Some of the more general surveys of

---

[8] The same monographic principle, on a much more reduced scale and with entirely different criteria of selection, is applied by Mrs Vera Alexandrova in her recent book, *A History of Soviet Literature: 1917–1962* (New York, 1963); its title is therefore a misnomer, despite the two short survey chapters, which cover, respectively, the periods before and after the second world war.

periods, such as George Reavey's *Soviet Literature Today* (Yale, 1947) and Vyacheslav Zavalishin's *Early Soviet Writers* (New York, 1958) are much less satisfactory.

There is still a shortage of books about individual authors of the Soviet period, though quite a number of brief studies have appeared in various journals, both academic and general, and there have been some volumes containing essays on several writers, such as Ernest Simmons's *Russian Fiction and Soviet Ideology*, and Helen Muchnic's *From Gorky to Pasternak: Six Writers in Soviet Russia* (New York, 1961). Among books devoted entirely to one writer, Vladimir Markov's excellent study of Khlebnikov (*The Longer Poems of Velimir Khlebnikov*, University of California Press, 1962) stands out. This volume has aroused great interest in the Soviet Union, where the name of Khlebnikov still has a great appeal, both among the young poets and among some of the older literary scholars. Unfortunately, there is as yet no similar study—similar in its scholarly quality and in its literary perceptiveness—of any other Soviet writer. D. J. Richards's little book on Zamyatin, published in England (*Zamyatin: A Soviet Heretic*, London, 1962), is both slight and not always accurate. There is no doubt that the expansion of Russian studies in American and European universities makes an important contribution to the dissemination of knowledge about Soviet literature. If at present many of the published studies in the field of Soviet literature tend to be politically and socially oriented, the blame for this should fall on Soviet literature itself: its destinies are too closely interwoven with politics, and it is almost impossible to study it *qua* pure literature.

In speaking of Western *Sovietica* one should not overlook the publication in the original Russian of the works of those writers who, for one reason or another, are on the index in the Soviet Union. Several such volumes were published, between 1952 and 1956, by the Chekhov Publishing House in New York, which unfortunately had to close down when the grant it was receiving from one of the American foundations was not renewed. Among the works published by it were Zamyatin's novel *My*, a two-volume edition of Nikolay Klyuev's poetry, edited by Boris Filippov; a volume of unpublished works by Gumilev; a volume of stories by Zoshchenko; a volume of stories by different writers banned from literature under Stalin (including Pasternak's *Safe Conduct*); an anthology of ' unpopular ' poets of the Soviet period, edited by Vladimir Markov; the first edition of the collected works of Osip Mandelstam, edited by Boris Filippov and Gleb Struve, etc. After the closing down of the Chekhov Publishing House such publications became more sporadic. They included, however, the three-volume edition of the collected poetry and prose of Boris Pasternak (University of Michigan Press, 1961; edited by B. Filippov and G. Struve). This first quasi-complete edition of Pasternak's works (the same publisher had earlier brought out *Doctor Zhivago* in Russian) was something of a literary event, and is said to be used now by Soviet scholars in preparation for a new edition of Pasternak's poetry, more complete than the 1961 volume of selected poems. A four-volume edition of Nikolay Gumilev's complete works is now in progress in Washington, D.C. (the first volume appeared in 1962). A volume of Marina Tsvetaeva's unpublished poetry, entitled *Lebediny stan*, was brought out by Gleb Struve in Munich in 1957, with an introductory article by Yury Ivask. Somewhat apart stand the publications of works by living Soviet writers, which are being smuggled out of Russia, such as Abram Tertz, Nikolay Arzhak, Valery Tarsis, and others. In having access to these works, readers outside the Soviet Union have another advantage over Soviet readers.

THERE is no doubt that in the last few years Western writings about Soviet literature, having become more easily accessible to some Soviet literary scholars and critics, have come to exercise a certain influence on them. A reflection of this may be seen in some of the controversies in which Soviet scholars and critics have been engaging, especially with regard to the literature of the 1920s, and in the criticism of the three-volume *History of Soviet Russian Literature* that was voiced a couple of years ago. One of these discussions was triggered off by the book entitled *Formirovanie ideynovo edinstva sovetskoy literatury, 1917–1932* (Moscow, 1960), by V. Ivanov. Ivanov represents the more orthodox faction among Soviet literary scholars, and his treatment of the literature of the 1920s provoked a number of retorts from the liberals.[9] Of course, none of those who took part in the discussion would dream of making common cause with Western 'revisionists', but the views they expressed sometimes coincided with those voiced by independent Western scholars. The official attitude towards the Western conception of Soviet literature—its richness and diversity in the 1920s, its subsequent decline in the 1930s—remains wholly negative. It was restated recently by Professor Roman Samarin in his contribution to the volume dealing with contemporary literature in the United States.[10] The title of Samarin's article ('The Distortion of the History of Soviet Literature in Literary Scholarship in the USA') speaks for itself. To make his thesis sound more convincing, Samarin opposes American studies of Soviet literature to those of the pre-Soviet period: while the latter often pursue purely literary objectives, says Samarin, books and articles about Soviet literature partake of anti-communist propaganda and aim at creating a false idea of Soviet literature. This, insists Samarin, is not a case of some individual distortions, but a systematic expression of views 'at the root of which lies the desire to utilise this falsification

[9] See articles by A. Metchenko, L. Timofeyev, V. Ivanov, D. Blagoy, N. Dzhusoyty, and V. Kneycher in *Voprosy Literatury*, 1961, Nos. 4, 5, 7, and 8, and the report of the discussion on the same subject organised by that journal in No. 9. Another discussion of the problems of Soviet literary history was held in the Gorky Institute of World Literature in the autumn of 1961; it was reported in *Voprosy Literatury* (1962, No. 3), under the title 'Kakoy dolzhna byt "Istoriya russkoy sovetskoy literatury"'.
[10] 'Iskazhenie istorii sovetskoy literatury v literaturovedenii SShA', in *Sovremennaya literatura SShA* (Moscow, 1962).

of Soviet literature for sorties against the Soviet regime, against Soviet people and their moral and esthetic ideals '. Samarin accuses the American scholars of bringing to the forefront writers ' who had little to say in the general development of Soviet literature ', of exaggerating the importance of Zamyatin, and of tracing the main line of development of Soviet literature through the names of Babel, Pilnyak, and Pasternak. To these he opposes the work of some ' sincere friends of Soviet literature ', citing such periodicals as *New Masses, Mainstream, Masses and Mainstream, New World Review*, etc. Two sins of which, according to Samarin, many American literary scholars and critics are guilty are their reluctance to discuss Maxim Gorky in the framework of Soviet literature and their tendency to ignore non-Russian literatures of the Soviet Union. It does not apparently occur to him that many of those who feel competent to discuss Soviet Russian literature would not have the cheek to tackle literatures of whose languages they are ignorant.

Western studies of Soviet literature are discussed along the same lines in another recent collective publication, entitled *Soviet Literature Abroad: 1917–1960*.[11] Here, too, we find some venomous sallies against Struve, Slonim, Lettenbauer, *et al.* Here is a typical passage:

> . . . in the fight against Soviet culture, against the principles of socialist realism, international revisionism made common cause with reactionary bourgeois criticism. And it is difficult to distinguish the voice of H. Fast from the slanderous discourses of the emigré G. Struve, the ' critical ' comments of the ex-communist André Léfèvre from the fabrications of that old enemy of the Soviet country, Maurice Nadeau, the utterances of G. Lukacs from the malicious invective of certain West German literary scholars. Their long-range target always turned out to be not our literature, but Soviet reality (p. 142).

The distinctive characteristics of this book are, however, its more detailed and systematic treatment of its subject (the book is divided into five chapters, chronologically arranged), the inclusion of a discussion of Russian emigré views of Soviet literature and of the relation between the two branches of Russian literature, and an extensive, though onesided, bibliography, arranged by countries and occupying fifty pages.

---

[11] T. Balashova, O. Egorov, and A. Nikolyukin, *Sovetskaya literatura za rubezhom, 1917–1960* (Moscow, 1962). The book is dedicated to the memory of the late Tamara Trifonova, the well-known Soviet literary critic and scholar.

WORLD COMMUNISM

Bernard S. Morris

THERE are a number of possible approaches to this subject: a biblio-
graphical essay; a comprehensive review not only of books and
articles, but of periodical policy, book publishers, university curricula,
and research institutes as well; or a review article, taking as its point of
departure the leading books in the field. But perhaps for the United
States, where more often than not it has been treated as mythology, an
impressionistic review is perhaps the most suitable.

The degree of mythopoesis was at times so great that one might
wonder whether there was such a thing as ' world communism ' at all.
Did it exist in any more substantial sense than ' world capitalism ',
which the communists conceptualised in categories strikingly similar to
non-communist views of world communism? Thus, for ' world communism ', read ' world capitalism '; for the ' Kremlin ', read ' Wall
Street '; for ' communist ideology ', read ' monopoly capitalism '; for
' communist parties ', read ' imperialist lackeys '; and for ' two camps ',
read ' two camps '. If both versions seem crude and cabbalistic, especially
in the light of recent events, they nonetheless helped to shape the post-
war political environment in both the USSR and the United States.

Similarly disconcerting was the tendency to view the communist
movement through communist glasses, a process known in the trade as
' reverse Bolshevism '. What the communists said and what they wrote
were all too often equated with what they were. They could not, of
course, be called fighters for peace, as they claimed, but it was readily
granted that they were revolutionary, that their unity was indissoluble,
and that they were ideological brothers-in-arms, if that was what they
said they were. We, the primitive and the sophisticated alike, were
victimised by the tyranny of words to support a myth dear to the
communists. Myths are notoriously easier to deal with than reality.

Even more insidious was the effect communist propaganda apparently
had on the non-believer who subconsciously fell for the myth of communist invincibility. Did he perhaps feel that the communists had
something; that they had found the key to social organisation in the
20th century; that they were the wave of the future, and that time was,
in fact, on their side? Some such psychological mechanism may have
been involved in the hysterical denunciation of all things communist, in
the cries for preventive war, and in the refusal to credit the communists
with legitimate accomplishments (spies or German scientists did it).

The question, then, whether world communism exists was a provocation with a point; it required answers to explain what the phenomenon
was and where it was going. The answers were neither readily forth-
coming nor highly satisfactory.

COMPARED to the plethora of works on Soviet affairs and on particular aspects of communism, very little has been written by Americans on world communism, *considered as a political movement*. Indeed, while 'international communism' is a household word in the United States, thanks especially to the late John Foster Dulles, American scholars have not shown much interest in it, though the subject has of course been touched upon in books on various specialised topics and in area studies.

The best and last significant book on world communism was written in 1938 by the erstwhile Austrian nobleman and one-time communist, Franz Borkenau.[1] The most useful history of the movement in the post-war period was the work of an Englishman.[2] Another comprehensive, but far less successful, attempt was made by Günther Nollau, a German with official connections.[3] Apart from Martin Ebon's *World Communism Today* (1948), put together largely from newspaper clippings, and a few others, it seems that the only American with the temerity to tackle the job systematically was the late Chairman of the Communist Party of the United States of America, William Z. Foster, in his *History of the Three Internationals* (1955).

If, in retrospect, the main conclusion from a survey of the literature is that there has been a striking contrast between the propaganda and the scholarly output on world communism, no less striking is the fact that, for better or worse, most of the systematic work on world communism has been done by various departments of the United States Government.

Why has so little been written on the subject in the United States, particularly when there has been such a proliferation of works on Soviet affairs? It is, of course, an immense and complex subject. Not only are there the usual inadequacies of documentary materials and memoirs, unavailability of key figures, and systematic falsification of history by the communists; the technical demands are far greater than the requirements for research on (say) communist ideology or Soviet civil defence. To study the Popular Front of the 1930s or communist insurrectionary activity in Asia in the late 1940s, it is necessary to know the Soviet sources, to investigate particular and complex situations in a number of countries, to unravel the story of their communist parties, and to establish the inter-relationships between all these. This requires a prolonged period of research, unusual linguistic competence, and some familiarity with the structure of different societies; and, of course, the patience and imagination without which such undertakings cannot yield fruitful results. Who

---

[1] *World Communism* (New York, 1939); Published in England under the title *The Communist International*. An updated version of the book called *European Communism* (London, 1953) was not up to the standard of the original.

[2] Hugh Seton-Watson, *The Pattern of Communist Revolution* (London, 1953). The American edition was called *From Lenin to Malenkov*, amplified in a second edition in 1960 called *From Lenin to Khrushchev*.

[3] *International Communism and World Revolution*. Translated by Victor Andersen (New York, 1961).

can do this? An American E. H. Carr? The Ford Foundation? Or someone as big as the United States Government?

IN a rare disclosure to the public, the Department of State announced that ' For 15 years a small group of key experts in the Department's Bureau of Intelligence and Research (INR) has been quietly meeting to discuss the zigs and zags of international communism '. This group of ' specialists—known as the Committee on World Communism (CWC)— has prepared or stimulated preparation of scores of global papers and intelligence reports for the guidance of US policy planners '.[4] The scope of this Committee's interest, spreading to local, regional, and world communist affairs, and its connections with other government agencies, suggests a wealth of resources that the private research worker cannot hope to match. The technical competence, quality, and range of coverage, however, cannot be judged, since most of the Department's output is not available to the public, though a few reports of a propaganda or statistical nature have been released. In this respect, the British have been more generous.

The size of the question has not been the only reason for the relative neglect of the study of the world communist movement. The mood in the United States after 1945 also served to shape training in communist affairs, and hence the published output.

World communism was proclaimed to be a menace, a conspiracy directed by Moscow to conquer the world.[5] The Word was given. What was required was documentation of conspiracy, not investigation of the condition of the movement and its possible trends after the war. This conspiratorial and mechanistic view of world communism, not entirely mistaken of course, but essentially misleading, was reinforced by the atmosphere (to use a polite expression) of McCarthyism. It was not a time to say what you thought. Nor can it be unconditionally maintained that the academicians as a group were more courageous than their bureaucratic brethren. Perhaps the dialectic of the bureaucracy provides a freedom of its own.

Then, too, the preoccupation of American scholars with communist ideology and the nature of the total state reinforced the rigidity of approach to the world-wide communist phenomenon. If the Soviet Union was totalitarian, if it exercised absolute control over a rigidly defined ideology, it followed that national communist parties had as much freedom of choice and manoeuvre as a man in a strait-jacket. Any deviant hypothesis on the subject was bound to be unpopular. It could be argued that the most intelligent authors and provocative books on

[4] Department of State *News Letter*, No. 24, April 1963, p. 20.
[5] In 1946 William Henry Chamberlin edited a number of Comintern documents designed to make Russia's aims clear to the American public. The reasoning here, and all too frequently elsewhere, was that Russia's aims never change. (*Blueprint for World Conquest*, Washington-Chicago.)

ideology and totalitarianism served largely to reinforce cliché-ridden ideas of communism.

There is no intention here to be wise in retrospect or to distinguish one author (including this one) from another. Rather it simply appears that world communism was treated largely as a political movement outside history, so to speak. Analyses in terms of socio-economic forces, nationalism, geo-political factors, counterforces, senility of people and ideas, etc., etc., were less satisfying than plausible tracts on totalitarianism, ideological rigidity, unprincipled flexibility, and organisational mastery.

If the press and magazines are now studded with articles on the divisions and disarray in the communist camp, this does not signify that the communist experts, taken as a whole, have been prescient. They are merely recording current developments in the communist movement. How the impact of current events will affect the pattern of thinking on communism remains to be seen. In retrospect, the commentators who gave due value to such factors as nationalism and national interest are proved to have been closer to reality than those who concentrated on ideology and organisational magic.

But old habits of thought die hard. It is simpler and more convenient to regard what is happening in the communist movement as merely a tactical dispute over how best to bury the West. If all the ferment in the communist orbit amounts to no more than a quarrel about the choice of undertakers, there has indeed been a change from the ' monolithic ' days, but not a very comforting one.

On the other hand, what has been happening in the communist movement has stirred up interest in the development of new concepts, as if the failure of analysis were due to the use of out-of-date methodologies. Now subjected to exercises in model-building and play-pen versions of games theory, world communism is no longer outside the mainstream of American sociological research.

THE greatest recent stimulus to the study of the world communist movement has been given by the Sino-Soviet controversy. Faintly visible on some issues in 1956, by 1960 the controversy had come into full public view. The two communist giants, indissolubly linked, as we had been taught, by a common ideology and purpose, had somehow come unstuck. Moreover, the so-called monolithic communist movement, if not already polycentric, was displaying unaccustomed signs of internal divergence and independence. Clearly, these developments required scrutiny *de novo*.

Once again, the initiative was taken by the US government [6] and also by those who, at one time associated with it, had left its service. The outstanding case was Donald S. Zagoria, whose *Sino-Soviet Conflict (1956-1961)*, published in 1962, is the best book so far on the subject.

---

[6] *News Letter, op. cit.*

Its great merit is to have presented to the scholarly community and the lay public an explanation of the Sino-Soviet break which left no doubt that it was genuine and serious. It deserves attention also for its aggressive defence of Kremlinology.

Kremlinology, as the initiated know, achieved respectability when Beria's failure to accompany his peers to a performance at the Bolshoi Theatre was proved to have nothing to do with his taste in ballet. Yet, like the psychoanalyst who still suffers a feeling of inferiority in the presence of the publicly accepted branches of the medical profession, the Kremlinologist is still fighting for acceptance. Thus William E. Griffith comes to its defence in the preface to his book on Albania: ' Last [of five reasons for writing so much about Albania], the methodology used in this book, that of the intensive deciphering and analysis of esoteric communist communications, is still under dispute; this book will hopefully provide more evidence of its effectiveness '.[7]

Why the breast-beating? Some years ago Daniel Bell, in his irreverent tour of the methodologies of the Soviet specialists, pointed out that Kremlinology is practised by every foreign office and by most journalists.[8] And that is to the point, for Kremlinology is useful for the day-to-day task of newspaper or official reporting. When the esoteric data finally add up to a story—as in Griffith's book on Albania, for example—the net result is a laboured and virtually unreadable collation that informs the reader of what is by publication time common knowledge. On the why's and wherefore's of the dispute, there is, by contrast, relatively little.

In short, what is useful for the foreign office and the newspaper is not necessarily of interest to the intelligent layman and the professionals, outside a limited circle. What the study of world communism does not need, at this time, is cultism and the incestuous professional relationships that go with it. What it does need is detachment from fashionable opinions and the application of historical and political perspectives to current situations.

THE communist movement today and the world within which it functions have changed drastically from what they were when Borkenau sat down to write his *World Communism*. The USSR is one of two world powers, not merely one of the major European powers. The communist movement is composed in the main of a number of states with their own particular interests; it is not a collection of impotent sects attached to a Moscow centre. It is even doubtful whether one can speak any longer of ' an ' international communist movement. A number of parties out of power are mass parties, or parties able to exert considerable political influence within their respective countries. The durability of capitalism and the revolt of the underdeveloped areas have in some degree shifted

[7] *Albania and the Sino-Soviet Rift* (M.I.T. Press, Cambridge, Mass., 1963), p. vii.
[8] ' Ten Theories in Search of Reality ' (*World Politics*, April 1958), reprinted in Alexander Dallin (ed.), *Soviet Conduct in World Affairs* (Columbia University Press, N.Y., 1960).

the focus of communism from Europe to the outlying areas. Probably one of the more interesting facets of communist studies is the effect of communist power and ideas on the organisation of societies which, for one reason or another, eschew western capitalist ideas. The development of Soviet society and the revolution in weapons technology call into question all cold war formulas. The persistence of the nation-state system both perpetuates some aspects of East-West relations and alters others. Communist behaviour in the Sino-Indian border dispute is worth brooding about.

The field of world communist studies is wide open. In the immediate post-war period, trained cadres on the Soviet Union were in short supply. Following a sensible order of priorities, universities, research institutes and foundations concentrated their efforts on the training of specialists on the Soviet Union. That was as it should have been. Now, an oversupply of students, the boredom of the USSR specialists and developments in the communist world itself, have combined to put the study of world communism on the map—and in the market-place.

The pursuit of Soviet studies in the United States has stimulated the interest of graduate students and of certain professors in various aspects of international communism. There are a number of universities offering courses and seminars in the field, and the inevitable institutes have sprung up on the campus. There is, for example, the Institute for Sino-Soviet Studies, which offers graduate work in ' Sino-Soviet Bloc Affairs ' at the George Washington University in the nation's capital. This Institute claims to conduct ' . . . integrated research on the ideological, political, economic, sociological, psychological, geographic, legal, and military aspects of communism and communist political systems, especially as manifested in the Soviet Union and communist China '. How can you lose?

A more promising innovation is the Research Institute on Communist Affairs at Columbia University. This benefits from the well-established Russian Institute at the same university, and has already attracted a number of capable senior fellows.

Still on the East coast, M.I.T.'s Center for International Studies has undertaken to publish a series of works on international communism, of which Griffith's book on Albania is the first. The Center has also published a series of interesting monographs by Ernst Halperin, formerly of the *Neue Zuercher Zeitung*.

On the West coast, Stanford's Hoover Institution on War, Revolution, and Peace has a series of studies going, including a long overdue history of the Comintern.

The Sino-Soviet dispute has stimulated the publication of the single most useful source available to the public on the current situation of the communist parties. This is the series on ' International Communist Developments ' which, together with translations of other communist materials, is available through the Joint Publications Research Service (JPRS) of the US Department of Commerce. Perhaps the time has come for the US Government to consider opening its archives on communism more readily to scholars, and to make current materials more easily available. It is also possible that scholars have not taken advantage of—if they indeed were aware of—the sources already available in Washington.

Although writing on current communist affairs obviously has its attractions, it would probably be more useful to study the relationships between individual communist parties and Moscow, and to elucidate the history of the communist parties themselves. All too often the cliché 'control by Moscow' has been taken for granted, without an enquiry into the nature of that control. And 'control' is but one cliché that bears re-examination. What did the 'left' strategy of the 6th Comintern congress amount to? How does a communist party in the underdeveloped areas set about being 'subversive'? Is an international front organisation really a 'front' organisation? Who is fronting for the communists? Communists? What happened to all the intellectuals who used to join such organisations? And just what is a communist these days, my colleagues ask, and how does he differ from a radical nationalist in some areas of the world? It is high time to undertake systematic research into the world communist movement, if only to dispel some of the fog that has surrounded the subject in academic and public discourse.

THE HYBRID ART OF SOVIETOLOGY

Arthur E. Adams

BEFORE embarking upon some new campaign in Gaul or Britannia, Roman generals used to consult their augurs. Salaried Etruscan *haruspices* pored over the steaming entrails of slain animals, studied code books on the meaning of signs, and foretold disaster or success. Other eras have employed a great profusion of oracles, soothsayers, prophets, and fortune tellers. The present is little different. Today we have the electronic computer, which does all and more than haruspication could do, and without bloodshed; generals fight global nuclear wars on computer paper, calculating the number and character of the new weapons that will be needed to win a real war. But robot brains are not yet omniscient; because there are subtle political, moral, and psychological factors that defy exact formulation, we continue to base decisions concerning such matters as our national security on evidence so elusive that it cannot be fed into machines. Man must still depend upon man for much of his most vitally needed divination. To say this is to explain a great deal about the nature and practice of sovietology.

Sovietology is the study of all matters that help us to understand the meaning of current, politically significant Soviet-communist behaviour and to forecast its future course. There is great need for such study. Since the end of the second world war a paramount problem for the Western world has been represented by the dynamic growth of the Soviet Union and by the continuing spread of world communism from what was, until recently, its Soviet centre. In response, Western governments and their peoples demand reliable estimates of communist intentions and capacities.

Seeking to answer such demands, sovietology works against a number of odds not common to the research of social scientists in most other areas. While we know a great deal about communist ideas and various aspects of Soviet life, cardinal political facts are hidden. Too often Soviet documents are designed to mislead and the student of Soviet affairs must use an elaborate set of lie-detectors to extract their significant elements. Almost all inter-communist affairs are clothed in secrecy, so that the relations of the Soviet Union with its allies and with the communist parties of Western Europe, Latin America, and Asia, are largely matters for conjecture. Nevertheless, the sovietologist persists, and the past twenty years have witnessed a great deal of (sometimes rather wild) experimentation, with all the social sciences lending a hand.

The British cultural anthropologist, Geoffrey Gorer, argued that tight swaddling of Russian babies tends to make Great Russians unduly submissive to autocratic authority, yet ever ready to erupt in violent explosions. Irreverent observers have since dubbed this theory *diapero-logy*, and some Soviet refugees questioned on the subject for the refugee study of Harvard University contemptuously refused to answer the question when they understood its implications. Psychology, too, has had its day, for example in the work of Nathan Leites, who suggested that the key to Bolshevik character (and therefore to communist behaviour) is the Bolsheviks' fear of their own latent homosexual proclivities and an exaggerated emphasis upon the father-image, Lenin. Bypassing sound efforts to explain the determining factors of Soviet conduct on the basis of ideology and power, some sovietologists have devised and published theories quite at odds with known facts: the regime's imminent collapse is regularly prophesied by men who exaggerate the degree of influence exercised by popular dissatisfactions; and at least one renowned kremlinologist believes that what he writes about the Soviet Union influences the decisions of Soviet policy-makers. Such theories have created a bad image for sovietology by making it seem to be a field of study where irresponsible guesswork and the wildest theorising are standard practice. It so happens that sovietology does welcome guesses and theorising (though only when based upon much sound knowledge and careful analysis), for it looks into what is essentially unknowable—the future.

IT is not possible to talk about *the* method of sovietology because there are many methods available to the individual practitioner, and naturally each man's training, whether in economics or politics, in literature, anthropology, journalism, or statistics, has much to do with the particular combination of skills he may develop for his work. Yet it is both necessary and possible to sketch at least in outline the methodological framework within which every sovietologist carries on his research.

Since the ultimate purpose of sovietology is to chart the course of political decision-making and to predict the future, the sovietologist is interested above all in the policy-making processes at the apex of the party-state pyramid in the Soviet Union and in the inter-relations of party leaders around the world. Within the Soviet Union events inside the Presidium and Secretariat are of the greatest significance, for these bodies alone make the decisions that determine Soviet conduct; here also are the men who make the policy and whose struggles for position, prestige, and power directly influence every decision. But while it is a truism that sovietology is concerned primarily with decision-making and the power struggle in the highest circles of the party, it is just as true that such decisions and struggles do not take place in a vacuum. Policy decisions are made on substantive issues—economic problems, administrative difficulties, military affairs, and foreign relations. Leaders support one or another side of each issue for a variety of reasons. A man may defend the point of view that seems to have the most merit; he may use the issue to attack an opponent or to mend his fences by supporting a factional group that may help him in the future.

Clearly, to one who hopes to comprehend the all-important events in the Kremlin, virtually anything concerned with communist party and Soviet affairs may be of use. The sovietologist must be thoroughly familiar with all that is known about the structure, organisation, and operation of both party and state. He must know the history of their development, keep abreast of structural changes, and estimate their intent and consequences. He must know the men in office, their professional abilities and factional relationships; and, since these change, such knowledge must be kept constantly under review: a rapprochement of two former enemies at the Presidium level may change the course of history.

While secrecy in high party affairs is extreme, the same cannot be said of other areas. The volume of economic information published by the Soviet Union and made available to the West is immense: the sovietologist must master economic facts, the latest budget figures, the current plan, the causes and consequences of agricultural failure. He must understand, as exactly and concretely as any military strategist or professional economist, the stresses created by the conflict between limited resources and ambitious economic and military plans. So, too, he must be familiar with opposing theories (sources of conflict) within the party on such matters as the proper emphasis to be given to heavy industry, nuclear testing, or collective farm reorganisation. He must be an advanced student of Marxism-Leninism, familiar with fresh developments in theory as well as their probable significance in the minds of party leaders. He must have a profound knowledge of the social system, of the past and its traditions—the Orthodox faith, the writings of Pushkin, Tolstoy, and Dostoevsky, the revolutionary tradition, and the early history of the party.

There are some who argue that to be thoroughly grounded for his work the sovietologist must have been at one time or another an active communist, preferably in one of the communist-ruled countries. This is not the case. While lengthy party experience can be immensely helpful, early enthusiasm for the Marxian deterministic outlook and communist utopianism has in some cases proved a permanent hindrance to rational analysis. The crux of the matter lies with the knowledge, objectivity, and analytical capacity of the man.

It is self-evident that the sovietologist must be deeply informed on matters of Soviet foreign policy and that here, as in other fields, his information must be up to the minute. This latter requirement is one of the essential characteristics distinguishing the sovietologist from the expert in Soviet politics or economics, or the scholarly historian of party affairs—the sovietologist's information is up to date and he has some idea of what is coming next. His job is to inform and advise foreign ministries, prime ministers and presidents, the scholarly community, and a vast world of newspaper readers. Most of these clients are peremptory in their demand for immediate interpretations of current events. Therefore, the sovietologist reads and analyses Khrushchev's latest speech the moment it becomes available; he keeps up with *Pravda, Izvestia,* and

Kommunist, with the Chinese *Red Flag* and *People's Daily*, and with a mass of other materials.

ALL this study is possible and finite; it deals with information that can be acquired by intelligent industry. But there is a second and far more difficult part of the sovietologist's work, which is to learn what ranges from the less knowable to the almost totally unknowable, to reach conclusions about important matters for which only little direct evidence is available or for which there are no sources of direct evidence.

Although both phases go on concurrently, the sovietologist's work with what is knowable is preparation for the more demanding work in the less knowable areas. By learning everything he can about the known areas, he narrows the limits of the unknown, eliminating some of the empty squares on his chart, identifying within others precisely what it is he doesn't know and what he needs to learn before he can answer certain questions.

Given his operational model of the Soviet Union, which provides most of the information needed for run-of-the-mill analysis and prediction, how does the sovietologist make his approach to the less knowable areas? For this he has developed special techniques, whose usefulness and reliability are often questioned because they have been mishandled. The nature of the problems these techniques are fitted to solve and the question of their proper application deserve careful attention.

Foremost among the problems is the subject of policy-making and the concomitant power struggle that we assume is taking place among the top policy-makers. We know almost nothing about how Soviet decisions are reached; nor do we know what roles are played by the various members of the Presidium and Secretariat. We seldom learn what issues are debated while some new policy is being made, for, with rare exceptions, extreme care is taken to suppress every hint of dissension. When policies are announced as decrees or resolutions of the Central Committee and/or the Council of Ministers, we are given to understand that the decision was unanimous, the implication being that the truths of communism are not only superior but also manifest, to which there is always only one way of doing practical justice. But are these decisions really unanimous? Is it true, for example, that all members of the Presidium equally approved Khrushchev's decision to place intermediate range missiles on Cuba and then agreed with equal unanimity to pull them out in late October 1962, after President Kennedy's warlike demonstrations? Is it true that all members of the Presidium unanimously approve the first secretary's present policy vis-à-vis China?

Given our fairly extensive knowledge of the past history of power struggles among communist leaders, involving dissension over a variety of issues, it is necessary to assume that in fact unanimity rarely exists, that on the contrary the rivalry for place and power among communist leaders is constant and intense. For Western policy-makers the precise degree of friction and the exact strength of the party leader's authority are of tremendous interest. It is the task of the sovietologist to identify the issues, to anticipate the probable outcome, and to interpret the significance of the conflict in terms of its probable effect upon the strength or weakness of central authority.

Consider another example of a less knowable area. What is the real degree of unity between the Soviet party and its sister parties in the bloc? How does the Soviet leader exercise his predominance and to what degree? Does he possess greater personal authority in Sofia than in Warsaw? And, to reverse this line of questioning, to what extent, if at all, do the strongest leaders of the bloc countries influence the policies of the Communist Party of the Soviet Union?

Add another series of crucial questions: What is tomorrow's Sino-Soviet relationship to be? And how will this relationship affect the Soviet party's policies vis-à-vis other communist parties? Will the Soviet party slow down the revisionist pace, and move towards more rigid controls or will the opposite course be followed? What of the idea, widely discussed in the Western press, that the Soviet Union must ultimately turn to the West for an alliance against China?

Given the Soviet Union's limited resources and international political ambitions, will she continue to go all-out for greater nuclear armaments? Or is there a possibility that she will turn to disarmament in earnest? And what of Russia's desire for influence in Africa, Asia, and Latin America? Will the strain of economic assistance, both upon her own and upon the Eastern European economies, prove too great to be supported? Who will be the next supreme leader of the Soviet Union? Will his policies follow those of the present incumbent, or are there good reasons for believing that major changes of direction may be expected?

THE first special method the sovietologist employs in trying to answer these questions is that of analysing what he somewhat pretentiously calls 'esoteric communications'. It is a known and demonstrable fact that Russia's communist elite (as well as those of other communist countries) talk to each other in the press by means of a highly formalised and changing set of symbols which only members of the group fully understand. While some of this veiled language can be deciphered only by the most sophisticated members of the ruling group, the hidden messages in others may be brought to light by the outsider who has carefully learned as much as he can about the codes used.

The little signs the sovietologist must know how to interpret are innumerable. Of first importance are the party's many ideological formulas; whilst at any one moment they represent sacrosanct dogma, over a period of time many of them undergo evolution and reinterpretation. Assuming that the smallest alteration is never inadvertent, the sovietologist attempts to unearth its hidden significance, which in ideological affairs can be extremely exacting.

When Ilya Ehrenburg writes boldly in *Pravda* about the effect of Stalin's terror upon writers, the sovietologist surmises that Khrushchev has given the go-ahead signal for the literary exploitation of Stalin's purges and labour camps. When an economic theory, hitherto black-listed, is discussed at length in *Pravda* by a little known professor of economics, it is safe to assume that the party is either reviewing its theory or has already done so. Typically, this assumption would entail a search through learned and technical economic journals for corroboration and a scanning of industrial news to learn if the theory in its revised form is already in practice.

The sovietologist may need to know a whole detailed history of events simply to catch the full import of a single word or phrase used by a party leader. For example, during his visit to Bulgaria in May 1962, Khrushchev made a speech at Varna in which, speaking warmly of Soviet-Yugoslav relations, he clearly implied that he considered Yugoslavia to be 'building socialism'. Now from 1948, when the Soviet-dominated Cominform read Yugoslavia out of the world communist movement, until the Varna speech, good communists had said of Tito many a curious thing, but building socialism was not one of them, because that phrase had been reserved exclusively for nations with Soviet-approved communist regimes. Although Khrushchev had made efforts at rapprochement in 1955 and 1961, Yugoslavia was still condemned for deviations from orthodoxy in a number of official edicts. Khrushchev's statement that cooperation with the USSR would help the Yugoslav peoples to 'consolidate their socialist positions' and would 'redound to the benefit of all countries that are building socialism and communism', was a bold announcement of a new policy, an order to the bloc to fall into line, a slap in China's face, and a clear indication to Western governments that Yugoslavia might be leaning rather more heavily eastwards than they had suspected. The indirect acknowledgment that Tito's regime was building socialism formally reversed fifteen years of history.

These are but the briefest illustrations of what the analyst may find under the surface in the Soviet press, in documents and speeches, in the rare statements made by Soviet leaders to distinguished Westerners, or in the planted 'leaks' to Polish, Yugoslav, and Italian communists, who dutifully whisper them into the ears of Western diplomats and journalists. For the man sensitive to the political significance of slogans, catchwords, theoretical formulas, and the nuances of communist phrasing, the Soviet press, while not quite an open book, is full of information the layman cannot see. Carried out systematically, used always in conjunction with other sources of information, and guided by a sovietologist prepared to admit the role of accident even in Soviet political life, the interpretation of enciphered language is an invaluable aid to exegetics.

Certain of its practitioners tend to emphasise the difficulty of unscrambling esoteric signals and to resent the fact that their efforts are not sufficiently appreciated. It is true, of course, that the scrap of evidence presented by a change of formula is often difficult to recognise and interpret; yet the process of ferreting out the hidden meaning of an official document, a literary work, or a rumour is certainly not new to scholarship. Every good British constitutional historian, piecing together a picture of England from the Anglo-Saxon laws and the *Doomsday Book*, has carefully extrapolated his way to what he believes to be the true meaning of his texts. So, too, every competent interpreter of the Bible, whether his approach be literal, or mystic or allegorical, has practised with varying success the technique of deciphering the hidden implications of his text. So, too, the young lover, who reads the answer to his hopes in the flushed cheek of his maiden, is deciphering an esoteric communication, while the man who waits for an explicitly worded answer may live unrequited all his life.

The common man has long had to guess what it is his king is trying to tell him with those formal, awkward-sounding phrases kings use, and the king or his soothsayers must painstakingly examine the official communiqué of another ruler to judge whether its threats are inspired by bombast, fear, genuinely murderous intent, or the malice of some bilious clerk in the enemy's foreign office. The sovietologist, an outsider, seeks to fathom the hidden significance of what one communist leader or faction is saying to another, to various sub-sections of the party, to other communist parties, or to the West. The acumen and intuition needed for deciphering these coded messages, while undoubtedly considerable, is certainly not so great as to defy intelligent minds trained in the academic disciplines.

KREMLINOLOGY is another special technique used for plumbing the less knowable areas of Soviet life. It relies heavily upon the art of breaking the code of Soviet jargon, but its attention centres primarily upon the power struggle at the top levels of the party and government and upon the rise and fall of the party and state leaders. *Murder will out*; this is the working hypothesis of kremlinologists, who assume that prolonged struggles between members of the ruling circles must sooner or later surface in the Soviet press and in the actions of Soviet leaders. At its most macabre this activity verges on the ancient art of anthropomancy—divination by the entrails of a human sacrifice.

For the West the value of knowing who is rising and who falling in the central decision-making bodies is great. Internal dissensions may mean hesitant foreign policies; or in certain circumstances, over-aggressive policies; a ruling party torn by violent conflicts may become too weak to react intelligently or forcefully to domestic and external pressures; and since we are seldom able to perceive conflict and change in the Kremlin by other means until it is too late to matter, the sovietologist's ability to detect the struggle and foresee its outcome by using the technique of kremlinology is too valuable a trick to ignore.

While the Kremlin seldom publishes information on these struggles, scattered information is nonetheless provided, most often in what is called ' protocol evidence '. Who among the members of the party Presidium were present at Vnukovo Airport to welcome the head of the Polish party, and who was absent? Who stands atop the Mausoleum for the May Day parade, and where are others placed in relation to the First Secretary? While such evidence may seem at first glance too primitive to be of real value, it should be remembered that the sovietologist making use of kremlinological techniques brings with him the benefit of other know-ledge. There is more to kremlinology than *Pravda* photographs of men all wearing the same kind of hat and standing on Lenin's Mausoleum.

Day after day the names of party leaders are listed in *Pravda* and *Izvestia* for one reason or another. The order often varies, but it is seldom accidental, and the kremlinologist ignores it at his peril. Major revisions mean major changes in the leadership and probably in policy. Even minor changes may represent an alteration in the balance of forces within the ruling group. It is of course perfectly true that men age, become ill, retire, or simply do not measure up to a job; therefore, while assuming that the changes he records have political significance, the sovietologist reminds himself constantly that accident plays a role in all human affairs, and much that happens, even in the Kremlin, has little political import.

To be more specific, everyone seems to understand that in certain conditions, official reference to a communist leader without the word 'comrade' preceding his name, may mean that he has been disgraced. In his secret speech at the 20th congress in 1956, Khrushchev gave another excellent example of protocol evidence which even the lowest party member could decipher:

> I can remember how the Ukraine learned about Kosior's arrest.[1] The Kiev radio used to start its programme thus: 'This is Radio Kosior.' When one day the programme began without naming Kosior, everyone was quite certain that something had happened to Kosior, that he had probably been arrested.

Should a young careerist like Alexander Shelepin (appointed head of the important party-state Control Committee in November 1962) turn an obscure phrase that appears to attack a policy identified with a respected elder statesman, the sovietologist would look for other evidence that Shelepin had taken a new step upward. And if such evidence were discovered, there would be need to reconsider a whole spectrum of relationships in the Presidium, the Secretariat, and the higher echelons of the apparat—the permanent, paid workers of the party.

As with the deciphering of esoteric language, much has been made of the blackness of the art of kremlinology. Some hold this to be the least respectable of the techniques employed by the sovietologist, yet this method of research is neither new nor bizarre. The Kremlin is not the first court to decide its affairs in secret. Nor is it the first court where the middle and lower nobles have had to study incessantly the careers of their patrons, anxiously scrutinising protocol signs in order to know

---

[1] S. V. Kosior was First Secretary of the Ukrainian party until January 1938. Arrested shortly thereafter, he was probably executed the same year.

when to desert a loser and attach themselves to a new and rising figure. In this age-old struggle the ambitious noble has always known how to indicate to his supporters that his favour at court is growing. Nor is Moscow's the first court in history where men fall out of grace over-night, where the leader maintains his strength by surrounding himself with favourites and by playing one powerful baron against another. Finally, Moscow is hardly the first capital city to witness constant intrigue and strife between the cliques that hold power. That the kremlinologist's study has been considered unique in the history of scholarship reflects badly upon our memory of the past.

A THIRD technique of prediction upon which the sovietologist relies very heavily is common to all men. This is simply the technique of defining current trends of development, in order to estimate their probable effect upon related institutions, ideas, and men, and to envisage something of their future. Simple enough when it concerns the harvest, or an estimate of railroad freight with detailed statistics of past traffic loads at hand, such trend study and projection become infinitely complex in other fields.

Khrushchev's destalinisation, for example, has been accompanied by a limited liberalisation of the party's control over certain intellectual and artistic affairs. What will be the effect next year and the year after? By permitting men in the sciences, in literature and art a limited freedom to think and discuss, the party appears to be encouraging a process that must inevitably undermine its authority. Conceivably, at some time in the foreseeable future, the advance of intellectual freedom may so weaken the party's power to arbitrate in intellectual affairs that it might find itself unable to lay the ghost it has raised without more cost to itself than it would wish to pay. A reversion to earlier practices would probably find little favour with the leaders, for it could revive the dysfunctional tensions of Stalin's era. But can we believe that the party will voluntarily limit its right to step in and decide any intellectual or artistic issue it considers politically important? What, in short, will be the political and social consequences of intellectual liberalisation five or ten years from now?

Manifestly, such questions must be the subject of serious study. Men must do their utmost to foresee the future, but there are no particularly fine techniques for making such work easy or accurate. What is needed is intelligence and knowledge, patient industry, sound judgment, and recognition of the openness of history.

(This article is a considerably abridged version of one which will appear in Talking to Eastern Europe, edited by G. R. Urban, to be published by Eyre & Spottiswoode, London.)

IN DEFENCE OF
KREMLINOLOGY

Robert Conquest

Quis? Quid? Ubi? Quibus auxiliis?
Cur? Quomodo? Quando?
(medieval legal hexameter)

THE editor tells me that this issue will contain attacks on the practice
of Kremlinology. How these will run I cannot, of course, know. But,
if I cannot answer them directly, I can deal with arguments which have
been raised in the past, in the expectation that the essentials at least of
the case against the subject will not have changed substantially.

I took particular note of these arguments when they found expression,
a couple of years ago, in connection with my own *Power and Policy in
the USSR*. This was essentially a large-scale exercise in the genre, and
it naturally attracted (and I naturally read with particular interest)
reviews by numbers of scholars for whose opinion I have great respect,
and several of whom stated their reservations about the whole approach
in cogent terms.

I did, indeed, detect a certain competitiveness of approach, a certain
possessiveness even, which seemed to lead to exaggeration. Sir William
Hayter, for example, wrote of Kremlinology, that I ' would probably
argue that it is the only valid branch of, or indeed coextensive with,
sovietology '. But of course I would do no such thing. In fact, I have
myself written on several other sides of Soviet life. But it does not seem
reasonable to blame me when, in a book about the struggle for power, I
treat economic and other matters only, or mainly, for their relevance to
it. Sir William seems to be in the position of a man who criticises a book
on the climbing of Mount Everest because it ignores the—to him—more
important question of the geology of the Himalayas. In fact I had
written in the book under review (and I imagine this would be the opinion
of most Kremlinologists):

> Writings on the subject of questions of power in the USSR are often
> criticised roughly on the grounds that they ignore the existence of
> large-scale social forces. It should be said at once that although this
> book is not in principle concerned with these forces it does not for a
> moment deny or denigrate them. The Soviet leaders do not live in a
> vacuum, and however much the totalitarian apparatus is designed to
> enable a few at the centre to manipulate the mass social tendencies,
> this does not mean that those tendencies do not exist nor, particularly
> when there is dissension at the centre, that they can fail to be taken
> into account. But this study is concerned with those large-scale
> movements only in so far as they are given political expression. And,
> in Soviet circumstances, they are not given any direct political

expression: they figure simply as influences, competing with other and often more powerful influences, on the moves made in the only area where political change is possible—the central group of politicians.

In fact, the student of the struggle for power does not, as Sir William implies, deny the importance of sociological and economic developments within Russia. On the other hand, Sir William does appear to deny the significance of the political. But we are confronted in the Soviet Union not by a faceless society and economy but by an organisation of actual rulers operating in accordance with definite standards of behaviour and preconceived doctrines. Any approach which ignores this tends to reduce the USSR to an abstraction of social forces not very different from our own. I suggest that the ' value ' of the study of the struggle for power is that it shows how the political machine and the men composing it conduct themselves.

But the attitude of rebuffing the supposed pretensions of the study is, in a less extreme form, one widely taken. *The Economist* argued that ' The very excellence of his limited work confirms that Kremlinology is only a part—some will say a minor part—in the study of Soviet history '. Few writers could resent criticism couched in such friendly terms, and I hope, at least, that it will be clear that I am not moved by any personal pique or complaint, that it is my subject, not myself, that I am defending.

THIS divergence of view is, of course, to some extent a temperamental matter. One works and writes on the whole better about subjects one is interested in. Sir William Hayter says: ' Yet with all the merits of this book, doubts of the validity of Kremlinology persist. Mr Conquest rightly says in his concluding paragraph that the academic validity of a subject is unaffected by its uselessness " so long as the subject interests ". But does it interest? I confess I found it difficult to remain absorbed . . .'

And the temperamental reservations felt by many people against the study are not limited to the vague feeling that power on the one hand and personality on the other are nebulous subjects compared with the decent, impersonal, readily abstractifiable phenomena of general sociology and the homely and comfortable equations of the economists. They are also, I think, directed against the type of research worker who becomes involved in this unrespectable field. He is seen, perhaps, as a sensationalist—or, if not that, perhaps as a man who prefers an area in which speculation must remain the norm, just because this provides an opportunity for the construction of crackpot theories. And it is true that in its time Kremlinology has attracted such people. Yet there is another and different temperament which, I think, finds such subjects particularly fascinating. That is, the type of mind which is drawn to areas where the information is not adequate and a great effort has to be made to force the deductions from recalcitrant material.

That this temperamental distinction within the subject is not confined to Kremlinology may be illustrated in another field. The Vinland Problem —the attempt to deduce the location of the brief Norse settlements and their other place names in North America around the year 1000 from the available documents and the facts of geography—has recognisably drawn in two quite different types of enthusiast. One is concerned to prove, with immense and laboured detail, that favourite spots answer to each point; these usually work in a large amount of local evidence which could equally well prove anything. On the other hand, there are those who may reach virtual certainty on one or two points, high probability on others, and complete bafflement on still others: men who are truly concerned not merely to establish the truth but to consider the impossibility of establishing it, and to balance the claims of two alternatives, when the evidence does not answer. These latter seem to me to be admirable, perhaps the most admirable type of intellectual exercises in existence— just as Namier seems to me to be worth a hundred Toynbees.

Such a man, in the Vinland case, was J. R. Swanton, whose comment is extraordinarily apt to Kremlinology too:

> The fact of the matter is that the data are just strong enough to tempt one to theorise and just weak enough to open the door for an immense amount of speculation, especially if one has an undisciplined imagination and a plentiful supply of local pride or wishful thinking. . . . It is one of those investigations which enable men who pride themselves on their acumen to prove it by leaving the problems ostentatiously alone or by registering scepticism, the cheapest way there is to acquire a reputation for scientific ability.[1]

The temperamental objection to such an attitude comes out again, I think, in Sir William Hayter, when he writes:

> A classic specimen of the kind of thing I have in mind occurs when Mr Conquest describes the twentieth party congress at great length without ever mentioning what were, to my mind, its most important results, the revision of the doctrines about the inevitability of major wars and about the possible achievement of socialism by parliamentary means.

Now, in the first place, I was not especially concerned to decide in a general way what were the 'most important' results of the congress, but merely to deal with it as it affected the study I was engaged upon—just as it would be unfair to a writer of the history of the British Cabinet in the 1830s to say of him that he seemed to think the only important thing about the development of the railway engine was that one of them had killed Huskisson. But I feel, still, that Sir William shows very strongly the dangers of too great a revulsion from Kremlinology. Of the two points he takes as being the most important, one, the theorising about the attainment of power by parliamentary means, strikes me as very minor and largely concerned with verbal propaganda. Suslov, Mikoyan, and

---

[1] John R. Swanton, 'The Wineland Voyages'. Smithsonian Miscellaneous Collections, Vol. 107, No. 12.

the others who put it forward combined it with strong attacks on reform-
ism and gave as their example of a parliamentary evolution what had
already happened in Prague and elsewhere in Eastern Europe! (I have,
as a matter of fact, dealt with this elsewhere.) The non-inevitability of
war was, indeed, an important theme. And it may be taken as registering
the final acceptance by Moscow of the unacceptability of a nuclear clash.
But even on this one may perhaps doubt if it was more than the transformation into theory of what had already happened in practice.

But in any case, not to grant equal status as a major political event to
the attack on Stalin seems to be greatly overdoing things, on any view.
After all, it launched a series of vast political changes throughout the
communist world, which are still going on. (And is it irrelevant to note
that *The Observer*, in which Sir William's review appeared, had at the
time devoted an entire issue to the secret speech?)

A taste for what one might call anti-politics leads to the neglect of
matters not only important in themselves but often actually decisive in
the fields which anti-political man is trying to cultivate as autonomous
enclosures. As I said in *Power and Policy*:

> There seems to be a definite feeling among sociologists that the
> actual events of politics and war are in some way superficial. They
> believe that deep social tides are more basic to all change in human
> circumstances and that battles and *coups d'état* are somehow rather
> petty subjects. And it is true that to concentrate attention on them
> in such a way as to imply a denial of the existence of deeper move-
> ments would be absolutely wrong. Just the same, it is a little unreal
> to deal only with the deeper movements and ignore the visible politi-
> cal and military climaxes. It is rather as if a man interested in race-
> horses should study only their form and their general condition, with-
> out concerning himself with the actual race.

This view of history is dubious enough at the best of times. ' The best of
times ' was probably the nineteenth century, when economic forces were
exceedingly powerful and political ones comparatively weak—and, in any
case, often disoriented by the current theory that political intervention in
economic matters was bad doctrine. Even then Engels had been able to
point out that ' Force is itself an economic power '. It is the great discovery of the twentieth century that political and political-military technique and organisation can be developed to such a degree of power and
efficiency that they are able for the first time in history (if we except some
special cases like Inca Peru, as Plekhanov noted) to take the economic
forces head on and thwart and divert them. Sociologically, the totalitarian
state is a lever by which one man, or a small group, can exert the same
weight as whole social classes.

IRONICALLY, it was in the USSR that this discovery was given practical form. Stalin's collectivisation and industrialisation were the im-
position of policy decisions against the wish of the whole people and the
tendencies of the economy. Their dynamic, and it was one which defeated

the supposedly unconquerable forces arising naturally in the economy
and society, was a theory in the minds of a few policy makers, willpower
in the skull of a paranoid Georgian. For once, an Idealist Conception of
History was correct.

Our own epoch has been the scene of a number of attempts prematurely to erect into rigorous disciplines various studies which are not
yet prepared for this. The prestige of the true sciences has been so great
that there has been a rush to make some of it rub off on investigations
which cannot yet meaningfully absorb it. In part this has been abetted by
the creation of academic institutions to which the erection of ' scientific '
theory gives added *raison d'être*. Thus we have seen the pretensions of
' Literary Criticism ' blown up past bullfrog-bursting point. There is the
now crumbling structure of Freudian psychology. And, to my mind, a
great deal of what passes for scientific sociology is of similar nature.
(One of the distinctions between a scientific journal and one aping science
is that in the former the interest always lies in the anomalous, that which
appears *not* to fit existing conceptions, while in the latter, as in a theological journal, everything proves the theorist right all the time.) The, quite
bona fide existence of pseudo-sciences and semi-sciences masquerading
as fully established branches of knowledge is not a new one. The past is
littered with astrologies and phrenologies. But the tide now seems to be
running against the last batch.

But one of the saddest by-products of a dubious sociological attitude
has, in any case, been the persistence of historicism—of the notion that
there are forces assessable by economic or sociological means which are
determinative of history. That is, in effect, the formal denial that politics
are anything but an epiphenomenon on other processes. Or, even if the
' superstructure ' is permitted to react upon the base, it reacts according
to rules ultimately determined outside itself. This view is one which
typifies the over-tidy mind, the simplifier who has, moreover, already
oversimplified for himself even the ' base '. It arouses not only rejection
but also resentment, because it is in political action too often an excuse
for inhumanity, the theorist being prepared to accept the real and visible
sacrifice of generations and nations in the name of the, one would have
thought, less tangible future predicted by his patent method. I cannot
believe that this is an accidental correlation, that it is mere chance that
the idolater of the abstractions of System and History is also the wor-
shipper of Power and the shrugger-off of the suffering of the mass of
individuals.

What, in any case, is the nature of the Soviet polity? Professor
Leonard Schapiro has written:

> ' How little as yet (one cannot safely make predictions about any
> political system) public opinion of any kind can hope to operate on
> politicians who, over a period of forty years, have mastered the art
> of keeping all power safely in their own hands—even though they
> may fight to the death inside their own narrow circle,' and he adds

that the amateur is inclined ' to project on to the Soviet system political principles with which he is familiar in his own experience. They very seldom apply. For example, in democracies politicians quarrel over policies and if need be resign in the hope of making a comeback. In the Politbureau and the Presidium it is the other way round: politicians quarrel over power, using policies as a means of struggle ' (*The Listener*, 18 May 1961).

As *The Times Literary Supplement* pointed out, Kremlinology shows that the gap between East and West is one between political cultures. And I suppose it would be agreed, except by superficial and optimistic journalists and their readers, that the liberalisation which has taken place in Russia since Stalin's death has not registered any advance in the positive political power of the ruled. The *pays légal* is still limited to a few hundred, or a few thousand apparatchiks. The autocracy has shifted from repressionist to concessionist tactics as other autocracies have in the past, but it remains an autocracy. And the ruling class consists as ever of the cadres who got their training under Stalin. The characteristics of this class—philistine, hypocritical, shortsighted, bigoted, ruthless, totally indoctrinated with their own right to rule—do not change overnight. Though some may be better than others they are a special breed. And it is in the internal struggle that we can really see what they amount to.

The apparatocracy may, like previous ruling classes, crumble in the face of crises it is ill-equipped to deal with. But it is extremely tenacious, and meanwhile the politics of Russia consists of the moves and manoeuvres of its members. If the contestants were called Michael the Drunkard or Basil the Macedonian we would have no difficulty in making the emotional effort of understanding that their ways are not ours. Yet in Byzantium too, there was also doctrine—*filioque* and so on—on the one hand, and policy—taxation, or the defeat of the Bulgars—on the other.

IT is vulgar and regrettable that important historical crises should be decided by personal ambition, but it is also, unfortunately, true. Soviet sources themselves are perfectly explicit about the role played by personal ambition and malice in the struggle for power, though naturally only on the part of the defeated. After accusing the ' anti-party group ' of egoism and love of power, Kuusinen, in his speech to the 22nd congress, said: ' The main effort of the group was to remove from the Presidium of the Central Committee Comrade Nikita Sergeyevich Khrushchev '. Or again, ' Although the gingerbread was poisonous, Bulganin, being dissatisfied with his position in the party, nevertheless ran after it when it was promised to him ' (S. D. Ignatiev at the December 1958 Plenum).

Policy is bound to enter in, if only for the reason that a struggle for power cannot be conducted openly on the programme ' We want your posts because we want to rule '. Doctrine is an element by which power can get a purchase. Stalin would have been thought a moderate at the time of the struggle against the Left Opposition, and was doubtless praised as such in the Western press. Having destroyed them, he was in a position to steal their policies and use them against the Right. Similarly, Khrushchev ensured Malenkov's first defeat by sponsorship of 'Left' policies, and then turned Right himself. The struggle with the anti-party group in 1957 has almost always been misrepresented. In fact both the victorious and the defeated factions contained right and left wing elements. The tactics they objected to in Khrushchev were ones of style rather than policy proper.

> The anti-party group—Malenkov, Kaganovich, Molotov, Bulganin, and Shepilov—accused our Party's Central Committee and also Comrade N. S. Khrushchev of practicism and of being too engulfed in the practical tasks of economic construction. As is known, such accusations were also raised by the Yugoslav revisionists (I. I. Kuzmin at the 21st congress, *Pravda*, 5 February 1959).

A viewpoint shared by Molotov and Tito is scarcely one of policy.

This also reminds us that since, as we have said, the group contained the ' liberal ' Malenkov and Shepilov as well as the ' reactionary ' Molotov and Kaganovich, it could be attacked in connection with almost any policy which later became popular. Malenkov headed the list at first, and Molotov was transferred to top spot when, and only when, Khrushchev was directing his main fire against remaining ' conservative ' elements within the party.

Another important deduction from this way of looking at things is that there is no necessary connection between policies. During the height of Khrushchev's ' liberalisation ' at home, in 1962, we get the Cuban adventure, a far riskier piece of ' forward ' policy than anything of Stalin's —and understandably condemned, even by the Chinese, as ' adventurism '. What links Khrushchev's policies is their ' style ', as the Russians say—large, risky initiatives, looking as if they will bring big results on the cheap. Temper, personality, rather than coherent views, seems the common factor—a curious conclusion about a man who is widely taken as primarily just the locus of social forces. It may remind us of Canning's ' Away with the cant of measures not men! —the idle supposition that it is the harness and not the horses that draw the chariot along '. This is to put it very strongly; yet in politics, in the area in which the actual decisions are taken that will determine the Russian future, does anyone imagine that things would have been the same if Molotov had come to power? And does anyone think that his accession to power was impossible, under some Law of History? Politics proper, moreover, is the realm of the accidental, the run of bad luck, the chance concatenation. The death of Hugh Gaitskell transformed British politics. So it has always gone, from the assassination of Lincoln to Kozlov's heart attack. Accident is unpredictable, but its effects may not be. To put it at its lowest, if we neglect the elements of this level of Soviet phenomena, we will not understand the rest.

Professor Seton-Watson wrote in the *Financial Times*: ' Thus the study of Kremlinology is not opposed to, but is complementary to the study of Soviet society. Each is equally necessary to our understanding, and each illuminates the other '. And again, J. Miller, joint editor of *Soviet Studies*, wrote:

> I have a strong prejudice against Kremlinology because I know, through the accident of having lived for a year with several hundred budding young Soviet politicians, that they have far stronger political motivations than the desire for power; and because the decisive developments in Russia (or any country) are liable to be missed if attention is concentrated on the political leaders. Nevertheless, I recommend this book as an able exercise in Kremlinology, which— whatever its limitations and dangers—is certainly one of several ways into a knowledge of what is happening in the USSR (none of the other ways are, of course, without their own limitations and dangers).

Fair enough, but to take up Mr Miller's point about motives. Of course, no one would deny that there are other drives than mere power in the Soviet politician's motivations. Indeed, in any struggle of this sort, ' idealism, conviction, careerism, and factiousness form an inextricable blend '. And again, ' it is virtually impossible to clarify how far the communist leaders, or particular ones among them, are motivated by *odium theologicum* and how far by ambition, even in the struggle for power itself. This is more a psychological question than a political one ' (me). We do not need to discover the extent to which the other motivations are psychological ' justifications '. What we can say is that these qualifications apply to *all* political societies, but that, in any case, the power motive is more obviously compelling or less adequately sublimated in some cases than in others. Napoleon had it worse than Lincoln, and Stalin than Attlee. And under Stalin, in the USSR, by a process of natural selection, ' a hypertrophied type has been bred in which the motives that are sufficiently frenetic even in a mild Western office or university have become a full-time, consuming passion ' (me again). I would moreover add that of Mr Miller's hundreds of young Soviet politicians, I should expect those to rise to the top whose power motivation is higher, or becomes higher, than the average.

KREMLINOLOGY may be thought of, *mutatis mutandis*, as the Namierism of Soviet political history. In Namier's special period the political nation consisted of a limited number of men—those members of the nobility, the merchant and intellectual classes, and the squirearchy, who were interested in politics. He was able to revolutionise a study previously based on generalisations by examining the particular moods and opinions of numbers of those concerned. Similarly, in the USSR, the *pays légal* is a limited one. Until recently only the actions of very few people at the centre needed to be considered, and the bare record of the allegiances of minor figures was adequate. Even this was regarded as unnecessary by students attached to general ideas. And it is now suggested (for example, by Edward Crankshaw) that since a larger number of people are perhaps being admitted to the oligarchy, the method is no longer applicable. The contrary appears to be true: what is now required is large-scale research into the background of the lower level repositories of power.

For in speaking of Kremlinology as a sort of Namierism we must unfortunately qualify this by saying that on the whole it is an inadequately resolved Namierism. There is still, to my mind, too much that we do not know but could know with a good deal more effort. I was very conscious of this when working on the subject myself. To take a single point: Namier got his results by investigating the politics and the political weight of comparatively large numbers of people forming at least a reasonable cross-section of the entire *pays légal* of eighteenth-century Britain. My book, and most of the others in the field, seldom descend, and never fully or effectively, below the Presidium, or at most the Central Committee. The provincial secretary level and lower, and even the detailed backgrounds of all the Central Committee membership, are simply impossible without far greater and more widespread time, effort, and facilities. The research currently being undertaken at the Columbia Russian Institute will, one hopes, be something in the nature of a breakthrough in the whole field. Meanwhile, as Mr David Shapiro points out, 'We have no alternative method [to Kremlinology] for judging the course of Soviet politics at the level of the Presidium'. Anyone, he adds, who tries to explain the breakdown of the Summit talks in 1961 finds that they have to 'dabble in Kremlinology'. I have always noticed, indeed, that when it comes to talk about Russian politics, there is really no such thing as a non-Kremlinologist. Whoever remarked that the man who says he is not a philosopher is simply a bad philosopher, was making a point which may perhaps be taken as applying in this case to the study of Soviet politics.

But can results be obtained within the field itself? Yes. It was possible to give what proved to be a sound account of the June 1957 crisis before confirmation came with later revelations. Even without much in the way of deduction and extrapolation, assembly of known facts and statements often provides a clear enough picture of events, and one which sometimes goes usefully against false preconceptions, giving a desirable shock to lazy assumptions that Soviet politics are not so different from our own. It is true, indeed, that deduction—or even speculation, if carefully controlled—can give good results, and in any case better ones than those based on conservative assumptions about harmonious development. As to simple deduction, I may quote one of several cases from my own book. With no 'inside' information, but simply working from facts and probabilities of their interpretation, I wrote of the circumstances of Mr Khrushchev's secret speech:

> The impression remains strong that, although some sort of intention to disavow the purges had developed some weeks before the congress, the precise tactics had not been decided on up to the last moment . . . all this confusion and hesitation followed by a decision must have taken place within the presidium . . . a group determined to press the

issue regardless could possibly have threatened to appeal to the Central Committee, or even the congress, with facts which the others were in no position to deny, and the secret speech, unopposed, may represent a very reluctant compromise.

Five years later, Khrushchev, reporting to the 22nd congress, said:

Comrade-delegates, I want to tell the congress how the anti-party group reacted to the proposal to raise the question of abuses of power in the period of the cult of the individual at the 20th congress. The proposal was violently resisted by Molotov, Kaganovich, Malenkov, Voroshilov and others. We told them in reply to their objections that if they resisted consideration of this question, we would put the matter to the congress delegates. We had no doubt that the congress would express itself in favour of the consideration of this question. Only then did they agree, and the question of the cult of the individual was reported on at the 20th congress.

Is this really to be regarded as having been either obvious or unimportant?

EVERYTHING that we read among the accumulating revelations about the struggle tells us something, begins to define the nature of the Soviet polity—it is one where a police chief plans a *coup d'état*; where an Army leader is accused of 'Bonapartist aspirations towards a single-handed seizure of power'; where a Prime Minister throws his armed guards round the Presidium; where gross insults are hurled between leading figures; where policies are launched not on their merits, but to secure a power advantage, and condemned not on their demerits, but in theological terms; where one former terror operative can charge his fallen opponents with terrorism—but not secure their expulsion from the party; where the very party history is altered decisively from edition to edition. Kremlinology is an attempt to obtain now, when it can be most useful, the information about Soviet politics which is thought to be essential when it comes to writing a history of earlier years. If an adequate account of the past is found impossible without it, how can it be imagined that an account of the present can dispense with it? Without this information our interpretation of events is certain to be defective at best. It is true that we may not always be able to get enough data for our purpose, but surely we are bound not to reject the attempt to do so.

Mr. Leonard Schapiro, in a very sympathetic review, took me up on one suggestion when he rebuked me as follows: 'Mr Conquest even gets near suggesting that 'kremlinology should become a new university discipline. This is really rather far-fetched'. What I had said was:

It seems to me to be a pity that no journal exists solely devoted to the matter, and I trust that the foundation of one may be considered. It would, as I see it, cover two explicitly separate fields—the registration of relevant facts, and the setting up of speculative theory. As it is, there are many careful workers and collators in the field, together with others who, though they may play by ear, come across useful information and are the sources of interesting speculation. But the student has to pan an enormous variety of different productions, in which no particular standards prevail. Moreover, the researcher who simply comes across the odd interesting point, and is not writing an article or book on the particular subject, has nowhere where he can briefly register it : and this, to my knowledge, is not a rare occurrence at all, but one which is happening all the time. A journal which was open to such material, and which also abstracted or reproduced the main material produced elsewhere throughout the world, would do a great service.

I am not ashamed of this suggestion at all. In fact I urge it again, and hope the various students who have spoken of some attempt to implement it will go ahead and do so. We do need this information. For the essential importance of Kremlinology is this. We do not know enough about Soviet politics. We do not know the alignments, the political forces and motivations which produce the great policy decisions and lead to the enormous and important shifts, reversals, initiatives of the regime. We can all predicate, more or less, the choices open to the Soviet Government in a given field, but we have little idea of what will decide the final real action.

It is not that we can seek any finality, any data on which certain prophecy can be based. No more can we in any other country; but in most other capitals we can at least meaningfully discuss the forces at work, the party and factional alignments, the personal affiliations. In fact most political comment about the rest of the world is in such terms. When we attempt it for the USSR, we must either *call* ourselves non-Kremlinologists and just guess or intuit, or we must go to Kremlinology, which is merely the assertion that faction and divergence exist in Russia as in every polity, and the formal determination to discover or deduce as much as possible about it by a conscientious study of the relevant evidence.

THE USES AND ABUSES
OF KREMLINOLOGY

Alec Nove

THE object of this article is to discuss the relative significance of some methods of studying the Soviet Union, and it is convenient for this purpose to use 'Kremlinology' as a peg on which to hang the discussion. By Kremlinology I mean the method of analysis which lays great stress on a careful study of the promotion, demotion, and inter-action of personalities, and also on the exact wording of pronouncements of certain conventional or formal kinds. On the whole, I take the view that this can be greatly overdone, and once gave a talk under the title of 'Down with Kremlinology'. However, it must be emphasised that 'down' does not mean 'out', but rather 'down to the second division', to use football language. It is certainly useful to study the sort of things which Kremlinologists study. The problem is—how useful, relatively to other things.

A critique of Kremlinology involves two important points of principle. The first is the role of personality in history in general, in Soviet history in particular. The second relates to the validity of the technique of Kremlinology as a guide to personality struggles or to policy clashes. The two points are to some extent independent of one another. Thus one may well hold the view that the decision about who is to succeed Khrushchev is of vital importance to the entire world, and nonetheless argue that we cannot discover who will succeed him by watching the careers of the supporters of Brezhnev, Polyanski, Kozlov, or other pos-sible contenders, or the precise wording of *Pravda* editorials. We will discuss later on the extent to which the traditional methods of Kremlin-ology are helpful even within the narrower confines of power-struggle analysis. But first, what is the case for the Kremlinological approach?

On a naive level, it consists of variations on the theme of the well-known generalisation, 'history is about chaps'. The biographies of politicians, on this view, *are* political history. It would then not matter particularly whether two (imaginary) comrades named Bushkin and Kukushkin stand for different policies. A conflict between them, if such exists, is by definition both relevant and important. Such an approach is common enough among diplomats and newspaper correspondents, and rightly so. It is an essential part of their jobs to report the rise and fall of personalities. The promotion, demotion, and ambitions of politicians must be reported, whether or not there results any change of policy. This is at least as true of the Soviet Union as of any other country.

But the Soviet Union is a special case, argue the Kremlinologists. Political strife does not take place there in the open, it is conducted behind the scenes, and little hints appear in obscure ways. These may be connected with the rise and fall of individuals in the hierarchy, or with significant policy shifts. Hints may be found in obscure paragraphs or in some peculiar rewording of certain formal statements. This is the bit of the iceberg that shows above the surface. Rumours of conflict within the leadership are always denied even when the political battle is in full swing, as it was on the eve of Malenkov's fall and in the struggle with the ' anti-party ' group. Yet acute observers did spot some tell-tale signs. Then it is also argued that policy issues in the USSR are in a special way subordinated to the power struggle, that it shows a misunderstanding of Soviet political realities to study issues in themselves. This view can readily be supported by evidence which shows that pronouncements on policy, ideology, and philosophy have been repeatedly used as missiles in political in-fighting. It is also said, again with justice, that the penalties of defeat in Soviet politics have been exceptionally severe, and that this has affected the behaviour of the actors on the political stage. It is also undeniable that the decisions of politicians affect many more aspects of the lives of the people in the Soviet Union than is the case in western countries. It may also be legitimately argued, though this point is often pushed too far, that in the Soviet Union politics controls social-economic reality, making nonsense of any analysis based on economic determinism. Thus, for example, forcible collectivisation and the first five-year plan represented a politically inspired attempt to change drastically the then existing economic and social milieu; these policies could hardly be regarded as a reflection of the class structure of Soviet society in 1928. All this does seem to add up to a powerful case for Kremlinology. The more intelligent practitioners of the art would presumably not deny that many things happen in the Soviet Union which have no causal connection with the power struggle, or that real problems do not exist. They would surely also agree that the power of the Soviet totalitarian state is not absolute, that it is limited not only by physical fact (a quart will not go into a pint pot, in Moscow as in London) but also by certain social and economic realities. In fact, the discussion between sensible Kremlinologists and their sensible opponents is concerned with emphasis. Neither side would assert that the preoccupations of the other are nonsensical. Both would admit that it is possible to go too far in either totally ignoring the power struggle or in considering nothing else. In the one case one abstracts from an important aspect of Soviet political life, in the other the analysis becomes one-sided and superficial. It is likely that we would all agree that the emphasis which one places on Kremlinological analysis is partly related to time-scale. The more one is concerned with ' micro-history ', the greater the role of the manoeuvres of individual politicians. Conversely, developments over a longer period tend to have causes of a less personal kind.

WHAT weaknesses are there in the Kremlinologists' case? In the first place, I feel that they tend to overestimate some of the differences between Soviet and western political systems. No-one would deny that there are important differences, but in virtually all countries politicians are ambitious men who intrigue against one another, who in the course of their intrigues do not always say what they mean, and are known to adopt policies with one or both eyes on the consequences of these policies for their political ambitions. An unambitious politician would probably be in another profession. A desire for power and a capacity for intrigue are a common denominator. As I am writing these words, I have in front of me an article by the *Evening Standard's* political correspondent, published on 25 June 1963, which contains the following words: 'It is a truism that politics is concerned with power. Equally its motive force is ambition to wield that power, directly or indirectly.' It is sometimes necessary to remind over-enthusiastic Kremlinologists that such words as these can be used, as they were used, about Great Britain. It follows from the above that politicians, in pursuit of their own ambitions, may adopt policies which are suggested to them by circumstances, in which case it is the circumstance rather than the ambition which explains the course of events. Thus Disraeli extended the franchise to the urban artisans in 1867 'to dish the Whigs', as he himself said. One notes this fact, but presumably no serious historian would assert that the extension of the franchise in the second half of the 19th century was 'caused' by Disraeli's understandable desire to carry out a political manoeuvre. One could assert with some justice that the pursuit of greater power is for politicians what the pursuit of profit is for the business man, a motive for action which causes men to take opportunities, but which is common to so many men that it ceases to be an underlying cause of events. Of course differences of setting and opportunity make for wide differences of tactics and throw up quite different kinds of politicians in different countries. Mr Maudling and Lord Hailsham do not strive for success by methods which served Beria and Malenkov, and it did not occur to George Brown to have his rival, Harold Wilson, arrested for counter-revolutionary activities. However, reasons for such striking contrasts in political behaviour must be sought in impersonal factors—institutions, traditions, political atmosphere, etc.

Are real issues and doctrinal arguments in the USSR subordinated to the power struggle in some special sense which does not apply elsewhere? That they are mixed up in varying degrees with the power struggle is not denied. The problem is of finding a method of analysis which most usefully enables us to see the causes of events. Let us take some examples. Malenkov's fall was preceded by politically inspired attacks on his alleged economic heresies. He was accused of doctrinal error in overstressing consumer goods as against producer goods. The arguments were put in the official and technical press in a dogmatically one-sided way. There was no debate in any serious sense. This was part of the process of removing Malenkov from the premiership, conducted in a certain conventional manner. Yet, underlying the formal verbiage there were some very real problems. Malenkov's abandonment of traditional priorities led to some confusion in planning, since shortages persisted. He had demagogically reduced retail prices, lowered taxes, halved forced savings, increased wage levels and peasant incomes, a policy which adds up to inflation. There was also a conflict with those who, like Khrushchev, desired a substantial increase in investment in agriculture. We may be sure that these things were debated behind the scenes. Issues and personal conflicts were intermingled, as they nearly always are, but the economic problem was quite plainly present, and it is wrong to treat this as a mere by-product of the power struggle.

Yet, from another standpoint, it was just such a by-product. There is no need to overstress the purely economic aspect of the story. It is not my purpose to argue for economic determinism, but rather to stress the importance of issues, circumstances, the logic of events. This logic may or may not relate to economic factors; the point is that it is impersonal. Kremlinologists seem to overlook even the logic of the power struggle itself. Let us take the position at Stalin's death. His successors faced a longing for relaxation of terror, an urgent need of agricultural reforms, an immense desire for more houses and consumer goods. *Any* successor was likely to compete for support by adopting policies which reflected this situation. The danger clearly existed that competitors for the leadership would try to outdo one another, to go beyond the possible in efforts to achieve popularity. Even Beria was reportedly aware of the need to act on these lines; Malenkov certainly was. (One could treat this as a Soviet version of a British ' election budget ', but because of the much greater economic powers of the Soviet state the dangers of such a policy are greater there.) There was an urgent need for deflationary measures in 1955. The immediate cause of these measures must be seen as the overstrain which had to be remedied. In other words, Khrushchev's economic policies of 1955 should not be explained *directly* by the power struggle. But it is true that the logic of the succession problem was itself part of the explanation for the overstrain.

WHILE the above analysis is to some extent independent of any particular personalities (save that the situation might not have arisen if Stalin were immortal), it is not argued that all the leaders would adopt the same policies or that their decisions are at all times situation-determined. No-one can assert such things about many important elements of Stalin's career, for instance. Some leaders can and do adopt drastic policies from which some of their colleagues would have shrunk. Others can commit grave errors. We must at all costs avoid a ' what happened had to happen ' approach. Or perhaps not quite at all costs, since to find the rationale of what did happen is usually a more fruitful way of writing history than attributing major events to the power struggle or to accidental decisions of great men. At any given moment the past is past, and the men at the top have before them a range of choice which may be small or substantial. Sometimes the general lines of policy are indicated by the already existing circumstances. It is a

myth that the choice of the Soviet ruling group is infinite. It is cir-
cumscribed not only by the objective situation but also by the ruling
group's own thought patterns. This remains the case despite the lack of
institutional checks on the exercise of power. Political scientists sometimes overstress the importance of institutional factors in decision-
making. After all, there are many things which a Conservative or
Labour government in this country would not do which it would have
the *power* to do. But the role of an individual leader remains great in
Russia, and consequently some decisions and reorganisations bear the
imprint of Khrushchev's personality. Thus his attempts to overcome
inefficiencies in economic planning are greatly influenced by an oversimplified picture of party trouble-shooters, a picture which is quite
irrelevant to the solution of the real problems. Thus we have here
an important personal element. Yet any serious analysis would have
to take account of three things:

(a) The problem of industrial planning is real and has a life and
logic of its own, independently of Khrushchev's view of it.

(b) Khrushchev's view of it is itself a product of his experience of
party life in the last 30 years.

(c) Because his solution is no solution, the problem will continue
to plague him and his successors, compelling them to try out other ideas,
which are being actively discussed.

Economic organisation is an area where policy, efficiency, ideology,
and power considerations overlap and interact. The Sovnarkhoz reform
of 1957 was both a genuine effort to correct real defects of planning, and
a blow dealt by Khrushchev against his enemies. The precise shape
of the reform was certainly affected by Khrushchev's political position
(such things are of course not unknown in other countries!). Thus,
to take one example, the size of the Sovnarkhozy was much too small
for economic convenience, and must have been influenced by Khrushchev's need to secure the support of the local party secretaries; this
led him to preserve in most cases the existing administrative boundaries. But the reform had causes and logical consequences which
transcended the power struggle and which made it unavoidable that
Khrushchev would make further changes. Thus the built-in tendency
towards ' localism ' on the part of Sovnarkhozy made recentralisation
the only alternative to a kind of decentralisation (to market forces)
which neither Khrushchev nor the party machine is yet prepared to
contemplate. The inevitable recentralisation placed impossible burdens
on Gosplan and this led to the multiplication of state committees and
other co-ordinating bodies. Whatever Khrushchev's intention was,
effective central control could not be exercised by local party organs
because these inevitably identified themselves with the economic interests
of their locality, i.e. with obtaining maximum investment resources from
the state and fulfilling local plans regardless of the effect on others. The
small size of the Sovnarkhozy led to experiments with coordinating
committees and large regions. There was plenty of evidence of stresses

and strains, which had a reality quite independent of the will of particular politicians and which called for urgent remedial action. Early in 1962, the author of these lines wrote an article (published in *Soviet Studies* in July) which forecast imminent changes. When these changes came, the pattern of reform was again affected by the political interests of individuals and of groups.

Khrushchev tried in November 1962 to strengthen centralised party control, while weakening the position of the *Obkom* secretaries. The solution adopted in March 1963 may be a compromise, since it differs in several significant respects from the ideas submitted to the November 1962 plenum. Of course, different leaders may have had different ideas about just what should be done. It would be amazing were it otherwise. The point is that the problems these men dealt with are complex and intractable, and have a logic and reality of their own which should be analysed as such, though economic organisation and the political aspects of planning also interact with the ' balance of power ' between individuals and groups.

In fact it is possible to forecast with some confidence that there will be a political and personal conflict on this very issue. It may already be in full swing. It is possible to interpret the otherwise obscure elements in the industrial reorganisation of March 1963, and in particular the appointment of Ustinov as a planning overlord, as evidence of just such a conflict. Perhaps this explains the otherwise peculiar outburst of Khrushchev in his speech to the ideologists in June 1963, in which he sought to assert the superiority of the party over the planners; the context was most unsuitable, and he seemed to be arguing with someone whose opinions have not so far been reported. Far from denying the power struggle, it may be asserted that the adoption of reforming ideas by power-seeking persons or groups is a vital part of reality, but the issues here help us to explain and even forecast what the struggle is likely to be about.

IT may not be unfair to assert that Kremlinologists are quite ready to see impersonal logic of events when they write about the sector of Russian life which they themselves know. Thus, Robert Conquest is able to see the logic of socialist-realism in the general context of the totalitarian system established by Stalin, and I feel sure that he would not attribute the repressive policies of the period in any fundamental sense to the personalities or ambitions of Shcherbakov or Zhdanov. He would doubtless agree that the two above-named comrades, as well as their views on art and their means of enforcing these views, were an integral part of the Stalin system. Similarly, while he and other Kremlinologists may note that Kozlov seems to be associated with a tough cultural line in 1963, they would doubtless admit that the hesitations of the leadership over the consequences of cultural liberalisation have a very real objective basis. (Also that Khrushchev's own taste in art is similar to that of most small-town politicians of his generation, and not only in Russia.) What

Conquest does seem to overlook is that virtually every separate sector or aspect of Soviet reality has its own inner logic, and that the role of the power struggle as an explanation of events is generally greatest in the spheres of which the given analyst is most ignorant. Whether one discusses the general pattern of Soviet diplomacy, the quarrel with China, legal doctrine, fuel policy, or whatever it may be, almost every expert on *that* sector will tend to devote his serious work to analysing the circumstantial logic of events, and while the decisions of politicians must be fitted into the pattern, they will only occasionally emerge as a decisive part of the explanation. Thus Kaganovich may have favoured the steam locomotive, and this may have delayed the introduction of diesel and electric traction on the Russian railways, but no one writing on transport would take very seriously a Kremlinological explanation of the advent of diesels and electrification.

In recent years Kremlinological methods have also suffered a blow from the gradual erosion of certain conventional procedures. The names of the leaders are now generally given in alphabetical order, though indications of relative status do continue to appear occasionally, as, for instance, in lists of localities wishing to adopt a given leader as a candidate for the Supreme Soviet. The absence of any individual from an official function is no longer an indication that anything is afoot. In 1953 the Kremlinologists rightly noted the significance of Beria's absence from an operatic performance. It was indeed a sign of his downfall and could not possibly mean, within the then existing conventions, that he did not like opera or even that he had a cold. Lists of leaders attending formal functions were a signal, read and understood as such by local officials. Presumably if a leader really did have a cold, his name would still have appeared as attending the Bolshoi Theatre, to avoid confusing the local comrades. But in recent years we have had repeated instances of prominent leaders absenting themselves, without any significance attaching to their absence. Similarly, it is no longer true, though it once was true, that a critical or unusual statement by a scholar or technician is likely to be officially inspired. Under Stalin statements which diverged from the official line involved so much risk that they would only be made with powerful political backing. Therefore even the opinion of an expert on a technical matter could be an important indication of changes in policy or the relative positions of politicians. Quite plainly this is no longer the case. As Herbert Dinerstein rightly put it, ' It seems that discussion . . . does not necessarily indicate a dispute over policy in the party. A debate may be just what it purports to be, an expression of differences of opinion by experts who hope that the cogency of their arguments will compel party leaders to retain or modify official policies.' [1]

PRESUMABLY all serious scholars would agree that, to borrow a sentence from an unpublished paper by Raymond Garthoff, ' the

---

[1] *Soviet Doctrine on Developing Countries: Some Divergent Views*, Rand Corporation, March 1963.

Communist Party is a dominant but not the omnipotent element of Soviet society ', that great importance attaches to a study of interest groups and to the voices which speak for them within the party. Clearly, since the party does hold the levers of political power, all kinds of pressures for action, conflicts over priorities, alternative policy proposals, are argued within it. Disagreements inevitably arise. Under Stalin this process was muted by fear and was only allowed to spill over into print (if at all) after the matter had been decided. Now the conventions have radically altered. It is thus no longer true that public criticism of a minister, a policy or an institution is either a reflection of the power struggle or implies that some decision has already been taken about what to do. It could be so, but frequently is not so. No one can doubt that arguments in recent years about all kinds of topics, from literature and criminal law to the role of mathematical economics, were quite evidently genuine and should be treated as such. The issues and the arguments, and the circumstances which gave rise to them, must surely be studied independently of the personalities of the protagonists, or of those political figures who may or may not be supporting them. By contrast, even dismissals of ministers in recent years have had little meaning in terms either of policy or the power struggle. For example, while agriculture is certainly an area in which Khrushchev's personal policies have played a most important role, analysis of the careers of and published attacks on successive ministers of agriculture would tell us very little about anything. One could write a long and detailed work on the many serious problems of collective and state farms without mentioning the name of a single minister. This is not to deny for a moment that the deliberate weakening (since 1959) of the Ministry of Agriculture was a political act, and the obscure episode of the creation and apparent abandonment of an all-union state committee on agriculture in 1962 (and the fall of Ignatov) had real political as well as Kremlinological significance. This seems to be part of a struggle over the role of the party machine in which Khrushchev himself is heavily involved. It could be objected that ministers of agriculture are relatively poor and insignificant creatures, so that their replacement has no major political effects. However, several very prominent leaders have been retired from political life in recent years, and this too seems to have made no appreciable difference to anything. What about Kirichenko, Aristov, Belyaev? Whom or what were they plotting against, or for? With what issues were they associated? In what respect did their rise or fall affect Soviet policy on farming, China, culture, the cold war, investment priorities, or even posts and telegraphs? If the answer is ' we have no idea ', then how does their demotion matter, except to themselves, their friends, and their relations?

Admittedly this is putting it a bit strongly, but it is surely reasonable to ask of any analyst of the Soviet scene that he explain the practical value of his researches in terms of explanations of the past or prediction of future events, and not just of political biography. To repeat, it clearly does matter to the world who will succeed Khrushchev. If, as seems to be the case, Khrushchev suffers from some loss of coherence and confidence, if on various issues he appears to be in conflict with colleagues, these are matters which must be watched and studied. If we can find indications as to the views on significant questions of Brezhnev, Polyanski, Kozlov, then their changing relative positions in the succession stakes would be a really important political indicator. Yet, while not for a moment denying the importance of personalities, and without subscribing to determinism, it is again worth emphasising that choices by politicians are often much more limited than we suppose. Some 'power' analysts have been known to argue that the fact that politicians have adopted their opponents' policies after achieving power lends support to their viewpoint. On a superficial level it could be said that such behaviour proves the primacy of the power struggle, but on reflection it tends to prove the opposite; that, after all, perhaps there was only one thing to do.

CRYPTO-POLITICS

T. H. Rigby

THE subject-matter of politics has been defined as 'who gets what when how'. Its essence is conflict, a struggle for material and non-material values waged between individuals and (much more) between groups of individuals, groups large and small, formal and informal. In liberal-democratic societies politics is the profession of some, the constant or occasional concern of many, and a daily public spectacle. Entire institutions—parliamentary assemblies, party conventions, the mass media, journals of opinion—exist primarily or incidentally to provide a forum for this conflict, while others—trade unions, employers' and professional associations, and innumerable voluntary organisations—exist primarily or incidentally to wage it.

It is natural in such societies to draw a fairly sharp distinction between 'politics' and 'administration'. Although it is acknowledged that jurisdictional and other conflicts may occur within an administrative set-up, and that interested groups may exert a direct influence on administrators ('properly' or 'improperly'), the issue of who gets what when how is supposed to be fought out mainly in the political sphere, leaving the administrator the technical task of implementing the resultant decisions. While in practice the boundaries between politics and administration may often be harder to establish than is commonly thought, the existence of these two separate spheres is one of the major features of liberal-democratic societies.

This distinction cannot be drawn in the Soviet Union. To argue in public over who gets what when how is regarded there as behaviour appropriate only in class-antagonistic societies, and organisations and occasions like soviets, party congresses, elections, trade unions, the press and so on, rather than figuring as arenas or protagonists in the public political process, are mobilised to endorse and disseminate with one voice the views of the executive leadership. Here we have 'public relations' on a massive scale, but no public politics. The Soviet 'political system' is in effect an administrative machine.

Of course, the communists did not invent government without public, institutionalised politics. Rather has this been the norm for most times and places. That politics of a sort nevertheless are conducted in such societies is attested by innumerable empirical studies, though the important task of generalising from this material has received scant attention. On the analogy of other non-liberal-democratic states, we might reasonably hypothesise that conflicts of interest and aspiration in the Soviet Union, denied a special political sphere of operation, tend to give a political coloration to processes ostensibly executive and administrative in character, that is, to generate a distinctive *crypto-politics*.

There are, it is true, a number of features found in the USSR (along with other communist countries) which we would expect to give a distinctive character to their crypto-politics:

(a) the tremendous scope of activities subject to direction by the state (though this has always fallen well short of ' total ');

(b) the thoroughness with which open or semi-open politics are suppressed; and

(c) the elaborate facade of pseudo-political institutions.

These not only lend a peculiar complexity to the hidden political life of such countries, but render it singularly difficult to uncover and interpret.

UNTIL the second world war serious study of Soviet crypto-politics in the West was practically confined to emigré political circles possessing personal experience of the methods of the Soviet communists, their leaders, and the conditions in which they were working.[1] While often well-informed and intelligent, this was heavily focused on the single problem of the emergence and consolidation of Stalin's personal rule and the destruction of oppositions. Through the writings of Souvarine, Trotsky, and other former figures of the communist left, we gradually became familiar with the intra-politburo manoeuvres, the organisational manipulations and the policy zig-zags which gave Stalin victory in the succession struggle of the twenties, and (for those who had ears to hear) with the successive steps from party ' cleansing ' to the Yezhov terror through which he first disarmed and then annihilated all those, whether former foe or former supporter, who represented an actual or potential limitation to the extension of his dictatorship. All this was invaluable, but in concentrating its attention on the one broad issue, and in employing a meagre explanatory armoury practically confined to Stalin's personality, the class-struggle concept, and the analogy of the French Revolution, it left vast areas of Soviet political life both empirically and theoretically unexplored.

Meanwhile academic study of the Soviet system, unsophisticated and insular (at least in English-speaking countries) throughout this period, gave us either highly formalistic or apologetic volumes [2] whose points of contact with emigré accounts of the politics of Stalinisation were negligible.

Soon after the war, a new topic of research and speculation emerged: the succession to the now ageing Stalin. The Soviet press was combed for hints of status shifts (the order of names in official listings of leaders and proximity to the Old Man at ceremonial appearances on Lenin's tomb quickly becoming favourite guides to

---

[1] The best sources of factual information and qualified comment on the Soviet political scene between the wars were the Menshevik *Sotsialisticheskii Vestnik*, and (during the thirties) the Trotskyite *Biulleten Oppozitsii*.

[2] Samuel N. Harper's *The Government of the Soviet Union* (N.Y., 1938), was perhaps the most ambitious and influential example of the former, and the Webbs' *Soviet Communism: a New Civilization?* (2 vols., London, 1936), of the latter.

'form'), and the search to identify protégés and policies restored intense political interest to areas of ideological and economic activity which had been little studied for their power aspects since the consolidation of Stalin's dictatorship. These first ventures in Kremlinology were confined for the most part to a crop of 'Russian specialists' among Western journalists nurtured on Soviet experience during the war. However brilliant and knowledgeable its practitioners, this new 'discipline', in the narrowness of its empiricism, its inadequately controlled speculation, and its invocation of a mystical intuition of the *cognoscenti* (perhaps often justified), frequently revealed a *lack* of discipline which has tended to discredit the study of Soviet intra-leadership conflict in the minds of many people ever since.

Meanwhile the academic study of Soviet Government was coming of age. Towster's hybrid but useful *Political Power in the USSR* (New York, 1948), teething-ring for a whole post-war generation of budding Sovietologists, was followed in 1953 by Fainsod's *How Russia is Ruled*,[3] the first mature account of the Soviet polity which could bear comparison with standard scholarly studies of other political systems. At last we had a detailed, realistic, and integrated picture of the system as a going concern, with the various parts—soviets, terror, ideology, and so on— assuming their due place and proportion, instead of being presented as the 'essence' of the system (like the blind men in the Indian fable who meet an elephant and argue about what it is like, one of them feeling a leg and saying the elephant is like a tree, another feeling the tail and saying the elephant is like a snake, and so on).

The four or five years following Stalin's death were the heyday of Kremlinology. Not only was it now plain to all that there *was* a succession struggle taking place, but this clearly had acquired implications, both for policy and for institutional structure, which greatly enhanced its practical and theoretical interest. The newspaper columnists now found their field invaded by 'Soviet specialists' working in the universities and in government departments. Informal cooperation and a certain amount of emulation among the various groups of Sovietologists in different Western countries encouraged a sharp rise in the levels of knowledge and argumentation at which Soviet politics were discussed.

A valuable job undertaken in this period was a re-examination of the crypto-politics of Stalin's last years. Armed with sharper methodological tools and some new scraps of information, Sovietologists succeeded between 1953 and 1955 in reconstructing a series of important case

---

[3] Merle Fainsod, *How Russia is Ruled* (Harvard University Press, 1953). Subsequent university texts, notably Derek J. R. Scott, *Russian Political Institutions* (London, 1958), and John N. Hazard, *The Soviet System of Government* (University of Chicago Press, 1957), while possessing particular virtues of presentation, have not really broken new ground. One work which approached Fainsod's in the quality of its analysis actually preceded it by two years. This was Boris Meissner, *Russland im Umbruch* (Frankfurt a/M, 1951).

histories—the 'Leningrad Case', the dispute over agricultural policies, the Georgian purges of 1951-53, and so on—which are of fundamental value in studying power relationships and the methods of struggle within the Soviet leadership in the early post-war years. Many of the hypotheses then arrived at were subsequently confirmed and further documented in Khrushchev's secret speech and other official revelations. So enriched, these case histories have been admirably presented to the lay reader by Robert Conquest, in his *Power and Policy in the USSR* (London, 1961).

By this point we possessed both good general textbooks on Soviet government, and a number of relatively well-documented case histories of crypto-political conflict in the upper reaches of the Soviet bureaucracy. But the two were still virtually unconnected, and they remain so today. There is a pressing need to abstract from our now quite considerable empirical data some general conclusions as to the issues and methods of Soviet crypto-politics, and to integrate these with our general picture of the dynamics of the Soviet system. This task was not really attempted by Conquest; nor, reasonably enough, was it attempted by Leonard Schapiro or John Armstrong in their invaluable political histories.[4] Nor, finally, was the gap filled in the course of those waves of general theorising about the nature of the Soviet polity, which were prompted by the changes of the post-Stalin era and the desire to estimate how 'essential' these changes were.

MEANWHILE, as I have said, Kremlinological research was in vogue; its aim was not only to explain the recent past, but to interpret current developments with a view to forecasting the future. In retrospect, the objective of working out Kremlinological techniques that would give it a high level of predictive power may seem naïve. How good are we at predicting political developments in political systems immensely more open to study? Yet even on this plane there was the occasional breakthrough. There were those who, reading the signs at the end of 1954, forecast an imminent show-down between Malenkov and Khrushchev, and considered the advantage had moved sharply in Khrushchev's favour. There were those again who, comparing what happened at the December 1956 and February 1957 Plenums of the Central Committee, and studying the conduct of the subsequent discussion on Khrushchev's decentralisation proposals, concluded that the First Secretary had now alienated a majority of Presidium members, and that they would have to make an early bid to unseat him or else reconcile themselves to his domination. On the whole, however, Kremlinology tended to follow one step behind 'life itself', which eventually disillusioned some of its sponsors (unjustifiably, to my mind) as to its practical or scholarly value.

---

[4] Leonard Schapiro, *The Communist Party of the Soviet Union* (New York, 1960); John A. Armstrong, *The Politics of Totalitarianism* (New York, 1962). The same comment applies to the two more general histories to appear in this period: Georg von Rauch, *A History of Soviet Russia* (New York, 1957), and Donald W. Treadgold, *Twentieth Century Russia* (Chicago, 1959).

As Khrushchev consolidated his dominating position following the defeat of the 'anti-party group', the time again seemed ripe for summings-up. A series of books appeared tracing Khrushchev's rise and reviewing empirically the developments of the post-Stalin era.[5] Since then, Kremlinology has lost something of its momentum. What sustains it now is a sporadic guerrilla warfare between those who believe that Khrushchev is well in the saddle and those who consider that he still has to contend with a powerful opposition possessing influential spokesmen in the Presidium. Surprisingly enough, the succession to Khrushchev, and the current fortunes of possible contenders, seem to have received less concentrated attention than did the Stalin succession before 1953. If the assumption is justified that the question whether A or B or C comes to the top has little importance for the determination of Soviet policies or the politico-administrative structure, this flagging of the Kremlinological impulse is rational. But *is* this view justified, *as an assumption?*

One impression that I hope will emerge from this article is that the future value of studying political conflict within the Soviet leadership will largely depend on our success in building up a *general* picture of the conditions of crypto-political activity in the USSR, and that, in our efforts to construct such a picture, we can derive enormous help from experience acquired in studying bureaucratic politics in other systems. Before leaving the Kremlinological dimension of the topic, however, and by way of drawing some interim conclusions from our trial-and-error efforts to date, it might be useful to list some of the more obvious errors which we have made on the way:

(1) Failure to distinguish between the conditions of intra-leadership struggle when that leadership is (a) basically monocratic, and (b) basically oligarchic. In the first case, for example, the good will of the 'boss' is of vital importance, and no amount of organisational strength at lower levels can ensure this; while in the second case, where no one reserves a veto-power over organisational strength, the latter becomes an autonomous force. Again, in the monocratic situation, alignments within the leadership are strictly limited in importance, since there is always one man who has the last word and whose links with each lesser leader greatly overshadow their links with each other; whereas in an oligarchy majority decisions turn alignments (whether stable, shifting, or *ad hoc*), into a basic determinant of action. Yet for long after 1953 people often discounted certain moves as relevant to the succession-struggle because they had possessed no such significance under Stalin. After the triumph of Khrushchev some observers continued to interpret the actions of other Presidium members as if they remained fully autonomous, freely-aligning

---

[5] Wolfgang Leonhard's *Kreml ohne Stalin* (Cologne, 1959), was the best general study of the period. The English translation, *The Kremlin Since Stalin* (London, 1962), brings the story forward to 1961. Myron Rush, *The Rise of Khrushchev* (Washington, 1958), is mainly valuable as a brilliant (if sometimes controversial) exercise in the exegesis of Soviet esoteric communication. Lazar Pistrak's *The Grand Tactician —Khrushchev's Rise to Power* (London, 1961), offers a careful and readable reconstruction of Khrushchev's political career, but gives little space to the post-Stalin era.

agents. In extreme cases this error verges on what the psycho-pathologists call ' perseveration ', and the sociologists ' trained incapacity '.

(2) Failure to realise that conflicts in a monocratic situation may vary greatly in character because of the degree and nature of the ' boss's ' power, which in its turn will be affected by a variety of factors, including his own personality and values, the institutional and informal relationships established in the course of his acquiring and consolidating power, and the domestic and international environment in which it is exercised. Lenin, Stalin, and Khrushchev were not only very different men, but, despite a striking continuity in some aspects of the Soviet polity, functioned in very different situations. On the nature of the ' boss's ' rule depend the stakes in the intra-leadership struggle (if these include life itself, as they did under Stalin, this may make a difference to the lieutenant's behaviour in a conflict situation), the way power is devolved and distributed among the lieutenants, and what sort of moves they (a) are encouraged to make, and (b) can get away with, in intra-leadership politics. All this would appear axiomatic. Yet, to take a current illustration (at the risk of appearing obsessive), the basically monocratic character of the present leadership sometimes fails to gain acknowledgment, on the ground that Presidium members do not behave, and are not treated, in exactly the same way as Stalin's lieutenants in the good old days.

(3) A sterile opposing of ' policy ' and ' sheer power ' interpretations of political moves. (This error is now rarely encountered in an extreme form, but it often confused discussion of Soviet politics in the early post-Stalin period.) ' In a bureaucracy ', writes a contemporary political sociologist, ' ideas do not stand on their merits alone. It is not only an opinion or an idea that wins, but also a man '.[6] It could equally well be put the other way about. Conflicts in decision-making bodies, even if originally generated by personal rivalries, and whatever other moves they may evoke, inevitably find expression in contradictory policy positions. Men cannot disagree in the abstract; they must disagree about something. Noting, then, that any conflict situation is likely to acquire both personal power and policy dimensions, we might further observe that (a) one may become the captive of policies, once adopted, or the line taken on one issue may limit one's choice of policy on others; (b) nevertheless, leaders sometimes find it possible and expedient to change their policies, or even (and this not only in the Soviet Union) to appropriate those of their rivals; (c) irrespective of the leader's own motivation, support for his policies may rest on disinterested agreement, or personal loyalty, or group interest, or any combination of these. While generally applicable, these considerations are particularly pertinent to the politics of 1953-57.

THERE remains a somewhat noisome red herring to remove: the notion that the key to policy, institutional, and leadership changes is

6 Victor A. Thompson, ' Hierarchy, Specialisation and Organisational Conflict ', *Administrative Science Quarterly*, Vol. V, p. 503.

the struggle between various political or social 'forces', identified as particular elite segments of society or major divisions of the party-state bureaucracy. To the extent that this view was generated from within the literature of Sovietology itself, perhaps the most influential source was Herman Achminow's's *Die Macht im Hintergrund* (Ulm, 1950). Achminow gives a Burnhamesque assessment of the importance of the technical-managerial 'intelligentsia', but whereas Burnham saw this group as already wielding power (the party leadership were their political agents), for Achminow they assumed the role of proletariat vis-à-vis the party's bourgeoisie; that is, being called into existence by the party as the necessary instrument of its purposes, they were destined to become its 'gravediggers'. No less influential in this connection was the force of analogy, conscious or unconscious, with other political systems: the pluralism we live in and tend to accept as normal, the authoritarian politics of the past, with their conflicting and circulating elites, and Nazi Germany, with its jurisdictional struggles between Gestapo, party machine, state bureaucracy, and so on. The job of articulating such analogies, of demonstrating their relevance, and of specifying under what conditions and in what respects they might be relevant, while accorded an occasional nod of respect, was never seriously attempted.

Whatever its genesis, the notion of Soviet political events as the resultant of a parallelogram of forces, applied by party, government, police, army, and so on, or of a tug-of-war between 'technocrats' and 'apparatchiks' (with 'ideologists' shouting esoteric encouragement), was all the rage among the newspaper Sovietologists by the mid-fifties, and exerted considerable influence over official and academic thinking as well.[7] True, enthusiasm flagged after a time, as it emerged that no two equally competent Sovietologists could ever agree on the correct identification of social force, leader, and policy. An explanatory tool that we do not quite know what to do with, but are nevertheless unwilling to discard, the 'social forces' theory, is still left lying around.

To illustrate the difficulty of employing this tool without confusion, arbitrariness, and self-contradiction, we might consider Roger Pethybridge's *A Key to Soviet Politics* (London, 1962). This is a study of the 1957 'anti-party group' crisis and its background. The background, focused on the Stalin era, is analysed in terms of 'interest groups' (the same old 'forces'), defined as 'those influential bodies of men within and without the Presidium and the Central Committee whose composite power makes them a force to be reckoned with in Soviet politics'. Along with these groups, Pethybridge discusses the early careers of the leaders figuring in the 1957 crisis, on the ground that, while they may often have shifted from one group to another, 'their position in the scheme of

---

7 'With some significant modifications, the sociologically oriented group theory of politics has been successfully applied to the interaction of such forces as the army, party, the managerial elite, and the secret police in a totalitarian system', D. A. Rustow, 'New Horizons for Comparative Politics', *World Politics*, Vol. 9, p. 531. The modifications are not specified.

political power was usually determined in the long run by their special adherence to one particular group'. Doubts as to the relevance of all this for the events of 1957 very soon arise, however, as it emerges that several of the 'anti-party group' themselves possessed long-term career associations with the party apparatus, particularly Khrushchev's main rival Malenkov, whose career made him almost the model apparatchik. This being so, one has to fall back on their actual behaviour in the 1957 crisis to discover which group the leaders 'really' adhered to, so that the 'interest group' theory, as an explanation for this behaviour, collapses to the ground. Pethybridge himself, in discussing the political developments of 1953-57, moves from a framework of interests to one of issues, on the ground that 'the ensuing quarrels illustrate their positions better than their connection with a particular interest group or groups'; and when he comes to his account of the crisis itself, which he handles very competently, the group theory is scarcely to be seen! If the reader emerges rather confused, this is not wholly Pethybridge's fault: try doing better with such a primitive tool!

My objection here is not to the notion that 'social forces' or 'interest groups' may play a part in Soviet politics, but to arbitrariness in defining the groups and to the assumption that all political events can ultimately be reduced to 'group' terms. A group hypothesis may often be warranted, but in framing such a hypothesis we would need to establish the following points:

(1) What is the common interest or other property defining your group?
(2) What are the pertinent contradictions with the interests or properties of other groups?
(3) What is the mechanism for forming and articulating group opinion on current issues?
(4) What is the nature of the bond between the group and political leaders? (In what sense do they 'represent' the group?)

Further cautions are indicated by the errors to which Kremlinology has been prone. Without proposing a revised and refined general group theory for Soviet politics—any such general theory would presumably constitute the most economical and consistent arrangement of special theories covering authenticated case histories—one prediction may be permitted as to the likely character of such a theory.

IN contradiction to what Pethybridge suggests, it seems probable that a group model, with the groups more or less corresponding with the major instruments of rule, would turn out to be more illuminating for the politics of 1953-57 than for the Stalin period. Under Stalin, not only did massive police and other controls inhibit the kind of communication necessary for those employed in such instruments to cohere as groups, but Stalin appears to have devoted considerable effort to preventing his lieutenants from becoming too closely identified with particular interests, by such measures as entrusting responsibility for particular instruments to two or more rival leaders, allotting each a variety of functional and territorial jurisdictions, and fairly frequent reallocation of jurisdictions.

Between 1953 and 1957, by contrast, while the last word on the most important issues seems to have been reserved to the Presidium acting as a committee, there was apparently a fairly clear distribution among Presidium members of administrative powers (and perhaps the right of initiative) in the various instruments of rule. (Khrushchev's increasingly blatant violation and appropriation of jurisdictions was what finally provoked the June 1957 crisis.) Moreover, the decline of terror probably facilitated a greater intensity and frankness of communication between these instruments and their Presidium representatives, while not only the Presidium, but, between 1955 and 1957, the full Central Committee meeting at its plenary sessions (and occasionally the press?), performed to some extent the role of a forum within which different points of view, and the interests attached to them, could compete. It seems probable that much in Soviet politics between the death of Stalin and the ousting of the ' anti-party group ' can be explained in terms of conflicts between party and police (March-June 1953), party and government (1954 and again in the first half of 1957), and party and army (July-October 1957). But we would need to add a few qualifications:

(a) the role of the leaders in these conflicts seems to have depended not on their past career-patterns, but on their current jurisdictions;

(b) the competing groups were not always identical with particular instruments of rule taken as a whole, as these might be divided along departmental, territorial, or other lines; for instance, in 1955-56 the various Presidium members amongst whom central government jurisdiction was split up did not apparently act in concert, while in the June 1957 crisis Khrushchev's decentralisation measures (the immediate provocation of the ' anti-party group's ' move against him) had produced a clear conflict of interest between central and regional government officials, the latter probably contributing significantly to Khrushchev's victory at the June plenum;

(c) factors other than group interests based on instruments of rule were also very important.

The period since 1957 may be less easy to characterise and I shall not attempt to outline my views here, except to suggest the general proposition that pluralistic elements have become less crucial, but continue to operate in a more diffuse way.

ALTHOUGH the purpose of this article is to review past achievements in the study of Soviet crypto-politics, rather than to mark out guide-lines for the future, it may be useful to make a few suggestions that might be worth following up when the marking-out starts.

1. The groupings best attested in our empirical material on Soviet

political conflict appear to be personal followings, which characteristically cut right across formal organisational lines.[8] The bond appears to stem from close collaboration in the same organisation at some time in the past, sometimes the remote past.[9] It is necessary to elucidate the character of this bond. While it is fairly clear what the patron has to offer the client, is it clear what the client has to offer the patron? Is it merely, as Macchiavelli puts it in Chapter X of *The Prince*, that ' it is the nature of men to be as much bound by the benefits they confer as by those they receive ' ? Has it something to do with joint implication in irregular informal practices (without which task fulfilment is rarely possible)? If so, the Soviet bureaucracy is not on its own.

Does the problem here come down to understanding the nature of *leadership* in informal groups? The following point is suggestive: ' leadership is a process of mutual stimulation—a social interactional phenomenon in which the attitudes, ideals and aspirations of the followers play as important a determining role as do the individuality and personality of the leader '.[10] And in any case, what is the reason for the tenaciousness and longevity of such associations in the Soviet situation? How many hierarchical levels can they, or do they, commonly embrace? Is the bond uniting them the same for all times and places? There is obviously room here for a great deal of further empirical work and comparative study.

2. Has the relative ease of identifying career connections led us to exaggerate their importance in group formation? I personally think not, but it is hard to prove. How can we assess the importance of such bonds as common opinions, common non-official interests, compatibility of personality, family friendships? Bonds based on age, education, social background, and local origin may be easier to study, but have received scant attention.

3. Can the chronic conflict observable between ' line ' and ' staff ' officers in Western industrial bureaucracies be regarded as in any sense paralleling *party-government* tensions in the USSR? Remember that the party apparatus, and particularly the hierarchy of secretaries, functions as a coordinating mechanism for the whole administration, from top to bottom. One writer's adaptation of the staff-line contradiction in terms of a clash between the principles of hierarchy and specialisation [11]

---

8 The cases discussed in Part II of Conquest's *Power and Policy in the USSR*, particularly the Leningrad and Georgian cases, illustrate this point very well. Many of us could supply impressive lists of officials who have come up on the coattails of Khrushchev, Kozlov and Brezhnev (for example) in recent years, relating their fortunes to the successes and setbacks of their patrons.

9 One of the victims of the ' Leningrad Case ', the RSFSR Premier Rodionov, never served in Zhdanov's Leningrad satrapy, but fifteen years before his arrest he had worked under Zhdanov in Gorki.

10 Cecil A. Gibb, ' The Principles and Traits of Leadership ', in P. Hare, E. F. Borgatha, and R. F. Bales, *Small Groups* (New York, 1955), p. 93. See also P. Pigors, *Leadership or Domination* (Boston, 1935); R. Dubin, ' Stability of Human Organisations ', in M. Haire, ed., *Modern Organization Theory* (New York, 1959).

11 Thompson, loc. cit., pp. 485–521. Cf. M. Dalton, ' Conflicts between Staff and Line Managerial Officers ', *American Sociological Review*, Vol. 15, p. 342.

has many points of contact with the suggested apparatchik-technocrat polarity discussed above. If there is a parallel here, a perusal of the literature on Western staff-line conflicts may well afford valuable clues for the Sovietologist.

4. Have we sometimes been too ready to dismiss pseudo-democratic institutions and procedures as irrelevant to the Soviet political process? In 1955-57, as suggested earlier, the full Central Committee, meeting at its plenary sessions, tended to become a court of appeal from a divided Presidium. On a more humdrum level, the Budget Commissions of the two houses of the Supreme Soviet and the Economic Commission of the Soviet of Nationalities may make some contribution towards articulating and accommodating conflicting departmental and especially local interests. There may be a law of inverse proportion between the political significance of such bodies and the degree to which their proceedings are publicised, due to the theoretical inhibitions to disagreeing in public. The political significance of Supreme Soviet sessions is negligible, while that of Central Committee plenums had obviously declined sharply by December 1958, when stenographic reports began to be published. On the other hand, esoterically expressed public criticism is also, at times, a weapon in the Soviet political game, and this raises the further question whether the press may sometimes play a more independent role in influencing the outcome of internal conflict than is generally believed. Who determined, for example, what got published during the heavy industry—consumer goods dispute at the end of 1954, or during the discussion on Khrushchev's decentralisation proposals in 1957? Clarification of the crypto-political functions of the press is one of the more urgent tasks for the student of Soviet politics, but this is a topic that will require patience and ingenuity.

5. As the present survey shows, our work on political conflict in the Soviet Union has been very top-heavy: it has concentrated too much on Kremlinology. The Soviet press is replete with case material on conflict at the regional and local levels. This reveals a great variety of causes and types of conflict and of crypto-political tactics, and provides much evidence on the points raised in the preceding paragraphs. Take the Anokhin case (1950), for example, an incident in what was evidently a continuing conflict between the Kharkov *obkom* and the Political Directorate of the Southwestern Railway, and involving (a) two rival patronage networks zig-zagging across formal organisational lines; (b) excitement of rank-and-file intransigence, expressed in a wholly formal fashion, through voting procedures normally applied and made possible by contradictory pressures from higher instances; (c) clear evidence of some autonomous participation in the conflict by press organs at different levels.[12] This material not only has great intrinsic interest, but promises illuminating insights into political processes at higher levels. It is practically virgin soil.

[12] See *Pravda*, 2 February 1950.

6. As well as studying the reasons and mechanisms for crypto-political activity in the USSR, we should think more about how it is related to the Soviet political and social system as a whole. In particular, to what extent is it functional and to what extent dysfunctional? It has been argued that conflict is an integrative, rather than a disruptive force, so long as there is consensus on fundamentals.[13] It has also been suggested that 'effective, virile organisations are bound to have conflict. A good case can easily be made that conflict is necessary to provide the stimulation required to achieve the high motivation and creative ideas which are present in a successful organisation.' Nevertheless, 'conflict can only be productive when the organisation is equipped to use it constructively. Bitter, unresolved conflict can immobilise or destroy an organisation.'[14] How far are these generalisations applicable to the Soviet Union? Is the Soviet consensus adequate to prevent conflict becoming disruptive? Is the Soviet political system equipped to use conflict constructively? These questions are as urgent for the Soviet leadership as for the foreign student.

[13] See Lewis A. Coser, *The Functions of Social Conflict* (London, 1956).
[14] Rensis Likert, 'A Motivational Approach to a Modified Theory of Organisation and Management', in Haire, ed., op. cit. p. 205.

ORIGINS OF PEACEFUL COEXISTENCE

A Historical Note

Franklyn Griffiths

TROTSKY APPARENTLY ORIGINATED the slogan of peaceful coexistence on 22 November 1917, when he first called for *mirnoe sozhitelstvo* (*lit.* peaceful living together or cohabitation) between peoples.[1] *Mirnoe sozhitelstvo* was part of a battery of slogans including ' brotherhood of peoples ', ' a United States of Europe ', ' peace without annexations or indemnities ', which were utilised to promote socialist revolution in Europe in accordance with Lenin's revolutionary peace policy. After using the expression on several occasions, among them the ' neither war nor peace ' declaration, Trotsky evidently relinquished it with the termination of negotiations at Brest-Litovsk in March 1918. By September 1918, Chicherin, Trotsky's successor, was privately seeking to convince the German Government of the Soviet desire for good-neighbourly relations and *mirnoe sozhitelstvo*.[2] Trotsky's slogan continued to be used with varying connotations by Chicherin, Lenin, and later Stalin until December 1927, when the present term, *mirnoe sosushchestvovanie* (*lit.* peaceful coexistence) received official sanction and came into sole use. The difference between *sozhitelstvo* and *sosushchestvovanie* is essentially that of living or existing together: *sozhitelstvo* suggests more active participation, but *sosushchestvovanie* is more stable, less transitory.

Chicherin was apparently the first to speak of *mirnoe sosushchestvovanie* when on 17 June 1920 he called for ' peaceful coexistence with other governments, no matter what they are '.[3] According to the materials so far published by the Institute of Marxism-Leninism, particularly those esoteric documents supporting the Soviet position on peaceful coexistence in the Sino-Soviet dispute, Lenin does not appear to have referred to *mirnoe sosushchestvovanie* as such. Nonetheless, on 17 May 1922 the Central Executive Committee adopted a resolution on the Genoa Economic Conference, which included the statement that ' the whole course of international relations recently bears witness to the inevitability, at the present stage of historical development, of the temporary coexistence (*sosushchestvovanie*) of the communist and the bourgeois systems of property ' (*Izvestia*, 18 May 1922). This characterisation of the epoch was not

---

[1] Trotsky, *Sochineniya*, III, part 2, pp. 163 (21 November 1917), 165 (22 November 1917), and 326 (12 February 1918). Some time ago Bertram D. Wolfe made this observation (Tamiment Institute Public Forum, New York, 1956), which was kindly brought to my attention by Professor Frederick C. Barghoorn of Yale University. Appropriately enough, in view of the connotations of ' living together ' and the secret diplomacy of the time, Trotsky's preliminary formulation was *chestnoe*, or honourable *sozhitelstvo*.

[2] Note of 18 September 1918 to the German Government. First published in A. A. Gromyko *et al.*, eds., *Dokumenty vneshnei politiki SSSR*, I (Moscow, 1957), p. 488.

[3] *Vestnik NKID*, No. 4–5, 1922, p. 2. Statement to Central Executive Commitee.

contained in the draft proposed by Lenin on 15–16 May.[4] Recently it has been altered to read 'temporary existence (*sushchestvovanie*) of the communist and bourgeois systems of property '.[5]

A closer look at some of the processes involved in the replacement of Trotsky's expression by Chicherin's, and the parallel transformation from slogan to doctrine, may provide insight into the meaning of 'peaceful coexistence' today.

ACCORDING TO THE ORIGINAL Leninist prescription for party action on questions of war and peace, the 'fight for peace' was regarded as part of the broader struggle for the elimination of capitalism. At international socialist gatherings prior to and during the first years of the first World War, the Bolsheviks called for the exploitation of mass peace sentiment in the interests of revolution, by means of propaganda exposing those governments contemplating or involved in major war. Later, as the experience of the war began to create a mass desire for peace, Lenin also urged a systematic propaganda to expose bourgeois and socialist slogans for a democratic peace, disarmament, and international arbitration. Such proposals he regarded as inimical to the organisation of revolutionary mass action, in that they fostered illusory hopes that the sufferings of war could be eliminated without major social transformations.

Propaganda of exposure played a leading part in the revolutionary peace policy elaborated by Lenin in 1915–16 in conjunction with his analysis of imperialism. According to this plan, once the Bolsheviks obtained power they would seek to ignite socialist uprisings in the West by openly proposing to the belligerent governments a 'just and democratic peace ', based on full self-determination and colonial liberation. In necessarily rejecting this proposal, Western ruling groups would lay bare their policies to their war-weary peoples. The Bolsheviks would then wage just and revolutionary war, and simultaneously the socialist proletariat in Europe would rise in indignation against their governments.

The first official act of the Soviet regime was to initiate Lenin's plan by issuing the Decree on Peace and undertaking to publish the Tsarist secret treaties. However, Lenin soon became convinced of the need for a separate peace. Although Trotsky, unlike the left communists, recognised the impossibility of waging revolutionary war, he insisted on continuing the propaganda struggle. While Lenin sought support for his change of tactic, the Soviet Government, and Trotsky in particular, conducted an extraordinary propaganda of exposure that stopped short only at the brink of national self-immolation. It was thus under conditions of acute non-military struggle against imperialism and for lasting peace that the peaceful coexistence slogan was born.[6]

Implicit in Lenin's decision to obtain a breathing-space to 'ensure the socialist revolution the possibility of strengthening or maintaining

---

[4] *Lenin*, 4th ed., 33 (1952), pp. 319–20.
[5] *Gromyko*, V (1961), p. 384. Cited in V. A. Zorin *et al.*, *Kommunist*, No. 4, 1963.
[6] Rather than consider the existence of Trotsky's line on peaceful coexistence, which ⁓ems, moreover, to have its modern proponents, V. A. Zorin regards the 22 November 1917 statement of the Commissariat for Foreign Affairs, calling for peace on the basis of the '*chestnoe sozhitelstvo* and cooperation of peoples ' as reflecting the immediate commitment of Soviet foreign policy to 'the Leninist principle of peaceful coexistence of states with different social systems ': *loc. cit.*

itself in one country until other countries are added '⁷ was the necessity
to cope, for however long, with the unforeseen condition of a vulnerable
Soviet Russian state existing together with capitalist states without the
assurance of immediate revolutionary assistance. Accordingly, when the
German terms were accepted at Brest-Litovsk, a new and contradictory
dimension was added to the 'fight for peace'. In the longer term it
involved delaying and, where possible, preventing the use of military force
by bourgeois governments against Russia. More immediately it meant
putting an end to intervention and, as the international situation permitted, the establishment of economic and diplomatic relations necessary
both to inhibit foreign military adventures and to facilitate Soviet internal
consolidation. For these purposes two interrelated categories of tactic
were developed, seeking to exploit on the one hand divisions between
capitalist states, and on the other divisions within each capitalist country.
The more distinctive features of the policy of peaceful coexistence are
to be found in early Soviet practice in the second category.

Quickly adapting the techniques of Bolshevik peace propaganda to the
demands of the new situation, the Soviet Government began to issue
a host of peace appeals and exemplary declarations designed to inhibit
the policies of the intervening governments by exposing them and by
cultivating favourable sentiments among pacifists and progressives in the
West. These activities were expanded in 1919–20, so much so that the
NKID annual report for the period begins with a consideration of Western
reactions to what had been called the Soviet 'peace offensive'. Increasingly Soviet peace propaganda was focused on the neighbouring states
and on Britain, where a powerful pacifist reaction to the war and external
differences with France offered leverage for improving the Soviet international position.

On 2 February 1920, the first peace was signed, with Estonia.
Chicherin called it 'the first experiment in *mirnoe sozhitelstvo* with
bourgeois states' and 'a dress rehearsal for understanding with the
Entente'.⁸ Lenin attributed the treaty, the first breach in the *cordon
sanitaire*, to the 'policy of peace'.

> The development of capitalism in different countries proceeds at a
> varied pace, under different circumstances and by different means
> and methods. . . . A socialist republic in one country exists side by
> side with capitalist countries of the whole world and forces their bour-
> geoisie to waver . . . the separately existing and, it would appear,
> feeble and weak proletarian republic has begun to win over to its side
> those countries which are dependent on the imperialist countries. . . .
> That is why our peace with Estonia is of world historical significance.⁹

This reference to Soviet efforts to make sections of the Western middle
classes waver was amplified by Chicherin in his account of the events
leading up to the treaty. Among the 'broad peasant and working masses'
there had been sufficient desire for peace to 'exert the most serious
pressure on the Government' in response to the Soviet peace proposal.

⁷ *Lenin*, 26, p. 404 (7 January 1918).
⁸ *Vestnik NKID*, No. 3, 1920, p. 1. Statement of 4 February to the Central Executive
Committee.
⁹ *Lenin*, 30, pp. 295–96 (2 February 1920).

However, this pressure alone was ' inadequate ', and it had been necessary to reassure and propitiate the Estonian bourgeoisie, taking into
account differences between the representatives of a pacifist tendency,
those who stood to gain financially, and the ' war party '.[10]

Where Chicherin was soon able to call for ' *mirnoe sosushchestvovanie*
with other governments, no matter what they are ', Lenin in a foreign
press interview described Soviet policy towards Asia as ' *mirnoe sozhitelstvo* with all peoples, the workers and peasants of all nations awakening
to a new life, a life without exploitation, without landowners, without
capitalists, without merchants '.[11] Several weeks after this gradualist
formulation of Trotsky's slogan had been made, ' *Left-Wing* ' *Communism : An Infantile Disorder* was written.

AS FURTHER TREATIES WERE SIGNED with neighbouring states, and as the
Polish campaign ended in failure and the Civil War and intervention drew
to a close, a turning point in foreign policy approached. In November
1920, Lenin expressed the view that ' a new period in which our basic
international existence in a network of capitalist states has been won '.[12]
The spring of 1921 saw the initiation of the NEP, necessitating trade with
and technical assistance from Western countries, and the *débâcle* of the
March action in Germany. In June 1921, the third Comintern congress
acknowledged the failure of the revolutionary wave in Europe and moved
to develop the tactics of the united front. Reflecting a corresponding
increase in the importance of Soviet diplomacy, Chicherin soon gave the
first Soviet endorsement of disarmament negotiations, in connection with
the proposed Washington Conference.

Uninvited to Washington, Russia was asked early in January 1922 to
attend a conference for the economic reconstruction of Europe, to be held
at Genoa.[13] The offer was promptly accepted, and for some weeks the
ailing Lenin was expected personally to lead the Soviet delegation.

Analysing the temper of the West prior to Genoa, Lenin discerned
three major tendencies at work in ' the bourgeois camp ', of which the
first two sought respectively to disrupt and to proceed with the conference.
The third existed in all bourgeois states as pacifism. On the relation of
bourgeois pacifism to Soviet policy at Genoa Lenin observed :

> As communists we have definite views on this pacifism, the exposition
> of which would be entirely superfluous here. . . . Of course when we
> go to Genoa as merchants, it is not a matter of indifference to us
> whether we deal with those representatives of the bourgeois camp
> who are pressing for a military solution to the problem or with those

---

10 *Vestnik NKID*, No. 3, 1920, pp. 1–6.
11 *Lenin*, 30, p. 340 (18 February 1920).
12 *Lenin*, 31, p. 385 (21 November 1920).
13 The invitation was extended from the Cannes Conference of the Supreme Allied
Council, where Lloyd George had managed to secure French acceptance of the
proposition that ' Nations can claim no right to dictate to each other regarding the
principles on which they are to regulate their system of ownership, internal economy
and government. It is for every nation to choose for itself the system which it prefers
in this respect '. Lenin attached considerable importance to this resolution. *Leninskii
sbornik*, XXXVI (1959), pp. 409–10 (26 January 1922). Cf. *Lenin*, 33, pp. 319–20.

representatives of the bourgeois camp who are attracted to pacifism.
. . . It would be a poor merchant who could not master this difference
and, adapting his tactics to this end, achieve his practical objectives.[14]

Consequently the Politburo drew up a detailed plan of action for the
Conference. Among other things it called for the Soviet delegation to
bring forward ' the broadest pacifist programme '. Since the Soviet
Government had no such programme, Chicherin wrote to Lenin, proposing one in detail. He believed that it should add novel elements to contemporary pacifism and economic practices so as to hinder their use,
in his vivid phrase, as ' fig leaves for imperialist rapacity '. He suggested
that the Russian delegation make thirteen proposals, including a general
reduction of armaments, which would not be acceptable to Western
governments. Lenin received this extraordinary programme with
enthusiasm, declaring that it would aggravate divisions in the bourgeois
camp, being both attractive and unacceptable to the middle classes in
the West.[15]

At Genoa Chicherin presented this programme in his first statement,
which moreover asserted that ' in the present historical epoch, which
makes possible the parallel existence of the old and the nascent new
social structure, economic cooperation between states representing these
two systems of property is imperative . . .'.[16] Several days later, having
successfully pursued another order of contradiction in the capitalist camp,
Russia signed the Rapallo treaty with Germany.

Less than a fortnight before his first major stroke, Lenin outlined the
Central Executive Committee resolution on the Genoa Conference for the
Politburo. Here he observed that ' the real equality of the two systems,
though a temporary condition until the whole world passes from private
property and the *economic chaos* and war engendered by it to the higher
system of property, is present only in the Rapallo treaty '.[17] This oblique
statement suggests assumptions more explicit than those underlying his
occasional references to an ' unstable equilibrium ' in relations with the
West, the ' period during which socialist and capitalist states will exist
side by side ', or a future transformation from a ' national ' dictatorship
of the proletariat ' existing in one country and incapable of determining
world politics ' to an ' international ' dictatorship ' of at least several
countries capable of having decisive influence on the whole of world
politics '.[18] It seems to mark the limit of Lenin's willingness to generalise

[14] *Lenin*, 33, p. 236 (27 March 1922).
[15] *Leninskii sbornik*, XXXVI, pp. 451–5 (10 March 1922). First published in 1959.
This far reaching correspondence has repeatedly been cited by Soviet spokesmen in
the Sino-Soviet debate as ' Lenin's directives for the Genoa Conference '. It is
conspicuously absent from recent collections of Lenin's works on foreign policy,
and the recent authoritative symposium on peaceful coexistence: A. A. Gromyko,
ed., *Mirnoe sosushchestvovanie—Leninskii kurs vneshnei politiki Sovetskovo Soiuza*
(Moscow, December 1962). To dispel any doubt the original documents were partially
reproduced in *New Times*, No. 11, 1962, as the eighteen-nation committee on disarmament was convened, and in *Pravda*, 24 August 1962.
[16] *Materialy Genuezskoi konferentsii* (Moscow, 1922), p. 78. Lenin apparently authorised
the formulations advanced by Chicherin (and possibly also the diplomatic over-
statement of his own views). Institut Marksizma-Leninizma, *Leninskie idei zhivut i
pobezhdaiut* (Moscow, 1961), p. 189. First publication of documentation concerned.
[17] *Lenin*, 33 (1952), pp. 319–20 (15–16 May 1922). The original document is said to
bear annotations by Bukharin.
[18] *Lenin*, 30, p. 21 : 31, p. 126 ; 32, pp. 412, 427, 455.

from post-revolutionary international experience. That a leading Party member or members chose to go beyond Lenin's position on the co-existence of the two systems in writing the final CEC resolution is suggested by the textual change of 1961, made in spite of continuing pressure to demonstrate the commitment of Soviet foreign policy to ' peaceful coexistence ' under Lenin's guidance.[19]

ALTHOUGH LENIN REFRAINED from an authoritative pronouncement on coexistence, he had by mid-1922 evolved a rich body of tactics to deal with the coexistence situation. In the absence of socialist revolutions in the West, the pressure that could be exerted by foreign working masses was insufficient to meet the long and short term needs of Soviet security. Thus, while Soviet statements and the united front tactics of communist parties could mobilise varying degrees of popular pressure on bourgeois governments, it was also necessary to exert direct influence on the middle classes. To this end distinctions between various bourgeois tendencies were emphasised. By means of peace propaganda and expressions of the desire to attenuate political and economic differences with Western governments, Soviet diplomacy sought to strengthen the position of the more ' reasonable ' elements, and thereby to inhibit the pursuit of anti-Soviet policies. At the same time the more aggressive elements would be deterred by the political cost of rejecting the cooperative proposals and ideal solutions put forward by Moscow, and also by Soviet statements of readiness for retaliation. A similar reasoning applied to agreements with bourgeois governments, which were regarded as strengthening the relation of the more moderate elements (to say nothing of the more favourably disposed governments) to the Soviet state while the struggle against the militant faction continued in other forms.

That steps in the direction of bourgeois pacifism and agreements with bourgeois governments compromised the continuing revolutionary struggle for socialism and peace was evident in the concern of the Comintern for the debilitating effects of disarmament propaganda on the ' revolutionary energy of the proletariat '. This problem reflected the fundamental contradiction of state and revolution coexisting within Soviet foreign policy itself: Lenin and his successors were faced with the dilemma of simultaneous relations with governments and with peoples, of coordinating tactics to avoid international war and to promote the international revolution. In the long term the problem was to reconcile Chicherin's *mirnoe sosushchestvovanie* with Trotsky's *mirnoe sozhitelstvo,* to unite in practical and effective action the fight for socialism and the struggle to maintain international peace where Soviet Russia was concerned. However, under the conditions of this early period Lenin clearly regarded the main problem as one of survival. His decision at Brest-Litovsk ' to preserve the possibility of the existence of proletarian power and the Soviet republic, even in the case of delaying the socialist revolution in the whole world ' [20] continued to animate the general line of Soviet tactics, while at the same time the doctrinal expression of this course was

[19] For example, Gromyko devotes considerable attention to an exposition of ' Leninism on the inevitability of the coexistence of the two systems ', and yet avoids reference to the CEC resolution: *Mirnoe sosushchestvovanie—Leninskii kurs,* pp. 13–22.
[20] *Lenin,* 2nd ed., 25, p. 484 (20 November 1920).

elaborated during the internal Party struggle following his incapacitation and death.

Thus, after a reference to *mirnoe sozhitelstvo* by Lenin in October 1922 which implied coexistence with bourgeois governments,[21] the next to use the term was Stalin at the fourteenth Party congress in December 1925: ' What we once considered to be a short breathing-space has changed into a whole period of breathing-space. Hence a certain equilibrium of forces and a certain period of " *mirnoe sozhitelstvo* " between the world bourgeoisie and the world proletariat '.[22] Then at the fifteenth Party congress, in the midst of a remarkable constellation of circumstances, which included the elimination of Trotsky from the internal political scene and the first Soviet proposals for total disarmament, Stalin ruled out *mirnoe sozhitelstvo* and affirmed the *sosushchestvovanie* of the two systems:

> . . . *the period of ' mirnoe sozhitelstvo '* is receding into the past, giving way to a period of imperialist attacks. . . . Hence our task is to pay attention to contradictions in the capitalist camp, to delay war by ' buying off ' (*otkupivshis*) the capitalists and to apply all measures to maintain peaceful relations. . . . The basis of our relations with capitalist countries consists of admitting the *sosushchestvovanie* of the two opposing systems. It has been fully verified by practice.[23]

The subsequent evolution from Stalin's ' acceptance ' to Khrushchev's active pursuit of coexistence was based on the organisational experience of broad antifascist and peace fronts, favourable changes in the world correlation of forces, the development of nuclear weapons, and a heightened capability for divisive agreements with capitalist states. Khrushchev's pronouncement of 1956 marked the replacement of the traditional view of the fight for peace as subsidiary to the fight for socialism by a coexistence doctrine aiming to demilitarise and in so doing to speed up the struggle of the two systems.

---

[21] *Lenin*, 33, pp. 348–50 (27 October 1922). In an interview to the London *Observer* he stated that lack of full Soviet participation in the Lausanne Conference would impede trade ' so that there would be either no grounds at all left for peaceful coexistence or it would be unusually hampered ', and that the League of Nations was without ' real equality of nations or real prospects of peaceful coexistence between them '.

[22] *Stalin*, 7, p. 262 (18 December 1925). The Congress accordingly resolved that ' the " breathing-space " has turned into a whole period of so-called *mirnoe sozhitelstvo* of Soviet and capitalist states '. Gromyko uses *mirnoe sozhitelstvo* in the same sense to describe the post-1921 period. *Mirnoe sosushchestvovanie—Leninskii kurs*, pp. 19 and 36.

[23] *Stalin*, 10, pp. 288–89 (3 December 1927).

SOVIET STUDIES, THE PRESS, AND THE PUBLIC

Leopold Labedz

A generation of the unteachables is hanging upon us like a necklace of corpses. George Orwell

IN his 1936 introduction to *The Revolution Betrayed*, Trotsky noted that 'the bookstalls of all civilised countries are now loaded with books about the Soviet Union'. He complained, however, that the reader 'would seek in vain on the pages of this literature for a scientific appraisal of what is actually taking place in the land of the October revolution.'

In the thirties—the era of the Left Book Club—scholarly works on the subject were indeed scarce. In the sixties this is no longer the case. Publications on the Soviet Union still flood the bookstalls, but after the war a new category appeared, no longer of the 'A Country With A Plan' variety, but which looks through the haze of ideology and propaganda at the actual details of the Soviet scene, or some aspect of it. Unlike their predecessors, these are a result of study and not of impressions or handouts. True, they would hardly have been praised as 'scientific' by Trotsky, who was not deeply concerned with 'bourgeois' academic virtues. But one immediate effect of the scholarly pursuit of knowledge on Soviet affairs has been to circumscribe the area in which solemn nonsense could be pronounced without any loss of intellectual respectability, particularly in the academic field.

No such limitations apply at less exalted levels. Even the serious press still occasionally serves up a mixture of sense and nonsense, as if the Soviet Union were indeed 'a mystery wrapped in an enigma'. Undoubtedly, the situation has improved in the quality newspapers, but even there a glance at back numbers can be a sobering experience. Even more instructive is it to look at the coverage of Soviet affairs in an earlier period, and to see 'what the papers said at the time'.

At all times there is of course a gap between better informed and more popular levels, and over a period of time there is a lag between the acquired and the disseminated knowledge. But in this case the gap was wider and the lag longer because the problem of bridging them was *sui generis*. It involved not so much the sociology of knowledge, as what may be termed the sociology of ignorance. To analyse its causes one has to look not just at the factors affecting positive knowledge, but at the obstacles preventing its emergence in the first place.

Prejudices distort knowledge. This particular gap was due to a special resistance to learning. To live with the Soviet myth was to encounter all sorts of pseudo-certainties, ranging from mild misconceptions to wilful ignorance. Only after Khrushchev's 1956 speech did things begin to change; but the legacy remained.

W̶HEN knowledge became more accessible and the myth began to
crumble, two tendencies began to manifest themselves: on the one
hand a slow erosion of the old attitudes, on the other a continuous
display of the familiar stereotyped responses, perpetuating themselves
in a more subtle and more attenuated form.

On the left, these attitudes were in the past expressed in their classical
form in the *New Statesman*; on the right, the American *National Review*
provides a good example of dyed-in-the-wool obscurantism; the third
category, the muddled middle, between the Bourbons of the left and the
Neanderthals of the right, cannot be identified with any particular journal;
it just pops out everywhere. It is not a question of the intellectual level,
which may be high, or of the lack of information, which could be obtained
with some effort, but of the unwillingness to learn.   Self-induced
ignorance thus forms an essential ingredient of their reaction to Soviet
developments.   Any number of illustrations can be given referring to
the past of the first category:

> *On the Soviet attitude to the West*: ' The whole attitude of the Soviet
> Government towards the West has changed since the exile of
> Trotsky and the adoption of the Five Year Plan.' *New Statesman
> & Nation*, 4 July 1931.
>
> *On the accused in the Moscow Trials*: ' Few would now maintain
> that all or any of them were completely innocent, though there
> may be many doubts both about the details of the charges and
> as to the motives or the precise degree of complicity of one or
> another in this tangled web of treason, assassination, and
> sabotage.' *Ibid*. 6 February 1937.
>
> *On the Soviet-Nazi Pact*: ' . . . It is not inconceivable yet that Stalin,
> who has captured the centre of the diplomatic stage, may himself
> take a hand in calling a halt to the war.' *Ibid*. 26 August 1939.
>
> *On the Doctors' Plot*: ' . . . There is little doubt that American
> intelligence was using Jewish organizations in Eastern Europe
> for its own ends in a fairly big way.' *Ibid*. 21 February 1953.

We are of course all anti-Stalinist now, and since Khrushchev's speech
this also includes the anti-anti-communist ' liberals '.   It may therefore
seem ungenerous to recall the pecadillos of the past.   After all, the *New
Statesman* has changed and is no longer so credulous about Soviet affairs
as it used to be.   But its present position cannot be understood without
the background of its past.

Here again, the *New Statesman* is fairly typical of a wider ' progressive ' audience.   It has dismissed the bad things in the past from its
memory; it has become better informed on the present; and it invests
in optimistic hopes for the future.   This is not unusual, but instead of
admitting that its past attitude on Soviet affairs was simply obtuse, it
concentrates its anger on those who were better informed.   In Stalin's
time it justified its apologetics largely by equivocation or denial of facts;
when the facts finally came out in an incontrovertible form, it adjusted

itself to the new situation by projecting its sense of guilt on to those who had the misfortune of being prematurely right. Edward Hyams' jubilee book on the *New Statesman* (1963) shows how little the ' progressive ' mentality can learn from the lessons of the past. The old reluctance to face the facts is now transformed into an internally contradictory position bordering on intellectual schizophrenia. Thus, it is admitted that the ' terrible aftermath ' of the Russian Revolution ' made it reasonable and necessary to be anti-communist ', but at the same time the contrary practice of the paper since 1931 is approved, with few exceptions for which extenuating circumstances are always present. ' This *New Statesman* attitude, critical but patient, was to infuriate the extremists on both sides.' Thus in retrospect truth itself appears as extremism and its absence as moderation.

The ' progressive ' nostalgia, however, coexists with the progressive realisation that the paper's ' failures have almost all been caused by the one single but overwhelming disaster . . . the adoption of Socialist ideas in Russia and the coming into being of the USSR '. If, according to expectations, socialist revolution had been victorious in Germany, he says, all these awkward problems would have been avoided. But history did not conform to editorial convenience, and it is no doubt easier to regret it and to resent the fact that others did not share the paper's illusions at the time, than to approach its past in the spirit of ' *amicus Plato sed magis amica veritas* '.

IF the past of the *New Statesman* was strongly affected by angelology, the present of the *National Review* suffers as severely from demonology. In neither case is it a question of the journal being on the left or on the right, but of their attitude to the facts. If the first case shows the necessity for Soviet studies in the thirties, the second shows how limited is their influence in the sixties on the prejudiced mind.

To illustrate this point one may take the coverage of Sino-Soviet relations by the *National Review* (subtitle: A Journal of *Fact* and Opinion). On 5 November 1960 it published a special supplement, ' Bear and Dragon ', devoted to relations between Moscow and Peking. The editor, James Burnham, explained in the introduction that ' the purpose of the symposium is not to debate issues of current practical policy, but to assemble and focus a body of relevant data, analysis and interpretation which will be of intrinsic scientific and intellectual interest '.

And indeed, it is of interest, as can be seen from the final paragraph:

> A careful study of the material forming the alleged grounds for concluding that there is a serious Sino-Soviet conflict proves the absence of any objective foundation for such a belief. . . . All statements regarding the existence of serious disagreement between Moscow and Peking on foreign policy, war, peace, revolution, or attitude towards imperialism are an invention. All are the fruit of fertile imagination and unbased speculation.

In the thirties the ' progressives ' would not believe in the existence of the Soviet forced labour camps; in the sixties, the diehards would not admit the fact of the Sino-Soviet rift.

It is not surprising that after it finally came into the open, the lessons drawn by the latter were no more impressive than those drawn by the former after Khrushchev's revelations. Burnham, for instance, concluded that the test ban treaty ' helps Chinese nuclear development . . . and leaves the way open for Soviet use of Chinese territory and facilities for its own further nuclear advance ' (*National Review*, 10 September 1963).

' Sovietology ' has to contend not only with the extremes, but also with the muddled middle.

It is difficult to define this attitude very precisely. It is vague, hazy, sometimes non-committal, and often undistinguishable from what finds its expression in a more forceful way on the left or the right lunatic fringe. But it is usually more sophisticated and much more concerned with its respectability. The developments of the last decade make this attitude attractive not only to the congenital centrists averse to sharp definitions, but also to the two other categories, who often camouflage themselves as the third, finding in it a more respectable refuge. On the whole, the muddled middle can absorb the information provided by Soviet studies more easily than the more fanatical categories. But it is in fact often less well-informed than its respectability and/or its sophistication would lead one to expect. It is just muddled.

Strictly speaking, one should not perhaps speak here about a single category; it stands sometimes simply for a kind of disarming ignorance unconnected with any special disposition in the realm of politics, which is however different from the ignorance of the earlier years, because the age of innocence is past. The muddled middle embraces a variety of attitudes. A few examples, all of them from 1963, will suggest the heterogeneity of this category:

A press tycoon on a TV programme asserts that Khrushchev secretly admires capitalists, while another expert assures the audience that he is establishing democracy in the USSR by returning to a more pristine form of Marxism.

A reviewer of yet another book on the forced-labour camps which, he says, ' adds significantly to our knowledge ', writes in *The Observer*: ' Unlike most other atrocities in human history, the Soviet forced-labour camps have become known in a curious way: official admissions first, individual testimonies later.'

A front-bench Parliamentarian declares in *The* (Manchester) *Guardian*: ' Perhaps it is the Russians, not the Americans, to whom we are destined to play the role of Greeks, and who will in return subject our democratic freedoms to the rule of universal law.'

BUT if Soviet studies have a long way to go to make a stronger impact on the public mind, this does not mean that they have had no appreciable effect on this level. In fact the contrary is true.

Most serious papers now have on their staff at least one specialist on Soviet affairs. Not all of them of course are equally competent, and some of them too often sacrifice straight reporting to esoteric speculation, more or less well founded. But there is little doubt that on the whole the amount of information on Soviet affairs provided in papers and journals since the war is greater than before, and its level is higher. Naturally there are exceptions, but by and large this is true, and the development of Soviet studies contributed to this, both directly and indirectly.

Western correspondents in the Soviet Union remain a frustrated lot, but here too progress has been registered, not only because censorship and secrecy are less strict, but because of a more competent performance by the correspondents. One only has to compare the journalism of Walter Duranty in the thirties with the reporting of Michel Tatu in the sixties to grasp the improvement. Admittedly, Tatu is in a class by himself, but many other Western journalists in Moscow, including even communist journalists like Giuseppe Boffa or Arturo Pancaldi, provide interesting factual information. Unfortunately, their conditions of work are such that they are often reduced to the study of the Soviet press, an occupation which can be pursued without travelling to Moscow. Here again, as some correspondents have pointed out, systematic studies of the Soviet Union in the West have helped to improve their work.

Western ambasadors in Moscow and their staffs have become better informed in the same way. When one remembers Joseph Davies and his *Mission to Moscow*, and compares it with the memoirs of diplomats more recently accredited to Moscow, such as for instance *Il Mondo Sovietico*, by Luca Pietromarchi (1963), one is struck not only by the gullibility of the American Ambassador, but by the knowledge of the Italian, who did his homework and read a large number of Soviet studies. Their impact in this sphere is of course more direct and immediate than on the general public, which also has less opportunity to learn and is more prone to be affected by stereotypes and myths.

The question is not so much the persistence of ignorance, which is after all normal, since the general public cannot be expected to know much about other countries, as the degree and character of this ignorance. Soviet studies can affect this only indirectly, and ' terrible simplificators ' will always be more effective than good popularisers, who are scarce anyway, so long as the subject remains highly charged politically, i.e. so long as the Soviet myth persists.

The attitudes of the general public are in fact likely to improve in this respect not when the number of popular books on the Soviet Union increases, but when it falls. Abnormally high interest is a symptom of a situation in which the public is still reacting to the myth rather than interested in reality. The generation of unteachables will probably disappear at the same time as the bookstalls carry fewer publications on the Soviet Union. This is not an immediate prospect, but as

angelology and demonology become things of the past, popular ' sovietology ' will be heading, if not for its own destruction, at least towards
a less prominent position in the public eye. Serious Soviet studies will
remain, to be read by a more restricted public.

That time, however, is still ahead. In the West, public ignorance
has shrunk, and so has its taste for myth. But different countries undergo
this process at different rates and in different ways. Mythomania itself
may diminish or be redirected. That, however, is another story.

CONTRIBUTORS

ARTHUR E. ADAMS is Professor of Russian History at Michigan State University and editor of *Readings in Soviet Foreign Policy* and *The Russian Revolution and Bolshevik Victory.*

ROBERT F. BYRNES is Professor of History and Director of the Russian and East European Institute at the University of Indiana.

ROBERT CONQUEST, poet, critic, and political writer, is author of *Power and policy in the USSR, Common Sense about Russia,* etc., and editor of an anthology of Soviet bloc 'Thaw' poetry – *Back to Life.*

VICTOR FRANK, writer and essayist, is of Russian parentage, and now lives in London.

ALEXANDER GERSCHENKRON is at present the Walter S. Barker Professor of Economics at Harvard, and was from 1948 to 1956 director of the economic work at the Russian Research Center there.

FRANKLYN GRIFFITHS is a Canadian doing research on Soviet disarmament policy at the Massachusetts Institute of Technology, Center for International Studies.

JENS HACKER is editor of the monthly *Die Politische Meinung* and a specialist in Eastern European politics, constitutional and international law.

EUGENE KAMENKA, a graduate of Sydney University, taught philosophy in Singapore and is the author of *The Ethical Foundations of Marxism.* He is now teaching at the National University, Canberra.

BASILE KERBLAY is director of Studies at the Ecole Pratique des Hautes Etudes at the Sorbonne.

GEORGE LICHTHEIM is the author of *Marxism: An Historical and Critical Study* (1961) and *Europe and America* (1963).

169

BERNARD MORRIS is Assistant Professor in International Relation at the American University, Washington.

ALEC NOVE is Professor of Economics in the University of Glasgow and author of *The Soviet Economy*.

THOMAS H. RIGBY is Associate Professor of Russian at the Australian National University, lectures on Soviet government, and has published several articles on the Soviet political system.

GLEB STRUVE is Professor of Slavic Languages and Literature at the University of California and was formerly Reader in Russian Literature at the University of London.

ADAM ULAM is Professor of Government at Harvard and Research Associate of its Russian Research Center. His most recent book is *The New Face of Soviet Totalitarianism* (1963).

PETER WILES is Professor of Economics at Brandeis University, a Fellow of New College, Oxford, and the author of *The Political Economy of Communism* (1962).

INDEX